MADAME TUSSAUD

AND THE HISTORY OF

Madame Tussaud

and the History of Waxworks

Pamela Pilbeam

Hambledon and London

London and New York

Hambledon and London

102 Gloucester Avenue
London, NW1 8HX

175 Fifth Avenue
New York
NY 10010

First Published 2003

ISBN 1 85285 283 6

A description of this book is available from the
British Library and from the Library of Congress.

Typeset by Carnegie Publishing, Lancaster

Printed on acid-free paper and bound
in Great Britain by Bath Press, Bath

Contents

Illustrations

Plates

Between Pages 50 and 51

Between Pages 146 and 147

Illustration Acknowledgements

The author and publishers are extremely grateful to Madame Tussaud's Ltd for permission to reproduce the illustrations in this book. In particular, they wish to thank Susanna Lamb at Madame Tussaud's for her help in suggesting and supplying suitable images.

To Stephen

Introduction

The modern history of waxworks originated with Philippe Curtius's two exhibitions in Paris in the 1770s. He trained Marie Grosholz, the future Madame Tussaud, whom he always introduced as his niece but who was probably his daughter. She inherited his business when Curtius died in 1794. She brought the best of the collection of wax models to Britain in 1802, running a travelling show until 1835, when she settled in Baker Street. Madame Tussaud's odyssey as a travelling showman in Britain between 1802 and 1835 was an extraordinary one, particularly when one remembers that she was forty-one when she began her touring career (with a four-year-old son), and seventy-four when she and the exhibition finally settled in Baker Street. Marie Tussaud had arrived in Britain with nothing but her models. In 1850, when she died, her exhibition was the most successful tourist venue in the country. The exhibition was owned and run by her descendants until it became a limited company in the 1880s, shortly after the move to its present site in the Marylebone Road. The last member of the family to be involved in running the show died in 1967.

Tussaud's success was based on the leadership and acumen of individual members of the family and the strength of the family firm as a collective, held together by inherited objectives. From an entertainment designed to appeal to an elite, Tussaud's transformed itself to a show that drew the largest audience of any tourist attraction in Britain. In an unlikely way, wax has survived into generations reared on photographs, film, television and the virtual reality of computers, and into an age when people no longer need wax images to tell them what heroes or villains looked like. Fortunately, the attraction and the fun of wax remains.

I am extremely grateful to Undine Concannon and her successors, Rosy Cantor and Susanna Lamb, for allowing me to work in the Madame Tussaud's archives, a very rare privilege because Tussaud's has no space for a public reading room. While my research days had to coincide with the archivists' days off or holidays, I have never before received such generous encouragement and help as they all provided. I am also very grateful to

Judy Craig, who runs the Tussaud's modelling studio, not only for showing me the studio and explaining modern modelling techniques but also for checking what I wrote about them. The Arts and Humanities Research Board generously funded a term of research leave in 2001, which enabled me to complete this book in time for the bicentenary of the exhibition's arrival in Britain in November 2002. Tony Morris, one half of my publishers, was very encouraging; Martin Sheppard, the other half, offered invaluable advice on a variety of things, including British history, which is new territory for someone who is primarily a historian of France. I also must express my gratitude for the enthusiasm, questions and encouraging laughter of academic and general audiences in Britain, France and America who have shared wax history with me. I hope the book lives up to their expectations of it. Above all, I thank my family for living with waxworks for an uncomfortably long period and, above all, my husband, who has read and commented on all of it.

1

The Origins of Wax Modelling

Wax has had a long history representing life and death, attesting to truth and facilitating deception. Wax models were used in the Indian subcontinent in 3000 BC. Wax has since then been associated with death and the after life, facilitating the relationship of the living and the dead with the divine. The ancient Persians and Egyptians used wax for embalming and making models of individuals. The Egyptians believed that the wax image, as well as the preserved mummy, retained the personality as well as the features of the dead. The ancient Greeks made models of living people. Both Greeks and Romans used coloured wax models in funeral processions. The Romans often put the wax head or bust of their dead relatives on display in the atria of their homes. Some buried their dead in the company of a wax model of the person, complete with real hair and glass eyes.[1] Painted wax figures were also an integral part of the ceremonies of the Roman Catholic Church. They have been used in processions, religious and other-wise, since ancient times. Wax was often used to make models of saints and of Jesus and Mary for use in churches. Although the Reformation eliminated them from churches in Protestant states, voluptuous and colour-ful full-size wax models continued to adorn Roman Catholic churches, especially in Italy. The Greek and Russian Orthodox churches also made use of wax models.

While Christian and most ancient civilisations made ample use of wax, others, especially the Jewish and Muslim cultures, rejected it emphatically, believing that all representation was demonic, leading only to the fires of Hell. Indeed the envoy of the Bey of Tripoli shunned the acclaimed models made by Benoît at the court of Louis XIV for precisely these reasons. Wax and magic were also linked because wax is a medium in which a mimetic representation of an individual can be achieved. Wax figures were part of the rituals of black magic.

The Roman custom of including a wax effigy in funeral processions was adopted for European royal funerals. In France from the thirteenth to the end of the seventeenth century models of kings were displayed dressed in their usual clothes, with a wax face and hands and a wood-framed body.

The Holy Roman Emperor, the doges of Venice, the dukes of Brunswick and other rulers met the same end. A full-size wax model of Henry III of England was made for his funeral in 1272. The custom grew up for the models to be kept after the funeral service at the relevant royal tomb in Westminster Abbey. In the seventeenth century they were all moved into one of the side chapels, but no one was responsible for their upkeep. By the end of the eighteenth century the abbey had an odd assortment of dilapidated and sometimes totally naked models. Only a ruff survived on the effigy of Queen Elizabeth. The boys of neighbouring Westminster School, whose attentions are unlikely to have improved their condition, referred to them as the 'ragged regiment'. There was another collection of more respectable remnants, consisting of later members of the royal family, described as the Abbey Waxworks. These included a model of Charles II, which was actually made after his funeral. William and Mary, Queen Anne and a new Queen Elizabeth were added. One of the last of the funerary models to be made was that of Charles II's mistress, the duchess of Richmond, modelled in 1703 by one of the leading experts of the day, Mrs Goldsmith, for £250. The duchess wanted her beauty to be remembered and paid for the model herself. She was standing, dressed in her green velvet coronation robes edged in gold and holding a fan. On her orders the model was stored in a glass cabinet. Her stuffed dog and parrot stood guard over what remained a lovely model even towards the end of the eighteenth century.[2]

In the seventeenth century it became common for wax models to be included in funeral processions of notable non-royal citizens. Charles II ordered a wax effigy for the funeral of General Monck in 1670, on the grounds that a model with wax head and hands for an important lying-in-state was an improvement on the wooden models previously made. Effigies of William Pitt the Elder, made by Patience Wright, and Admiral Lord Nelson, the work of Catherine Andras, were put in Westminster Abbey after their funerals. During the Second World War the Abbey Waxworks were stored in Piccadilly Circus Underground station along with the live humans who sheltered the during bombing raids.[3]

From the time of the Renaissance the accurate representation of the human body had been a prime concern for artists, including wax modellers and surgeons. Artists such as Michelangelo and Leonardo da Vinci visited dissecting rooms as part of their study of anatomy. Leonardo actually dissected corpses himself in order to represent the living body more accurately. Michelangelo and other artists of the time also made wax models. Anatomical wax models blended art and science. The first Italian to make anatomical models was probably Ludovic Civoli. G. G. Zumbo (1656–1710) was the first to use paint on wax. His coloured wax models of plague

1. The 'Ragged Regiment' at Westminster Abbey.

sufferers, 'Time and Death', were edifying, shocking and strangely popular. The Marquis de Sade admired his work. From the sixteenth century wax models were routinely made by surgeons for teaching human anatomy. Using real corpses was problematical for a variety of reasons. Preservatives then available damaged the body, but if a corpse were dissected without preservatives, even in cold weather, it became an impossibly smelly task long before it was finished. In addition opinion turned against the dissection of human bodies, stirred by illustrations such as Thomas Hogarth's *The Reward of Cruelty*, which showed the horror of cutting up a person in graphic and critical detail. The supply of actual corpses also dwindled as body snatchers, or 'resurrectionists', were stopped. In Britain the Anatomy Act of 1832 allowed only unclaimed pauper bodies to be used for dissection.[4]

More and more teaching was done with wax models. In the eighteenth century these became far from prosaic and utilitarian representations. The anatomical model maker consciously produced an idealised though accurate body, the appearance of which was delightful, even erotic. Art and science intertwined. The whole bodies that were produced were nearly all of women. Many of those made towards the end of the eighteenth century were sold in Britain, France and elsewhere as 'Venuses'. Their faces were beautiful, their 'skin' was coloured and they had eyelashes and flowing long hair. Their bodies opened to reveal body parts, particularly foetuses. The 'Venus' was displayed lying invitingly on silk or velvet cushions, and was often decorated with a pearl necklace. Few whole male bodies were made. Males had no wax 'flesh' or clothes and were always shown upright to demonstrate the position of muscles and bones. Perhaps the difference was intended to show that men were good for action, but women only to reproduce and be ornamental.

The most celebrated anatomical wax modeller of the eighteenth century was Felice Fontana (1720–1805). He made an extensive collection for the grand duke of Tuscany's Florentine museum, opened in 1775, which was used by military surgeons as well as being open to the public.[5] Typical of Fontana's work is the collection of anatomical models he and Paolo Mascagni (1752–1815) made for Joseph II, ruler of the Holy Roman Empire. In 1785 the emperor, an archetypal enlightened despot, founded the Institute of the History of Medicine at the University of Vienna to train his army surgeons. An Italian architect, Isidore Canevale (1730–1786) designed a complex of buildings, the Josephinium, devoted to postgraduate surgical training. At the centre was the collection of 1192 anatomical and obstetric wax models, made in Florence between 1775 and 1785 under the direction of Fontana and Mascagni. Mules were used to carry the models across the Brenner Pass to Linz, whence they were shipped along the Danube to Vienna.[6] The collection is still on public view in the Josephinium. It consists of elegantly crafted limbs and other body parts, whole male bodies, upright and without flesh, showing details of bones and sinews, all delicately coloured. In addition there is a Venus, complete with pearl necklace, blonde hair (head and pubic), blue eyes and an open abdomen revealing internal organs. She is prostrate on a silken couch, but is more coarsely cast, though still seductive, in a material not wax, perhaps plaster. There is no indication whether she is a later addition. The models are displayed in matching rosewood cases and the Venetian glass is edged with gold plate. Joseph II's contribution to medical training was generous and part of his determination to be a central figure in the Enlightenment. The collection was retained at the Josephinium when it was no longer needed to train doctors and surgeons.[7]

Today, when public exposure to the nude body is only too omnipresent in the media, the surviving models of this period still provoke a disturbing range of emotions, even when glanced at merely as book illustrations.[8] A wax model, however beautifully made, will always resemble a corpse, even if the purpose is not funerary. The observer is put mentally off balance looking at a model which is obviously also designed to be erotic. Were contemporaries uncomfortable when faced with these models? Far from it. At the time they were collectables for a wealthy elite. No collection was complete without some anatomical waxes. Wax erotica became popular among French courtiers; in 1715 the regent's collection, the work of Marc Antonio Raimondi and Agostini Carracci, went on display in the Palais Royal.[9] A later royal, the duc d'Orléans, who became Philippe-Egalité during the Revolution, was the leading French collector of anatomical wax models in the second half of the eighteenth century. Most of his 190 elegant models were the work of Pinson, a freemason patronised by the duke. Pinson was a close friend of Louis XVI and surgeon to his Swiss Guards.[10] These impressive, seductively erotic waxes were requisitioned by the Paris School of Medicine after the duke's execution during the Revolution.[11]

One of the most renowned French anatomical wax modellers of the earlier part of the eighteenth century, the surgeon Guillaume Desnoués, showed and sold his models in Britain. Twice, in 1727 and 1730, he brought exhibitions to London. The second time the exhibition was held at a chemist's shop on the corner of Pall Mall and the Haymarket. The entry fee was an astronomical 5s. Later the models were shown in Dublin. When they returned to Mr Rackstrow's Statuary, in London's Fleet Street, the viewing fee was a more modest 1s. Finally this set was bought for the university of Dublin. Benjamin Rackstrow was an excellent wax sculptor himself, a substantial London citizen and colonel in the Trained Bands (the London Militia). Rackstrow's museum was close to that of another wax entrepreneur, Mrs Salmon, and he was always keen to distinguish between their collections. He stressed that he ran a museum, not a waxworks. In effect his museum and Mrs Salmon's waxworks contained many duplicates; both had a famous London witch, Mother Shipton, telling fortunes, Bamford the seven foot four inch giant from Staffordshire, and a dwarf from Norfolk. Non-wax odds and ends were added – a whale skeleton, fish, skulls and fossils, and of course a mummy, inevitably a pharaoh's daughter. He also found room for two stuffed crocodiles. When Rackstrow died in 1772, the business continued until the main collection was dispersed in 1779.

Rackstrow's serious collection consisted of full-size anatomical wax figures. The star was a woman who was eight months pregnant. Liquid coursed through glass tubes to show the circulation of her blood, while heart and lungs moved correctly. Rackstrow added full size male and female models. The female, a woman who had been hanged, displayed all her muscles. There were also bottles containing actual preserved foetuses and placentas, the result of human and animal abortions. There were also moulds showing the position in the womb of the foetus at all stages of pregnancy, taken from women who died before giving birth. The museum contained wax representations both of the male urinary tract and penis and of female organs. It also housed the real preserved organs of both sexes, with the penis injected with a substance to keep it erect.

There was an accompanying scientific anatomical guidebook which was frank and totally lacking in prudery. There is no hint that either men or women might find the exhibits embarrassing, disgusting or titillating. The Victorians came to be less open in their attitudes to sex and the last Rackstrow handbill published assured clients that 'a Gentlewoman attends the Ladies separately'. Considering that scientists were still arguing whether the mother was merely the vehicle for a foetus which had been wholly created in the male, it is surprising that both sexes were expected to view this exhibition in a neutral fashion. Were the customers dirty old men or medical students? Horace Walpole admired Rackstrow's skill as a wax modeller, but there is no way of knowing if Rackstrow's collection, or any other, was used for serious teaching. Its location in Chancery Lane was close to several major hospitals, but it was also a stone's throw from Holywell Street, just off the Strand, which became notorious as the centre of the pornographic book trade in the mid nineteenth century.[12]

What of anatomical wax exhibitions in general? Eighteenth-century anatomical collections, whether for display, for paying customers or for teaching, customarily included spectacular and repulsive deformities as well as extensive examples of reproductive physiology.[13] There is sufficient indication in the way anatomical exhibitions were advertised later to appreciate that many had elements of the 'sex shop' alongside the educational role they claimed.[14] Masculine tastes cannot have changed so much for us not to believe that the seductively recumbent 'Venuses' were intended to titillate as well as inform.[15]

To be seen in Exeter Change in the Strand,

as well in Christmas and other Holidays, and at all other Times, tho' the Change be shut, only then you must go in at that end towards Charing Cross.

Just
finish'd,
and to be
seen. The present
COURT of ENGLAND,
in Wax, after (and as
big as) the Life, in the
Inner-Walk of Exeter Change
in the Strand, much exceeding, tho'
both made by the most deservedly famous
Mrs. MILLS, whom in that Art all ingenious
Persons own had never yet an equal. The Names
of the Chief Persons, are the Queen, his Royal
Highness Prince George, the Princess Sophia, his Grace
the Duke of Marlborough, the Countess of Manchester,
the Countess of Kingston, the Countess of Musgrave, &c.
As likewise the Effigies of Mark Anthony, naturally
acting that which rendered him remarkable to the
World: Cleopatra, his Queen; one of her
Egyptian Ladies. Oliver Cromwell in
Armour: the Count Tollemach: with ma-
ny others too tedious here to mention. To be seen from 9 in the
Morn, till 9 at Night. You
may go in at any of the
Doors in the Change,
and pass thro' the
Hatter's Shop in
the Outward
Walks.

Note.—The Prices are Six Pence—Four Pence, and Two Pence a-Piece.

There is the Effigies of a Comedian, walking behind the Queen.

☞ Persons may have their Effigies made of their deceas'd Friends, on moderate Terms.

2. A handbill for Mrs Mills's waxworks, undated.

Such models were intended for teaching purposes, but perhaps such stimulating visual aids made up for boring lectures. Anatomical models that could be taken apart reflected in a very simple way contemporary scientific experimentation as well as providing a new dimension on undressing at a glance. In the eighteenth century scientists were, as always, eager to understand the origins of life. Jean-Baptiste de Lamarck (1744–1829) investigated the layers of different forms of life and the role of inheritance. Geologists explored layers of rock to reveal their stages and ages of deposition. In his private classes as well as in his role as Professor of Anatomy at the Royal Academy, Sir William Hunter dissected women who had died in pregnancy to reveal the layers of their bodies and that of their foetuses. William and John Hunter, as well as Charles Bell and Joseph Towne, made wax anatomical models. Wax models that could be taken apart might be thought of as simple examples of the exploration of the layers of life.[16]

For most people wax models were not for scientific research but something to visit at a fair. The first mention of wax figures at one of the largest fairs in Britain, Bartholomew Fair, was in 1647. The fair had been held at Smithfield, in the city of London, each year for two weeks from 24 August since the time of Henry I, when it attracted both pilgrims and traders. By the time wax exhibits were first mentioned the fair was a wild, unruly occasion, dreaded by the lord mayor.[17] Representations of the grotesque, nature's freaks and dreadful murders were part of the stock in trade of wax shows in fairs and might be classified as the popular end of the trade, both in terms of subject and clientele. The wax side-shows included rulers, politicians, writers and biblical characters.[18] Towards the end of the seventeenth century there was a wax booth at the fair, the 'Temple of Diana' with a wax drummer outside to attract the crowds. He seems to have been fitted with a mechanical device so that he both drummed and appeared to be shouting. On either side of him were two wax babies.[19] Bartholomew Fair had an audience of artisans but scientists were drawn to the novel ideas on display. The fair was of course a tourist attraction. In *The Prelude* Wordsworth described the range of things to be seen.

> The Horse of knowledge and the Learned Pig,
> The Stone-eater, the man that swallows fire,
> Giants, Ventriloquists, the Invisible Girl,
> The Bust that speaks and moves its goggling eyes,
> The Wax-work, Clock-work, all the marvellous craft
> Of modern Merlins, Wild Beasts, Puppet shows
> All out-o'-the-way, far-fetched, perverted things.[20]

By the middle of the nineteenth century successive lord mayors had smothered the fair by increasing the rent for the stalls to prohibitive levels and only a tiny cluster survived.

Wax had begun to diversify away from the fair, church, laboratory and witches' coven in the seventeenth century, to provide a different, but familiar, opportunity for those with money to spare to flaunt their wealth. People were already accustomed to the ornate possibilities of wax in decorated candles in church, souvenirs of pilgrimages and prints cast from molten wax poured over carved wood. Secular versions of these prints became common and in the eighteenth century wax was used for nativity scenes for the infant Jesus, as well as for toys, dolls and table ornaments. Wax portrait-reliefs and medallions also became very popular throughout Europe, while in the eighteenth century wax was often used for decorating ornamental box-lids.

Miniature wax portraits, made by Abraham Smith, modeller for Queen Christina of Sweden, became fashionable in England. His customers ranged from the republican Henry Cromwell to Charles II. By 1672, however, the diarist John Evelyn was linking a fondness for wax figures with the covert reintroduction of Roman Catholicism into England. He related how he

> went to see the fopperies of the Papists at Somerset house and York house, where now the French Ambassador had caused to be represented our Blessed Saviour at the Pascal Supper, with his Disciples, in figures and puppets made as big as the life, of wax work, curiously clad, and sitting round a large table, the roome nobly hung, and shining with innumerable Lamps and Candles, this exposed, to the whole world, all the Citty came to see; such liberty had the Roman Catholics at this time obtained.[21]

Perhaps many British people were repelled by wax figures because of their association with the Catholic Church.

The models that made Evelyn uneasy may have been the work of Antoine Benoît (1632–1717), a member of the Académie Royale de Peinture et de Sculpture who was ennobled in 1706. Benoît perfected an already well-established fashion in wax modelling. He was renowned for the high quality of his coloured wax models. He was the first to make busts and hands from life, that is taking his mould from the actual body of the living person. He made medical wax models and wax puppets, and was one of the first to make models of people other than rulers and their courtiers. He made a famous wax haut-relief of Louis XIV as an old man.[22] He produced one of the first wax groups or *diorama*. It was a representation of the Sun King's court with the models dressed in the style of the time, sitting around in a circle. Benoît won a royal patent to display his work in public in the Rue des Ss.-Pères. His exhibition included models of the ambassadors of Algeria,

Morocco, Russia, Siam and of the doge of Venice.[23] The king and his courtiers paid a visit, as did Madame de Sévigné, La Bruyère and other aristocrats.[24] Public displays of wax models for private profit in an entrepreneurial setting were a novel idea. In 1684 Benoît modelled James II and some of his courtiers.

In 1685 a German, Johann Heinrich Schalch (1623–c. 1704), obtained a licence from the lord mayor of London to show royal figures. He produced a death mask of Queen Mary in 1694 and toured with a tableau of her on her deathbed. The standard of wax craftsmanship became very high. The art of colouring the wax produced delicate results. There were a number of other well-known wax modellers in the second half of the eighteenth century in Paris, including a Mademoiselle Biheron, as well as the anatomical modeller Bertrand and the surgeon Pinson, who had a wax exhibition in 1793.[25]

Wax dolls became popular, but one of the most popular forms of wax model, presumably because price and size made it accessible, was the miniature. Framed profiles of the famous were made in coloured wax. Wax miniatures, popular in Italy since the fifteenth century, became particularly desirable. A substantial number of these were made for the rich and famous by Catherine Andras, including representations of Nelson, George III and George IV and the Tsar Alexander I.[26] Their number attests to their popularity as collectables.[27] There were other money-making and fashionable uses for wax. Josiah Wedgwood employed John Flaxman junior to make wax reliefs for his wares.[28] Wax decorations were so popular that Wedgwood designed the final raised relief decorations to look as if they were made of wax, a style which is still the international hallmark of the firm.

While wax was being used by innovative entrepreneurs to exploit a burgeoning middle-class market, earlier uses of wax were in decline. In the sixteenth century the Worshipful Company of Wax Chandlers had a respected place in the City of London with its own hall and substantial resources. It gradually lost control of the industry and by the end of the eighteenth century the former aristocrat of lighting, the beeswax candle, was a rarity and the industry was far less flourishing thanks to the competition of oil lamps, long before the introduction of gas for lighting.

Candles bring us back to the paradox that wax attested to truth but often facilitated falsehood. Wax has traditionally been employed to seal and thus guarantee state and legal documents, and wax candles in churches had significant symbolic importance to ordinary people as part of church rituals. On the other hand, wax could be used to deceive. The world 'sincere', meaning literally without wax, derives from the practice in ancient Rome of masking a flaw in a pot by filling it with wax, or possibly to indicate that honey was entirely free of wax.[29]

As wax sculptures became part of an entrepreneurial culture, modelling in wax became a medium of choice for women. Perhaps this is not surprising as manipulating wax involves far less strength than working stone or other materials. Women also ran wax shows, sometimes carrying on a business they had run initially with their husbands. It cannot be claimed that Madame Tussaud was a pioneer as a woman sculptor and entrepreneur. Rather her distinction lies in being the last of such dynamic female showmen in England. In 1696 there were full-size wax models on show at Exeter Change in the Strand, made by Mrs Mills, who claimed to be the greatest artist in Europe. The models included Cromwell, Charles II and William and Mary. Her show ran from 9 a.m. to 9 p.m. at an entry fee of between 2*d*. and 6*d*.[30] Her striking handbill also said that 'persons may have their Effigies made of their deceas'd Friends on moderate terms'. There must have been fierce competition to model the living and the dead, because Mrs Goldsmith, who had made the admired model of the duchess of Richmond, had a show in Green Court in Old Jewry close by. She had also made effigies of William and Mary in their coronation robes.

The best known of the women wax modellers was Mrs Salmon (1650–1740), who was also a toymaker. She ran a show with her husband from before 1693 and continued when he died in 1718. She had an exhibition of 140 life-size figures spread through six rooms at the Golden Ball in the Strand. Some were fitted with clockwork and were advertised as moving. There was a model of Mrs Salmon herself with a child on her lap. She also had a show at Bartholomew and Southwark fairs. In 1711 she moved to the Horn tavern in Fleet Street and advertised with a sign showing a painted salmon. She remarried and became Mrs Steers, but retained her former professional name and the fish. The handbill for her Fleet Street show advertised, among numerous delights, 'Margaret, Countess of Heningbergh, Lying on a Bed of State, with her Three Hundred and Sixty-Five Children, all born at one Birth, and baptized by the Names of John and Elizabeth'. A representation of the frequently-modelled London witch, Mother Shipton, literally kicked out the customers at the exit. The floor of the whole show was booby-trapped with treadles which set off devices, including a raised broom to threaten the clientele. Mrs Salmon seems to have been somewhat odd as well as a joker. She apparently always wore a white crêpe cap, with coffin trimmings, and slept in a shroud.

When Mrs Salmon finally donned her own shroud at the age of ninety, the show was run under her name by a Chancery Lane surgeon-solicitor, Mr Clark, whose widow took over when he died. The royal family was kept

3. Mrs Salmon's Waxwork, Fleet Street, engraving 1793.

scrupulously up to date. The entry fee was 1s. Mrs Clark also held shows in the midlands, including at Birmingham, Wolverhampton and Walsall. The exhibition was obliged to move again in 1795 when the building which housed it was demolished. It was re-established on the opposite side of Fleet Street, in Prince Henry's room, above an archway leading to the Temple. Mrs Clark kept some of Mrs Salmon's humour, including the model at the exit which booted out the visitors. A wax beefeater and a woman selling matches stood at the entrance to attract customers. Upstairs there were the obligatory royals and leading politicians, including Charles James Fox and Pitt the Younger. There also were Nelson and General Wolfe, the preachers Whitfield and Wesley, Dick Turpin and other villains. A third room was filled with shepherds and shepherdesses, and lambs and goats copulating. When Mrs Clark died in 1812 the waxworks was sold for less than £50. The remaining models were shown in Water Lane. In 1827 thieves broke into the premises and destroyed some of them and the waxworks closed in 1831.[31] Dickens described Mrs Clark's 'perspiring waxworks' in *David Copperfield*. There were in addition numerous small and transient wax shows, in fairs and towns. In 1745 there was an exhibition at the junction of Shoe Lane and Fleet Street of a set of tableaux involving one hundred miniature figures showing the varied fortunes of Richardson's novel *Pamela*.

Mrs Bullock was another 'institution' in the world of wax, with a well-publicised 'Beautiful Cabinet of Wax Figures'. 'Mrs Bullock and Sons' toured and showed models in the midlands between 1794 and 1807. Her sons branched out into rice paste and plaster figures which they also sold. Eventually the sons, William and George, took over the touring shows, adding topical optical illusions and objects of interest. In 1789 the Sylvesters ran probably the best-known wax show, located at the Lyceum Theatre, where Madame Tussaud held her first British exhibition in 1802. They boasted models, just arrived from Constantinople, which were soon joined by a 'Cabinet of Royal Figures' from Paris. This included a model of the head of the governor of the Bastille, made for the English circus entrepreneur Philip Astley. In 1792 they went on tour in Manchester, then Aberdeen, to return to the Strand two years later. In 1801 their Cabinet of Royal Wax Works was on show in Mr Elstob's Coffee House in Hull. Full-length models had gone out of fashion for private purchase. On his handbills Mr Sylvester offered medallion portraits and promised 'Should the Portraits not be thought the most striking and correct Likenesses, he will not expect anything for his Trouble'.[32]

Wax modellers always liked to claim that their customers came out of the top drawer. Mrs Salmon said she moved to the Strand because St Martin-le-Grand was too narrow for the carriage traffic. Some of the references to aristocracy and gentry in her posters may be discounted, since wax modellers often claimed to be artists with noble patrons. In the second half of the eighteenth century, however, the market for wax changed. Wax became a plaything, not just for working people at fairs and royalty and their courtiers, but high fashion for anyone with money. Some bought and kept models in their homes, as well as visiting wax 'salons' to

4. Bullock's London Museum (the Egyptian Hall).

gaze at sculpted heads and whole figures, resplendent in court robes or rich garments. A wax show gave the well off middle classes the chance to see the latest fashions, a function fulfilled today by *Hello!* magazine and the Oscar and other media award presentation ceremonies, where a high proportion of the television audience is reckoned to be more interested in the frocks than the films. Wax became so fashionable that a minority of the very rich even took lessons in the art of wax modelling. Substantial numbers of these models survive, including those of Samuel Percy (1750–1820), who made Queen Anne and Louis XIV in wax.[33] Towards the end of the eighteenth century there were a number of outstanding women working in wax. Some were ladies, catering for their own kind. They thought of themselves as artists and would never have shown their work in a public exhibition. In 1801 Catherine Andras was made 'Modeller in Wax' to Queen Charlotte. A number of ladies learnt the craft, including Lady Diana Beauclerk, daughter of the third Duke of Marlborough and a friend of Dr Johnson.

There was a female wax expert from America, Mrs Patience Wright (1725–86), who had toured America until her show was destroyed by fire. She moved to Britain, operating first in Southwark (1772), and later in Pall

Mall and Bath. The wax housemaid she kept on the stairs of her house often fooled visitors. She visited Paris in 1781, where she failed to persuade Benjamin Franklin to help her set up a wax exhibition. He apparently told her there was too much competition. It was said she acted as a spy for Franklin, sending messages in wax heads.[34] Franklin certainly introduced her to friends in London and she claimed to have met the king and queen, and to have addressed them as George and Charlotte. Through such contacts this forceful woman, dubbed the 'Queen of Sluts' by Charles Adams's wife, secured well-heeled clients. Her model of the elder Pitt is still in Westminster Abbey.[35]

Wax models were included in the annual exhibitions of the Royal Academy and Society of Artists, and women modellers like Catherine Andras were among the exhibitors. For a short time wax models played a part in a relatively new entrepreneurial market in the art world, which liked to toy with entertaining sometimes politically radical concepts, perhaps mingled with slightly shocking and titillating novelty. Wax provided an accessible medium in which to display models which could be viewed as art, erotica or, when moulded into anatomical forms, as an ambiguous (but acceptable) blend of the scientific and the salacious. Along with another new form, the lithograph, a wax model could be endlessly, and inexpensively, replicated. Like music and painting, wax became part of a culture in which patronage was no longer limited to the official world or to the super wealthy. Wax models, quickly and deftly produced, satisfied the taste of the newly rich, as well as those with more established fortunes. Wax was to become part of the ceremonial of revolution in the 1790s, just as it had been part of religion. Nineteenth-century memories of revolution were also sometimes rendered in wax. In Nantes in 1833 a wax Napoleon and a representation of the battle of Austerlitz was ordered for the annual procession in celebration of the 1830 Revolution. Not inappropriately, the statue was commissioned by a local doctor, Ange Guépin, and was a neat mixture of invented relic in the style of the Catholic Church and the traditional anatomical surgical wax model.[36]

Contemporaries were unsure how to classify this old medium now translated into an aspect of elite culture and displayed more widely and publicly in polite society than had been normal in the past. The great and the good had been turned into wax for centuries and had been publicly displayed in churches and cemeteries. But the example of the Ragged Regiment in Westminster Abbey indicates that they had also been disregarded and neglected. What was novel in the eighteenth century was the proliferation of exhibitions which sought and attracted paying customers from all walks of life. Wax models of notable people typified the confidence of the

5. Frontispiece to *The Wax Work and Monumental Records in Westminster Abbey*, engraving 1792.

Enlightenment in the potential of the individual. Anatomical models proclaimed that science fully understood the rationality of how the human body functioned. Above all wax was presented as entertainment, but the figures, especially the anatomical models, must still have recalled the old links of wax to death, to representations of Christ and saints. Wax salons designed, located and priced to appeal those on the now fashionable Grand Tour of Europe were included in almanacs which provided details of theatres where popular live actors performed. Wax exhibitions were also included in almanacs that included pornographic images. It is hard to imagine today the appeal to an educated, rich market of wax as an item in a catalogue of erotica. We have to remember that these were the days before the video shop with its top shelf pornography. Anatomical models were sometimes ambiguous, deliberately exciting the eye by their exploration of the human body. The richer customer for wax could also buy his, or her, own unique, custom-made model of individuals in sexually explicit poses, an eighteenth-century equivalent of the home-made porn movie. These were confined to the boudoir, perhaps to excite a novice partner. Sadly, none seems to have survived; presumably heirs and prudes threw them out.

2

The Wax Salon

Long before Philippe Curtius arrived in Paris there were several wax shows open to the public in London. Curtius had the distinction of being the first to make a wax exhibition an irresistible part of elite, as well as popular, public entertainment. Philippe Curtius (1737–1794) made himself the most renowned exponent of the art and business of wax in Paris in the years before the Revolution of 1789. He shrewdly located his shows in the two most important and vibrant enclaves of popular entertainment in Paris, the Boulevard du Temple and the Palais Royal, the first catering to a broad-based clientele, the second to a more fashionable one.

Curtius was a native of Switzerland, although the French always thought of him as a German and often refer to him as Kurtz. He trained as a doctor, and, like other doctors, began to make wax body parts to help with his work. The prince de Conti (1717–1776), was apparently impressed by Curtius's small anatomical wax museum in Berne and encouraged him to move to Paris. Permanently out of favour with his cousin, Louis XV, because he supported the move to transform the absolute monarchy into a constitutional regime, the prince was famous for his patronage of avant-garde artists and intellectuals such as Rousseau. He created an artists' colony in the rue St-Honoré where he lodged artists including Curtius. He invited them to receptions in his palatial, but decidely bohemian, Paris home, the Temple, where they were able to meet potential clients.[1] By 1776, when de Conti died, Curtius had created a successful and highly fashionable wax exhibition. He was also a painter and sculpted in other materials, in which capacity he was admitted to the Academy of St-Luc in 1778.

Curtius began his career as a waxwork showman in a traditional fairground setting at the St-Laurent fair, near to the Temple, a fact that his niece, Marie Tussaud, preferred to forget. He had a permanent wax *salon* in a large upper room there. We know far more about this exhibition than one can glean from the usual advertising handbills because the exhibits were badly damaged when the roof leaked during a storm and Curtius made an insurance claim. The ceiling of the room collapsed and Curtius's precious collection was ruined by a combination of water and the weight of chunks of plaster brought down by the water. Many of the models were ruined. The damage was recorded in detail by Curtius's lawyers in June 1787.

The focus of this exhibition were the wax models and heads made by Curtius, but there was much more than wax. Curtius was an avid collector of precious and unusual objects, which he interspersed with the wax figures to produce an exhibition that, he was keen to emphasise, was unique at that time. Within a few years public exhibitions of paintings and sculpture would open in Paris, Vienna and other cities. Until then such precious goods were confined to private collections. There were numerous displays of unusual objects in circulation, especially 'oddities of nature'. Later, when part of Curtius's exhibition went on tour it was called 'Curtius's Cabinet of Curiosities'. He saw the entrepreneurial potential of wax plus art for a market of paying customers of all classes. His show included numerous large paintings, including several impressive seascapes and huge mirrors, which made the exhibition seem vast and imposing. There was also a map of Paris; accurately scaled maps were new and were fast becoming fashionable. There were Chinese lacquered cabinets, elaborate glass light fittings and a wicker elephant. The luckless elephant was squashed flat by rain and plaster. The room had been decorated with elegant and expensive wallpaper, all designed to make both the one-off customers, and those who came to order and collect private wax portraits, feel at home.[2]

By 1787, however, this was not Curtius's main exhibition, and none of his most famous models were among the damaged goods. His permanent establishment was nearby at 20 Boulevard du Temple and probably dated from the 1770s, although surviving records are imprecise. The boulevard was close to the Temple prison and the prince de Conti's palace. It was a new and bustling centre of entertainment. Always with an acute eye for business opportunities, Curtius had two sections to his exhibition. One was called the wax salon and included people who were considered famous and glamorous. The 'equally famous and glamorous' liked to wander around and inspect. The other was full of villains. This was the *Caverne des Grands Voleurs*, the forerunner of the Chamber of Horrors. People were accustomed to watch hangings and criminals being broken on the wheel. The *caverne* let them linger over the details of murder and the legalised violence of the subsequent execution, which in the flesh might be over too soon for those who liked to savour it. Curtius was happy to add imitation blood to the figures.

A principal attraction was the poisoner Antoine-François Desrues (1744–1777), whose murderous career is still remembered in France today. Desrues was a hardworking, ambitious but totally unscrupulous individual. He started life as a grocer's assistant in Paris. With determination and effort he bought the business and married the daughter of a rich coachbuilder, an heiress with brilliant prospects. He invented a title to match that of his wife's fortune and, by deception, acquired a château for 130,000 *livres*. He had neither the money, nor the intention, to pay for it. The seller, Monsieur de la Motte, accepted a bill of exchange, which his wife collected. Desrues offered her a cup of chocolate before she set off to cash the bill. It was laced with poison and opium. Desrues dumped her body in a chest in a large hole he had dug ready in his basement. A few days later the son turned up, to be told that his mother had collected the money and had left, saying she was going to Versailles for a few days. Desrues offered the son a lift and a chocolate drink 'for the road', doctored in the same way. They set off in a hired barouche, but the son died en route. Desrues made a big fuss finding a doctor. He insisted that the man was a total stranger with whom, because they were going in the same direction, he had decided to share transport. In tears, he assured the doctor and the police that the man had told him that he was very ill with venereal disease. The police let Desrues leave the scene to offer a prayer for the departed.

Fortunately Monsieur de la Motte was more suspicious than the rest of his family. The police searched Desrues's home and found the first body. Desrues was condemned to death by burning on 6 May 1777. His wife was also charged with the double murder, but her sentence was commuted to life imprisonment in the Saltpétrière, because she was pregnant. Later she became one of the victims of the September Massacres.[3] Curtius rapidly made a wax of Desrues which became a principal attraction in the *caverne*. Numerous illustrations, biographies, songs and ballads were composed about Desrues, helping to reinforce his desirability at the waxworks.[4]

The Boulevard du Temple building was also the Curtius family home and workshop. Models were made, dressed and stored there. Curtius did not designate specific rooms as workrooms, so all over the building there were models in process of construction, repair, being coloured, decorated and dressed. Curtius made enough money from the exhibition to buy a plot of land nearby in the Rue des Fossés du Temple, where he built a house which he let out to tenants.

One of the attractions of the boulevard for those in the entertainment business was there, in part at least, they escaped the legal stranglehold that the elite theatres, especially the Opéra, exerted over what they performed. Some of the entertainment, including Curtius's wax displays, also avoided all-embracing government censorship. The boulevard was an intriguing place to wander, to gaze at the crowd, to listen to music being played, and if inclined, make arrangements with one of the numerous prostitutes in the area. The city installed stone benches and chairs where older people played

6. Dr Philippe Curtius, wearing his national guard uniform. Engraving by Gilles Louis Chrétien.

chess or dominoes. In the 1780s the term boulevard was somewhat of a euphemism, the delightful, tree-lined avenue being churned to mud by carriage wheels in wet weather. The Boulevard du Temple, nevertheless, soon became the mecca for popular entertainment.

More theatres, seven in all, were built on this single boulevard than in any other location in Paris. Each was much smaller than the Opéra or the Comédie Française. It was the most concentrated centre of entertainment in the capital. Next to the Curtius exhibition was Astley's Circus, with its famous horse acts. Philip Astley (1742–1839), who had escaped from his father's trade of cabinet-maker in Newcastle-under-Lyme to become a sergeant-major in a British cavalry regiment, created the first modern circus. The central attraction was Astley and his wife dancing on galloping horses. He created circus venues in London and Paris and employed the first Grimaldi, Joseph, who set a tradition of clowns in the British circus. Marie-Antoinette visited his circus and Astley and his son, John, performed at Versailles.[5] Close by in the boulevard were the *ombres chinoises*: magic lantern shows came into their own in these years and this variety used illustrations of fashionable Chinese figures. Silhouettes were attached to oiled paper. Behind the paper was a light, whose heat made the images revolve, so that a range of silhouettes could be shown. Astley also included similar 'Chinese shadows' in his show. In the 1770s a Swiss showman, Séraphim, used clockwork to activate the silhouettes. In the 1780s came the Eidophusikon, which added sound to the images. Favourite scenes involved storms at sea, the storm being made by seeds shaken inside a cylinder, and wind, conjured up by pressing two silk-covered frames together. 'Pandemonium' was even noisier.

In the boulevard there were firework displays, jugglers and acrobats, animals in cages, performing bears, everything you would expect to find at a fairground, except that the boulevard was a permanent site. It preserved the atmosphere of a travelling fair with sideshows, people selling barley sugar sticks, oranges, liquorice water, roasted chestnuts, cakes and apple pies. Around the theatres rough and ready wine-shops, brasseries and cafés sprang up where people could play cards and billiards. The city authorities began to install street lighting in 1781 so that the boulevard its cafés, theatres and shops floated in an island of light. Contemporary engravings, and frequent litigation between rival builders, suggest that the establishments were hastily erected to capitalise on the growing popularity of the boulevard. Surviving illustrations remind one of the newly built 'towns' erected for American Westerns.

One of the charms of the boulevard was its social mix; you could not immediately discern whether an elegant young woman was a duchess or a whore. Curtius was located in a boulevard that for nearly a hundred years was the chief entertainment centre for Parisians, although more consistently downmarket than the Palais Royal. It was patronised by artisans from the adjacent Rue St-Denis and neighbouring streets, but it also attracted the wealthy to see special performers. Artisans were enthusiastic and regular theatre-goers, crowding into the pit. The police set prices at levels the poor could afford, from 6 to 24 *sous* a ticket. The hours of the Boulevard du Temple fitted the artisans' work routine. Performances started between 5 and 6 p.m. and finished in time for an early bed and work at the crack of dawn next day. Unlike the rich, who dined before they set off for the theatre, artisans took their food with them or bought it at one of the stalls. They ate their sausages, cold meat and bread, and drank enthusiastically during the performances, as well as in the interval. They were noisy participants and threw themselves with abandon into the melodramas that were the staple fare. The Boulevard du Temple was often referred to as the Boulevard du Crime, because so many murders and thefts took place on stage. Partly this corresponded to the taste of the clientele, but in addition more prestigious theatres, such as the Opéra, insisted that the little boulevard theatres could not imitate their dramas, but had to stick to mime, pantomime and melodramas.[6]

Curtius's most acclaimed wax show was in the Palais Royal. In the 1770s the gardens of the palace, home to the duc d'Orléans, the king's cousin,

7. Curtius's *Salon de Cire*.

were a well-established and fashionable spot in which the wealthy sauntered to chat and gossip. In 1781 the duc, head of a perpetually impecunious because perpetually spendthrift family, made over the building to his son, the duc de Chartres. Both palace and gardens were in desperate need of repair. The crown agreed to fund renovation, as long as Chartres matched the total spent. Thus began the commercial exploitation of the grounds. Plans were drawn up for enclosing the previously open gardens, initially to the anger of wealthy neighbours, although they were won over as property prices rose. Arcades were to be built on three sides, with public promenades running along the front of each. The ground floors were, as today, let as shops, cafés and theatres, while the upper floors provided workrooms and living space for the tenants. In return for a nine-year lease, the tenant agreed to pay all the construction costs and the lighting of his section of the arcade. A prospective tenant needed substantial funds, and the prospect of instant profit. A typical lease cost 37,500 *livres*, payable in four instalments, with an advance deposit of 3750 *livres*.[7] Curtius was one of the first tenants in the new building, an indication of the success of the *caverne*. His *salon*, in the same arcade as the Théâtre des Variétés, may have opened in 1783, before the whole arcade was completed.[8] His establishment was first publicised in 1784, when its neighbours were the Café des Arts and the Fantoccini Chinois (Chinese shadows).[9] In 1789 he moved to a different arcade and, according to a 1791 entertainment guide, he was still there in 1791, but a pamphlet written by Curtius in 1789, and Marie Tussaud's memoirs, indicate that Curtius had left the Palais Royal by July 1789.[10] Marie claimed that Curtius closed this *salon* because of the embarrassing expansion in the number of prostitutes, but that seems unlikely, as quite a number of these women patrolled the boulevard too.

The shops in the arcades of the Palais Royal looked much as they do today, but the gardens were longer and leafier. An additional underground level was dug out, initially with the hope of moving Astley's very popular equestrian circus from the Boulevard du Temple. There were objections that there was insufficient space, but the area was used for dances and games, then for a ménagerie, until it burnt down in 1799.

By 1784 funds to build galleries in stone were exhausted, and temporary covered wooden galleries were erected and leased at 49,247 *livres*, a massive price rise, but presumably indicative of their profitability. The majority of the units were let as boutiques to merchants, many of them far from honest. Used 'exclusive' clothing was sold at inflated prices, jewellery was advertised as being 'gold' and 'diamond', when, away from the dim lighting of the shop's interior, its inferior quality was only too apparent. There were confectioners, pastry-cooks, and shops selling imported foods, including English peppermints. A wine-shop sold overpriced wines from Cyprus and Madeira, as well as Bordeaux. Then there were pedlars, selling anything from stolen dogs, fancy men for lonely ladies and vice-versa, and expensive loans. A particular attraction were the pedlars-turned-booksellers who gravitated to the Palais Royal because it was so fashionable. Their numbers increased after 1767 when the government relaxed restrictions on the number of master booksellers in response to a growth in demand.[11] The chestnut seller was dressed as a Franciscan friar and sat on an ebony throne, shouting his wares. There were thirty-one gambling houses, including some where ladies offered cold English tea to accompany the gambling.[12] There was also a billiard hall and numerous restaurants and cafés, all at inflated prices.

The shops competed to make the Palais Royal the mark of entrepreneurial distinction at that time. It was a mosaic of elite and popular culture, of sparkle and sleaze, with clients from both high and low society. The promenades that fronted the wooden galleries, nicknamed the Camp of the Tartars, quickly became a favourite with young layabouts, thieves and a rapidly growing number of glamorously dressed whores who hustled for business. There were also the less expensive girls, who before 1789 began their parade around nine in the evening, with no attempt to hide their purpose. Before the Revolution they wore furs, satins and plumed hats, but in 1789 their hair was tied in blue ribbons and their gowns became much simpler. The young *courtisanes* could pass as very respectable ladies. At the highest level, about a dozen of these 'luxurious and hypocritical' females toured the gardens, ate at the best restaurants, recruited at the Opéra and the Théâtre Français, and were said to spend around an astronomical 50,000 *livres* a year each. Business was good; they lived, usually with a less attractive friend, in elegantly furnished apartments on the second floor of the new galleries. Their favourite catch was a foreigner, with whom they would do the rounds of fashionable society in Paris and the country.[13] After Napoleon's defeat cartoons showed them shamelessly offering their services to lonely Russian, British and other foreign officers and diplomats.

By 1815 the gardens were apparently almost submerged in whores, but in the 1780s the Palais Royal was the peak of fashion, the place where those who wanted to be seen having a good time paraded, drank coffee or chocolate, read and discussed newspapers and made assignations often at little tables under the trees. In the summer of 1789 they also listened to impromptu radical political speeches. One of the most influential and discriminating of those who publicised the charms of Paris, Mercier, enthused, 'This enchanted place is a small luxurious city enclosed in a large one ... It is called the capital of Paris. Everything can be found there'.[14]

Undoubtedly one of the great attractions for the rich was that pleasure was spiked with the thrill of illegality, even danger, while for the poor the gardens offered fun, and, for the unscrupulous, rich pickings. For high and low society there was the security that this seductive public space was in fact private. Police could only enter with the permission of the duc d'Orléans. Some of the shops verged on the wrong side of the law, there were illegal gaming establishments and booksellers who did a lively trade in obscene volumes. More than anything else the charm of the Palais Royal was the entirely novel way the royal owner welcomed and profited from the transformation of the gardens into a completely new and different type of venue for popular public pleasures. The duc d'Orléans was no absentee landlord and set a trend for royal marketing that we have grown to expect today, but which was new in the 1780s.

The Curtius exhibition in the Palais Royal has been acclaimed in recent years 'the greatest show in pre-revolutionary Paris, the centre of a renaissance of marketplace culture'.[15] It was arranged to resemble a gathering at a typical *salon*, hence its name. The rich and ambitious would meet to show off and talk at *salons*, often run by women. Calling his exhibition a *salon* was a clever marketing ploy to draw in customers who would never have a chance of meeting Voltaire or the royal family, or of being invited to an actual *salon*. Curtius would mingle with the more distinguished visitors, much as those who ran real *salons* circulated among their guests. There were floor-to-ceiling columns which marked off the central area, in which the Versailles dinner scene and other tableaux were displayed. Single figures stood behind the colonnades and busts were displayed around the walls.[16] Surviving illustrations of the Palais Royal exhibition show the way in which busts were mounted on short columns just as bronze or marble busts would be displayed around the walls of a wealthy private collector. Occasionally a critic would suggest that Curtius was deliberately parodying this tradition, but his desire to please his customers makes such subtle intentions unlikely.[17] Building on Curtius's success at the St-Laurent and St-Germain fairs the busts were interspersed with 'rare, precious and unusual paintings and sculptures'.[18] This added to the snobbish appeal of the collection to those who were keen to say they had seen this or that expensive work of art, but who did not have the connections to secure an invitation to view one of the private collections. Curtius was intrigued by light and specialised in devising innovative ways of illuminating the room, which was always brilliantly lit. Commentators invariably remarked on the exceptional lighting. People were used to theatres being lit during the performance, but dim in the intervals, and theatres were never as bright as Curtius's *salon*. Curtius's *salon* also appealed to respectability and family groups because whores were not allowed to ply their trade as they were at the theatre.

The Palais Royal was always part of the itinerary of foreign visitors, particularly the English, who tended to comment on its charms. Mrs Cradock, a wealthy middle-class English visitor, notched up two visits to the waxworks, both on after-dinner excursions. Her first visit was in February 1784, when her husband was voluble in his approval. Mrs Cradock herself was impressed by a tableau of Voltaire, Rousseau and Franklin, 'the workmanship was so good that the very character of theses famous, though baneful, men was conveyed by their appearance'. In July 1784 the Cradocks ate ice-cream in the Palais Royal and then went to look at the most talked-about tableau, the king and queen at dinner in Versailles. Mrs Cradock, a stickler for etiquette, noted that, although the king of Sweden was present, he was not seated, but standing at the king's side, because he was in France as a private individual not as the king. (Actually it was a model of the queen's brother, Joseph II, recalling a visit that had been very popular with Parisians.) She was bowled over by the model of Frederick the Great, 'All the busts were very good likenesses, but that of the king of Prussia, surpassed all one could have hoped for; you would have thought that it was actually living'. Mrs Cradock was entranced that the place was so crowded, but less thrilled by the heat and dust, so left before 10 p.m.[19] Like theatres, the waxworks closed early. Undoubtedly Curtius's *salon* was a recognised 'must' where bustling Americans, English and others had to go so they could boast about the experience.

For twelve *sous* rich visitors like the Cradocks could wander among the models and touch them, imagining they were in a real *salon* with distinguished guests eager for clever conversation. Less well-off clients paid a mere two *sous* for a view from a roped-off raised area at the rear. They got double value, pondering which of the notables below was wax and which real. For an additional twenty-four *sous* customers could go down to the basement and watch a ventriloquist perform twice daily. Following the fashion of the day, Curtius displayed 'natural history' exhibits. Alongside a collection of plants were also grotesque humans. Visitors could see this miscellaneous fairground stuff alone for a mere two *sous*. The waxworks were competitively priced; even the theatres frequented by the labouring classes on the boulevards charged between six and twenty-four *sous* a ticket. It must have been something of a shock to Curtius's elite customers to have to pay. They were accustomed to very different treatment at the theatre. On occasions only a tiny proportion of an audience in the more exclusive theatres paid for tickets, although working-class audiences in boulevard theatres like the Boulevard du Temple always paid. Playwrights and actors always had free tickets to distribute. Government officials did not pay. Even customers who had paid would ask for their tickets to be marked 'complimentary' because it made them feel important and won them kudos with their companions, especially their lady friends. One of Curtius's neighbours in the Palais Royal, the Théâtre Montansier, regularly handed out fifty free seats to the local prostitutes, who were placed in a prominent balcony at the front. They attracted customers to the play and used the interval to make, and sometimes complete, assignations. Boxes were good for such commerce.[20]

The late eighteenth-century entertainment business relied to a large extent on annually published guide books or almanacs for publicity.[21] Those with time and money on their hands would identify what to see and where to be seen in the almanacs. Unlike newspapers, which might give brief information on the current 'spectacles', almanacs gave detailed critical appraisals of theatrical presentations and exhibitions. They also supplied more than the basic news on the cultural life of the capital. Alongside information on items in the Curtius exhibition and others, some dealt in

8. The French royal family at dinner, a tableau in Curtius's *Salon de Cire*.

dirty ditties, gossip about theatrical matters and titillating tales of whores, flagellation and the most famous pornographer of the day, the marquis de Sade.[22] Curtius's exhibitions were lauded with praise by the almanacs and newspapers of the day.

> The Curtius *cabinet* is well worth a visit. The wax models are so close to nature you could take them for real. The display is constantly changed in response to striking and noteworthy events.[23]

Models were very different from the modern ones to be seen at Madame Tussaud's today. They consisted of wax busts with a very rough body shape in wood or leather covered in clothes. Some wax models, then as later, were made from existing stone or bronze busts.[24] If possible Curtius made the head and hands directly from life – hence he was inclined to describe himself as a wax modeller rather than sculptor, the term preferred today. He would begin by putting oil on his subject's skin and pomade to flatten any facial hair. Then he applied a fine plaster of Paris mask, putting straws or quills in his sitter's nostrils, to allow the person to breathe. These were not needed if he was making a model of someone who had died. Marie Tussaud forgot the straws on one occasion and almost 'lost' her subject, ironically a purveyor of patent medicines. The next stage was the one that required most skill if the model was to be lifelike. Curtius would make a clay 'squeeze' or model of this mask and carefully check and improve it to ensure it was the best possible likeness. A final clay mould would then be made in two pieces to allow the finished wax head to be extracted. Hot wax was poured into the mould, just the right amount so that the wax head would be hollow to the correct degree. As it cooled and set, surplus wax was poured off. This process depended on air temperature, and required considerable skill and judgement. The wax used was a not dissimilar mixture to that used by Tussaud's today: bleached beeswax and japan wax, which is a vegetable tallow, combined in the proportions of three to one. Some old wax would always be used, not just for economy but because it reduced shrinkage and coloured the wax.[25] When the wax was set, the pieces of the clay mould would be removed and any necessary finishing done. Then the head would be coloured and genuine human hair inserted one hair at a time. Finally glass eyes, tinted to match the subject, were put in place. Actual human teeth were often used. Curtius, and Madame Tussaud after him, always preserved the clay mould from which they made the final wax head of any subject they considered historically significant. If the person became controversial, which was often the case during the Revolution, the mould was kept hidden.

Then as now, there was no shortage of ambitious and eager models, willing also to supply a set of their own clothes in the cause of authenticity. One of the charms, or idiosyncrasies, of wax museums is the eclectic mix of people who in chronology or social ambience would never have associated with each other. Housed in the Palais Royal show were Voltaire, Rousseau, Necker, the duc d'Orléans and Benjamin Franklin. Keen to assert Curtius's credentials, Marie emphasised in her memoirs that Voltaire, Benjamin Franklin and especially Rousseau were frequent dinner guests, Rousseau attracted by her mother's Swiss cooking, but we have no more than her word that Curtius actually entertained such illustrious people. Marie described how the comte de Mirabeau, who later took the lead in the first phase of the Revolution, often ate and drank too much at Curtius's together with the duc d'Orléans.[26] The future violent revolutionary Marat was a close friend of Curtius, both being doctors and very interested in optics and light. Another visitor was the abbé Sieyès, who did much to shape revolutionary demands for political representation.

In 1778 when, shortly before his death, Voltaire apparently accepted an invitation to dinner to see the exhibition, Marie was given the job of making his wax model. The wax Voltaire was later put on display sitting at a table, surrounded by books. She also modelled Benjamin Franklin.[27] Marie took both busts and moulds to England, where they are still part of the display. Curtius himself made a miniature of Voltaire on his deathbed. The waxworks reflected an eclectic mixture of unreformed royalism and enlightenment combined with eroticism and violence. Wax philosophers and politicians hobnobbed with the ostentatious and salacious charlatan hypnotist Mesmer, presumably in the famous mauve robes in which he wafted around his consulting salon, charming the ladies. A model of the grand cascade at the royal palace of St-Cloud always drew crowds. Frederick II of Prussia set people talking because he looked so drab and down-at-heel, compared with the ostentation of most models. His model was wearing the king's own clothes which he had insisted on donating. At his side were three of his uniforms, also rather threadbare. To please male visitors, a very glamorous Louise Contat reclined on a coach. Recalling anatomical waxworks whose realism often verged on the pornographic was a tableau of Pyramus and Thisbe, the famous lovers of classical antiquity, in which Thisbe's body could be opened to reveal her inner workings.

What fascinated the crowds most of all was the tableau Mrs Cradock had admired showing the royal family at dinner in the palace of Versailles. This display caused a sensation. In true fairground tradition, Curtius employed a barker outside the exhibition to call out 'Come this way, ladies and gentlemen! Come and see the royal family at dinner! Exactly as at Versailles'.[28] Although anyone could go to Versailles and watch the royal family at dinner, visiting Curtius's tableau replicated and almost improved the experience. In some ways the *salon de cire* display went one better than driving out to Versailles to watch the real Marie-Antoinette eat her dinner and possibly being too embarrassed to have a good look or having to shuffle past rapidly in a queue of socially mixed citizenry. Then, as now, the waxworks gave ladies an unparalleled opportunity to examine in as much detail as they liked what the rich and famous wore and to gossip to gullible and less enterprising friends about intimate details of the queen's toilette. They could gaze, at close quarters and at leisure, at copies of the clothes and jewels Marie-Antoinette actually wore. Curtius commissioned Rose Bertin, the queen's favourite dressmaker, to reproduce her most loved gown.[29] Marie also modelled the king's two sons and surviving daughter. The sons are with their parents in the present-day exhibition. If the ladies liked to spy on the royals at dinner, presumably Curtius's tableau of the queen preparing for bed in a low cut nightgown had a direct appeal to the men.

What the royal entourage ate, and their furniture, seem to have been represented more cursorily, as were their actual bodies. Realism stopped short at the breast with full-size models. This was not the case with the small table top miniatures in erotic poses which were Curtius's speciality and which he made for private customers. These were a great success among the Parisian elite and, it was rumoured, were the biggest money-spinner of all.[30]

In the years leading up to the Revolution, wax models were so fashionable that when the ruler of Mysore, Tippoo Sahib, sent an embassy to the court, they visited Curtius's *salon*. Tippoo Sahib had a great respect for French culture, equalled only by his eagerness to employ French officers in his campaigns against the British army. His ambassadors were impressed by the Curtius exhibition. They were told by some courtiers that there were other wax effigies at Versailles, and were, it seems, taken in by courtiers posing in glass cases. Instead of being insulted by the trick, the delegation all ordered models of themselves to be cast, presumably by Curtius.[31] Tippoo Sahib ordered copies of the models of the king and queen at dinner. When Madame Tussaud took the exhibition to Britain, her catalogues included a model of Tippoo Sahib himself. Given the Muslim ban on representing the human form, the sultan and his ambassadors were breaking their own strict religious rules.

A particular favourite in the *salon* was the shirt Henry IV of France was wearing when he was stabbed by Ravaillac, with the tear (and blood) made by the dagger still visible and of course with certificates of its authenticity. Since the king's assassination was followed by prolonged civil war, the shirt

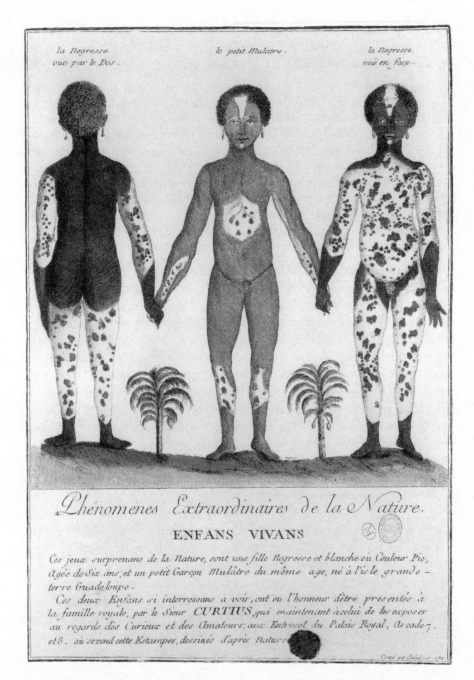

9. 'Extraordinary Pheonomena of Nature', in Curtius's *Salon de Cire*.

was a dramatic and popular item in the show. Madame Tussaud took it with her to England and her catalogue gave a gruesome account of the murder and Ravaillac's fate.

> A gloomy fanatic, and having conceived that Henri IV had given him offence, he mortally stabbed him while in his coach and surrounded by his guard. The act was of the greatest wickedness, but the punishment inflicted on Ravaillac was a disgrace to his judges; his right hand was consumed in a cauldron of boiling brimstone, his flesh was pulled from his bones with red hot pincers, boiling oil and resin, and brimstone was poured into his wounds, and melted lead into his navel. To put an end to his misery, four horses were fastened to the four quarters of his body and on the horses being whipped he was literally torn to pieces. Though he denied having any accomplices his parents were banished, and every person bearing his name was compelled to renounce it that the name of Ravaillac might no more be heard in France.[32]

While a very large part of the Curtius exhibition consisted of the royal, rich and famous, the mezzanine floor included standard fairground stuff, for instance 'Extraordinary Phenomena of Nature'. These were young children, neither entirely black nor white but piebald. Customers could see an Egyptian mummy, a princess of Memphis, who had died, it was claimed, three hundred years ago (so the almanac writer assured his readers). Then there was a wax nude, 'la belle Zulima', supposedly a Turkish harem slave or odalisque, who had, reputedly, been dead for two hundred years, but was still in good shape. Her hair partly covered her breasts but, for an extra fee, the customer could lift the tiny piece of material spread over her lower torso.[33] Even if few live whores frequented the exhibition, it was not entirely free of titillation. Finally, customers could gaze at Paul Butterbrodt, who weighed in at 238 kilograms. The renovated wicker elephant was also on show, plus a large map of Paris.[34]

Curtius's successor Marie Grosholz (1761–1850), the future Madame Tussaud, was trained by him and worked as his assistant. Born in Strasbourg, her written French always remained somewhat Germanic. Her mother, widowed before Marie was born, was Curtius's housekeeper in Berne and followed him to Paris. Curtius always treated the child as a close relative. As with almost everything to do with waxworks, Marie Grosholz's parentage was ambiguous. She always referred to Curtius as her uncle, but there is no baptismal evidence and he may well have been her father. When he died he left everything to her. There were even rumours that Marie was the daughter of the prince de Conti's son. This tale must have had its attractions for the mature Madame Tussaud. Years later in England, she liked to be able to claim that she had hobnobbed with the royal family and descendants liked to lay claim to the Bourbon nose. Dressed in her black bonnet and shawl, Marie at the same time clung tight to bourgeois respectability.

Although Louis XIV had established Versailles as the home of the monarchy, the court and nobility also dominated pre-revolutionary Paris. Curtius's waxworks reflected the appeal of kingship and its attendant display. The latter held a particular appeal to gentlemen visitors. The *salon* included invitingly horizontal ladies, including Louis XV's mistress, Madame du Barry. In her memoirs Madame Tussaud claimed that one of Curtius's first commissions when he settled in Paris was to model Jeanne Vaubernier, soon to be wed to Monsieur du Barry and become Louis XV's mistress. Madame Tussaud included this model in the collection of models she transported to England in 1802. Reclining on a bed, Madame du Barry, was given a mechanical beating heart, which could easily be seen rising and falling under her skimpy frock. 'Sleeping Beauty', whether or not actually the work of Curtius, and whether it not it really was Madame du Barry, is still on display in the historical French section of the Marylebone Road exhibition. The second odalisque displayed on a couch was the voluptuous Madame St-Amaranthe,

10. Marie Grosholz in 1778, Lithograph used as frontispiece to Madame Tussaud's memoirs (1838).

a renowned flirt who was executed during the Revolution, apparently after she rejected Robespierre's advances. Madame Tussaud also packed her onto the cross-channel boat in 1802.

The new king, Louis XVI, did not add to the collection of royal mistresses, real or in wax. In 1770 he married Marie-Antoinette, the fifteen-year-old sister of the Holy Roman Emperor. For seven years Louis was unable to consummate his marriage because of a condition which required minor surgery. Hunting was his consolation, but the queen found pleasure with other men and ladies. Finally Louis agreed to the necessary operation and in 1778 their first child was born. Popular at first, Marie-Antoinette's frivolity and particularly her extravagance were inappropriate in the severe economic crisis which hit France in the late 1780s. She bought elaborate diamonds and was accused, falsely, of procuring even more. She commissioned her dressmaker, Rose Bertin, to make amazing gowns and matching plumed head-dresses. In 1779 alone she ordered 136 frocks, including forty-three formal gowns.

Curtius began to teach Marie Grosholz how to model in wax when she was a small child. In her memoirs, dictated in old age in the 1830s, Marie described at some length how she had lived at Versailles for eight years while tutoring the king's sister, Madame Elizabeth, in the technique of wax modelling. The memoirs began

> The recollections of an individual, for many years the companion of the
> unfortunate Elizabeth, sister to Louis the Sixteenth, and of one who moved,

11. 'Changing the Heads in the *Salon de Cire*'. French cartoon of 1787 reflecting the rapid turnover of models.

both before and since the downfall of the royal family, amongst the most conspicuous characters of France ...[35]

There is no proof that she ever lived at Versailles. She is not listed in any of the royal almanacs, nor does she appear on any royal payroll.[36] Her claim that she lived in Madame Elizabeth's private apartments at Versailles and that the king's brother, the comte d'Artois, flirted with her, would not have conformed to court etiquette. On the other hand, it is perfectly likely, given the interest in wax modelling shown by the wealthy at the time, that Marie visited Versailles from time to time and coached Madame Elizabeth in wax modelling, especially as Madame Elizabeth is known to have made wax effigies of religious characters. If over the long time gap she embroidered her visits, no one in England was likely to bother to question her claim in the 1830s. Her memoirs give the decided impression that Marie's sympathies always lay with the royal family and aristocrats she observed at that time, rather than with the middle-class revolutionaries of the 1790s. The memoirs were ghosted in the 1830s in Britain when even invented royal links were appealing and it would not have been good for business to emphasise Curtius's involvement in the Revolution.

There is no doubt that Curtius made a brilliant entrepreneurial decision to develop his Boulevard du Temple establishment. Despite the low price of admission, Curtius took up to 100 *écus* or 300 francs on the door each day. The cultural mix of his two exhibitions was ideally suited to the new location. His *caverne* of the great criminals fitted admirably into this setting and attracted the artisan families who flocked to the melodramas, while the wealthy would enjoy the unspoken danger of roughing it at the *salon*. Curtius's wax exhibitions were among the most popular attractions in Paris on the eve of the Revolution. Mayeur de St-Paul, a much-read compiler of almanacs, who looked down on many of the new boulevard entertainments, gave Curtius an enthusiastic endorsement in 1782.

> This hardworking German produces coloured wax heads of such quality that one could imagine that they are alive ... with an entry fee of merely two *sous* they attract a mass of fascinated people from all ranks of society ... Curtius does not miss an opportunity to add something new to his show.[37]

On a later occasion he enthused at even greater length:

> This *salon* is always crowded, and with good reason. The artistic presentation and magnificence are a worthy setting for the superior talents of this outstanding artist. The figures are accurate representations, even down to the facial expressions. The crowds are overwhelmed by astonishment, surprise and admiration.[38]

Other almanacs were rather condescending about the lower tone and social ambience of the *caverne* compared with the *salon*. At the outbreak of the Revolution, however, Curtius was a highly successful entrepreneur who exploited the entertainment market effectively, capturing an elite and popular audience with a swiftly changing show that, as the accolades he received from Mrs Cradock indicate, guaranteed that the customer would come back for more.

3

Revolutionary Paris

At first the 1789 Revolution was an entrepreneurial triumph for Curtius. With the Revolution politics moved from the *salons* and court into the streets. Repeated episodes of conflict between troops and Parisians led to fear and uncertainty, creating unprecedented opportunities for those who reported events and for sure-footed operators of visual media, including both the theatre and waxworks. A waxworks had more of a chance to present up to date impressions of the events of the Revolution than the theatres, whose productions were, both before, during and after the Revolution, carefully censored in advance, making spontaneous and uncensored performances risky.[1] Newspapers were also strictly monitored. No such censorship existed on waxworks, presumably because, until this time, no one had thought to use a wax exhibition to reflect contemporary politics. The rapid and kaleidoscopic changes during the Revolution meant that people, particularly those who could not read the newspapers, were eager for news of who was in power and favour, and especially who had been recently guillotined. From the summer of 1789 waxworks became a vivid source of news for Parisians eager to follow the progress of the Revolution. What was real, what fantasy? Contemporary almanacs and newspapers reported with some envy how successfully the wax 'theatre' had transposed itself into a far more precarious and dangerous world.

The Revolution began in an attempt to solve the crown's imminent insolvency by a one-off consultation of the taxpayers in a representative assembly. The seriousness of food shortages and high prices provoked direct action among artisans and peasants, who did not consider that they had been adequately consulted. Artisan districts in the capital became effervescent. The crucible which helped to turn reform into revolution was the Palais Royal where the duc d'Orléans had always been at the heart of criticism of his royal cousin. People from all social groups were accustomed to mingle there and listen to impromptu political speeches. On 30 June the duc d'Orléans allowed companies of the *gardes françaises*, who had mutinied by refusing to fire on crowds rioting over food prices, to camp on the floor of the *Variétés Amusantes* music hall in the Palais Royal.

Two of Curtius's models became an integral part of the first armed confrontation between royal troops and an angry crowd. They provided a template for the display of more bloody popular violence a few days later. On the afternoon of Sunday 12 July 1789 the gardens of the Palais Royal were crammed with over six thousand people, middle class, peasants, artisans, all enjoying their day off and listening to speeches commenting on the lack of reform and criticising the king for dismissing Necker the previous day. Necker was perceived by people as their saviour, the one man who could solve the economic crisis. While Necker had personally guaranteed a shipment of grain with his own fortune, the word on the street was that the food shortages were due to speculation by merchants, not harvest failure. To show their solidarity with Necker, the crowd, led by the orator and journalist Camille Desmoulins, whose speech in the Palais Royal had stirred them to a frenzy, rushed to Curtius's waxworks in the Boulevard du Temple, where Curtius was closing the doors in response to a decree that theatres should shut because of the political crisis. The crowd demanded the loan of the wax busts of their two popular heroes, Necker and the duc d'Orléans. They also asked for the full-size model of the king, but Curtius insisted it was too fragile to be carried aloft around the streets. It is impossible to know how far this was a spontaneous request which came into people's minds because the models had been on display until very recently in the Palais Royal where they had been meeting. However the astute Curtius, sometimes referred to as 'artist and wax modeller to the duc d'Orléans', turned the event so much to his own advantage, that one wonders whether he had suggested in advance that the busts might be useful in any march or demonstration. Certainly the cost of repairing or renewing the models was minimal compared with their publicity value. They provided one of the most memorable early images of the Revolution. The scene, with the busts held aloft as Desmoulins addressed the crowd, appears in many histories of the Revolution.[2] Modern accounts of 1789 still mention the story of the busts as a dramatic turning point when popular protest escalated into murderous violence for the first time.[3]

When the crowd commandeered the two busts on 12 July 1789 the carefully contrived and controlled artistic illusion of polite enlightenment displayed in the wax *salon* slithered into terrifying reality. The wax heads were wounded around with black crêpe, as for a funeral, speared on pikes and paraded through the streets to the Place Vendôme to emphasise that the crowd identified with the desire for reform evinced by the real Orléans and Necker. Wax models may accurately represent reality, but no one dreamt that the real originals would ever have joined a demonstration; indeed Necker, when he heard of his dismissal, left for Brussels. Confrontation

12. Camille Desmoulins with Curtius's wax heads of Necker and the duc d'Orléans, 12 July 1789.

escalated between protesters and royal guards, struggling to keep order. The head of Necker was hacked about by one of the soldiers, a grim prelude to the fate of real heads two days later. The man carrying the head of the duc d'Orléans was injured and the one brandishing Necker was killed in the skirmishes. Sustained fighting continued between the royal regiments, mostly of German or Swiss origin and regarded as foreign by the crowd, and the *gardes françaises*, who had mutinied and were from similar backgrounds to the Parisian artisans with whom they had fraternised. The wax head of Orléans was returned undamaged that night, but it took six days for Necker to come back, his hair burned and face slashed, but at least wax can be repaired.[4]

Property-owners were alarmed, both by the popular protest and the response of the royal troops. The following day a citizens' militia, the forerunner of the national guard, was organised at the Hôtel de Ville in central Paris near Notre-Dame, not far from the where the skirmishes had occurred. It quickly recruited 48,000 men keen to check repression by royal troops, but also to quell further popular disturbances. Curtius was one of the first to volunteer and was made captain of a forty-strong squad, drawn from his local Pères de Nazareth district. On 23 July he temporarily resigned his commission because he was so busy, although he was careful at the

13. Rioting in the Place Louis XV, 12 July 1789.

same time to donate forty-eight *livres* to the district committee in response to an appeal. He was soon involved in the guard again, as captain of a battalion of *chasseurs* whose job was to guard the city gates to prevent smuggling and to collect revenue on produce entering Paris.

True to his calling, Curtius the entertainer reinvented his image adroitly. The modeller of royals and enlightened thinkers melted into the man of the people. The prosperity of Curtius, a foreigner who had always exploited his connections with the privileged elite, now depended on his ability to stay abreast of revolutionary change. Before 1789 political activites had been restricted to a tiny minority. Within a short time the Revolution made politics more a matter of the streets than of polite debate. All adult males could take the opportunity or accept the obligation to participate. Passively presenting a display of wax models, however politically correct, was no longer enough; those who did not participate in revolutionary events might be judged enemies, then made victims, of the Revolution.

By 14 July 1789 Paris was becoming increasingly lawless. Royal troops were no longer in control. The word spread that the fortress of the Bastille was the key to crushing the popular movement and that it had been reinforced with guns and powder. It was regarded by locals in the faubourg Saint-Antoine as a monstrosity of Gothic torture, where prisoners were held on the command of the government without trial. In reality, just before the Revolution there were government plans for its demolition because it no longer fulfilled any real function.

On 14 July a crowd of about nine hundred demanded that the big guns of the fortress be put out of action and the powder store handed over. The crowd included soldiers who had defected, the traditionally radical artisans of the area, cabinet-makers, joiners, hatters, tailors and owners of *cabarets*. The governor was indecisive. In reality, it was unlikely that the Bastille could have spearheaded a counter-attack on the popular movement, for the fortress had no independent water supply and rations only for a couple of days. Only its very vulnerability in the heart of a volatile artisan district made it a likely focus for popular suspicion and assault. The Bastille was attacked on 14 July not because it was a threat but because it was a soft target.

The Boulevard du Temple was not far away and Philippe Curtius led his squad of national guardsmen to investigate the fighting. At about the same time someone in the crowd cut the chains of the Bastille drawbridge. Some of those who swarmed across thought the drawbridge was being lowered by capitulating troops. Fighting became intense. The men later honoured as the leaders of the attack, Jacob Elie and Pierre-Augustin Hulin, two officers who had defected from royal regiments, arrived mid afternoon, together with other soldiers, *gardes françaises* and a supply of arms. At 5 p.m. the governor, de Launay, capitulated. His alternative was to blow up the powder store, which would have devastated a densely populated neighbourhood.

Ninety-eight of the attackers were killed or died from injuries, but only one defender, which enraged the crowd, who blamed the governor for the death of so many of their associates. De Launay was taken to the Hôtel de Ville where he was beaten to death without any chance to defend himself. Curtius insisted that he had had no part in the murder. At the head of his national guardsmen he escorted a group of the retired soldiers who had been among the Bastille's defenders, first to the Hôtel de Ville and then to a hostelry where they were fed and given beds.[5] Outside the Hôtel de Ville, de Launay's head was hoisted on a pike, surrounded by a crowd of singing and laughing citizens. Within a short time a second head was added, that of de Flesselles, the *prévot des marchands* who was accused of misleading people about stores of arms. He was shot as he emerged from the Hôtel de Ville and his dripping head was speared on a pike.

Although these were impromptu killings, they did not lead to uncontrolled mass slaughter. Displaying human, instead of wax, heads was apparently treated as almost a symbolic sacrament to confirm the victory of the people. Within an hour it seems that the human heads were also copied in wax. According to Madame Tussaud and Philip Astley, the owner of the circus next door, when the severed heads of de Launay and de Flesselles were pulled from the pikes, they were rushed to her at the *salon* for modelling. In her memoirs she claimed that she sat on the steps of the exhibition, with the bloody heads on her knees, taking the impressions of their features. The heads were rapidly completed and were a great success, and not only at the *salon*. Philip Astley ordered a copy of each for display at his circus in London. Astley's copies, advertised as modelled from the actual heads, drew bigger crowds than the drama at Sadler's Wells and the display at the Royal Circus dedicated to the fall of the Bastille. Astley later turned the whole of the stage of his Amphitheatre in Lambeth into a model of Paris, in which he showed the wax severed heads and copies of the uniforms worn by de Flesselles and de Launay, which he had also bought from Curtius.[6]

Horrific tales were told about the condition of the prisoners released from the Bastille. Madame Tussaud recalled, many years later, that after the fortress had been liberated iron cages, eight feet by six feet square, were discovered, in one of which lay a skeleton. In fact the *vainqueurs* found only seven prisoners, despite an extensive search of the vast underground passages, which, rumour claimed, reached as far as Versailles itself. Madame Tussaud made a model of one very confused elderly prisoner, assumed to be the comte de Lorge. His long white beard and emaciated body were held to epitomise the cruel way prisoners had been treated. He had been in the Bastille for thirty years, but was very reluctant to leave. His model was a great attraction in the *salon* and Madame Tussaud bore it off with her to London in 1802.

The Bastille itself was subsequently demolished, Mirabeau, the leading politician in the first stages of the revolution, taking the first ceremonial swing at the walls with a pick.[7] By the end of November most of it had been flattened. Symbolically the destruction of the fortress can be compared with the demolition of the Berlin Wall two centuries later. It became the patriotic focus of the Revolution. Like the Berlin Wall, the ruins immediately became a tourist attraction. A thriving Bastille industry was orchestrated by a friend of Curtius, Pierre-François Palloy. The single fortress mushroomed into hundreds of facsimiles. Bastille-shaped dominoes, paperweights and other mementoes were hawked throughout France. Curtius played the episode for maximum publicity. Madame Tussaud recollected in her memoirs that Curtius took her on a tour of the fortress the day after it had been taken and Robespierre caught her hand to stop her falling on the steps. Curtis displayed a chunk of the masonry from the fortress in his *salon* to authenticate his participation in its fall and to emphasise the glory of the event. A year later a map of the demolished fortress had been carved on this 'last stone from the Bastille'.[8] Madame Tussaud took it off with her to England, where it was displayed in the exhibition until it disappeared during the catastrophic fire of 1925. A wax tableau of the victorious citizens was made, headed by the leaders of the assault on the Bastille, Hulin and Elie.[9] The display also included representations of a number of the liberated prisoners, and two much esteemed cardboard models, one of the fortress before the attack and one of the partly demolished ruin. The taking of the Bastille was the high point of Curtius's role in the Revolution. He made sure he was officially honoured among the *vainqueurs* of the Bastille. He was anxious to publicise his role, presumably to try to wipe away the memory of his previous links with the monarchy. He published a short pamphlet, describing his contribution, together with a total of ten letters or 'certificates', signed by other participants, authenticating his patriotism between July and December 1789. He also joined the Jacobin Club, which at that time was a moderate group.

Within nine days of the fall of the Bastille, two more heads of government officials were speared on pikes, marched in procession and speedily rendered in wax. They were Foulon, named in the government to replace Necker, and Foulon's son-in-law, Bertier de Sauvigny, *intendant* of Paris. After an ill-judged remark that the hungry poor could eat hay, Foulon was strung up from a lamp post. This time it was Curtius who made the wax casts. Foulon's head, 'still dripping blood', was a particular attraction in the *salon*. Wax thus became a medium through which the controlled popular violence of the Revolution was displayed to Parisians, helping to make them accustomed to it and tolerant and complicit witnesses.

Wax models still continued to reflect more sedate and traditional reality. Ironically, in 1790 after the royal family had been obliged by the Paris crowd to move back from Versailles to the Tuileries in central Paris, the Constituent Assembly asked Curtius to display his famous models of the royal family at dinner in Marie-Antoinette's favourite miniature palace at Versailles, the Petit Trianon. The wax images were left to stand in place of the real. The real royal family was hustled back to Paris by a crowd of market women, eager to emphasise that food was dear and in short supply and to persuade the king and queen to take steps to solve the problem.

At first the Revolution was a marketing triumph for Curtius. The new National Assembly set to work to write a constitution and initially they were confident that a constitutional monarchy could be created. Hence

14. The taking of the Bastille, 14 July 1789.

Curtius's model of the king remained the leading attraction, followed by Madame Bailly, wife of the astronomer who was the first president of the National Assembly and, until November 1791, mayor of Paris. Everyone wanted to see the model of Lafayette and other leading figures in the Assembly. Lafayette was a radical aristocrat who had fought with the Americans for their independence. He became the head of the revolutionary national guard or civil militia and in October 1789 led the Parisian market women who marched to Versailles to demand food, and brought both bread and the reluctant royal family back to the capital. The National Assembly followed them and set up home in the Tuileries. To his annoyance, instead of leading his national guard squad to Versailles on that occasion, Curtius had had to keep order in the empty part-demolished Bastille. He had a large and rather self-important portrait made of himself in his uniform, which is still prominently displayed in the Carnavalet Museum. In June 1790 the Assembly officially acknowledged, despite some jealous grumbles, the significant role of the *vainqueurs de la Bastille*. Curtius, never one to indulge in false modesty, always signed his letters *vainqueur de la Bastille*. All the *vainqueurs* were presented with a certificate, a badge inscribed with a victor's wreath, and a gun and sword. Curtius's gun and sword had pride of place in his exhibition, but Madame Tussaud did not take them with her to Britain.

Curtius continued to market the Revolution to his own great advantage.

In place of the erotic waxes which had brought him so much profit, Curtius now secured orders to make wax funeral effigies in the style of classical Greece and Rome, the revolutionary alternative to Catholic imagery. On the orders of the National Assembly, he made a model of Voltaire to be part of the massive procession staged by the artist Jacques-Louis David in July 1791. A lengthy cortège accompanied Voltaire's body, and its waxen image, to the Panthéon. Voltaire lay on an impressive sarcophagus placed in a bronze-wheeled funeral chariot and drawn by twelve white horses. The effigy lay in vermilion robes, and a beautiful girl, representing Immortality, crowned him with a halo of gold-coloured stars.[10] Unfortunately it rained and the vermilion dye streaked the effigy, for which Curtius was roundly berated by a friend of David, the playwright Talma, and by George Duval, one of the officials in the Ministry of the Interior who helped to organise the procession.[11] Nonetheless, participation in such events was good for business. Foreigners still flocked to Paris and processions like the one for Voltaire formed part of their visit. A future British Prime Minister, Palmerston, mentioned the wax effigy in his diary entry for the day.[12] In April 1793 a wax portrait made by Curtius formed part of the huge funeral procession of the Polish patriot Lazowski, during which his tiny daughter of three lay asleep at the feet of the dead man.[13]

At first it had seemed that the movement for radical reform in France might secure almost universal support, including that of the king and of leading nobles and clergy. In August 1789 the Declaration of the Rights of Man and of Citizen and the decision of the privileged orders, the clergy and nobility, to abolish their tithes and feudal privileges, were well received. Immediately after the fall of the Bastille, however, the comte d'Artois, the king's youngest brother, and his cousins, the princes de Condé and de Conti, the heir of Curtius's erstwhile patron, fled into exile in Austria. Later in the year the comte de Provence, Louis XVI's other brother, and many leading aristocrats joined them as émigrés, as the Revolution moved in an increasingly radical direction. Their alliance with Joseph II, the brother of Marie-Antoinette, put Louis XVI in an increasingly difficult position.

The National Assembly set to work to write a constitution and prevent the crown's imminent insolvency. In 1790 the lands of the church (about 15 per cent of the land of France) were confiscated and sold as 'national land'. In future clergy were to be paid by the state, and in return had to take an oath of allegiance to it. Many refused and went into hiding. These policies did more than anything to turn large areas of southern and western France against the Revolution. In June 1791 the king, queen and the king's sister, Madame Elizabeth fled, although when stopped at Varennes they claimed that they had not really been trying to run away to join the émigrés.

Few were convinced. Subsequently it was impossible to believe Louis's claim that he wanted to be a constitutional monarch.

In 1791 Curtius secured a long-coveted honour when, thanks to his friendship with the famous painter, Jacques-Louis David, a coloured wax bust he had made of the Dauphin was admitted to the annual salon of the Academy of France. It was not long, however, before royal and aristocratic models in Curtius's own wax exhibition were mothballed and hidden from view. In 1791 the central theme of the exhibition remained the capture of the Bastille by the citizens of Paris. Sensational and novel displays retained their popularity. Perhaps in tune with growing republicanism, the shirt Henri IV was wearing when his fatal stabbing by Ravaillac in 1610 plunged the country into chaos was still a great draw.[14]

As the Revolution later escalated the different stages of the Revolution could be followed by a glance at the guests seated at the *grand couvert*, which previously had shown the king and queen at dinner in Versailles. Models of Necker and his daughter, Madame de Staël were followed successively by Bailly, Barnarve, Roland and the Girondins. Next came the turn of the popular military commander Dumouriez, then the Committee of Public Safety, with Danton, followed by Robespierre, Collot d'Herbois, Saint-Just and Couthon. The Public Prosecutor, Fouquier-Tinville headed a group from the Revolutionary Tribunal.[15] It was an endlessly adaptable dinner table, where only the wax fruits, table and chairs remained constant. Curtius also included exhibits praising more 'popular' aspects of the Revolution, including a group of bakers' assistants, representing the ad hoc committees set up by the Committee of Public Safety in 1793 to try to maintain adequate supplies of food.

Why did Curtius's exhibition continue to attract crowds? Compilers of almanacs now ascribed his popularity less to the quality or identity of the models on display than to his 'patriotism' and his enthusiasm for the Revolution. Only as an afternote did they recall that the models 'imitated nature to perfection', that they could easily be identified and were authentically clad in period costume. Finally the exhibition was topical. Models were changed every month, providing a unique visual update on the events of the Revolution.

> The honorable artist Curtius, who although a German, is a naturalised Frenchman by his many years residence and above all through the patriotism he has shown on numerous occasions during the Revolution, has for many years run wax exhibitions which imitate nature to perfection both in the Boulevard du Temple and in the galleries of the Palais Royal. On display are rare, precious and unusual paintings and sculptures. The entire exhibition is renewed every year and every month there is something new to see – some are models of fantasy, some full

of character, some beautiful – the ancient world Heroes are instantly recognisable because their costumes are so authentic.

The most popular models this year are those of the king, of Madame Bailly, of La Fayette and of many outstanding members of the National Assembly ... Curtius has taken care to satisfy people's curiosity and taste for new and sensational items.[16]

The exhibition was still so popular that one almanac even included illustrations of the interior of the *salon*, while another remarked that the wax heads were such good imitations of actual statues that you could almost imagine their brains were still intact.[17] You could sense immediately the mood of the times by the costume of the wax doorman: royal military uniform before 1789; then the uniform of the national guard. Finally, as the Paris crowd became more assertive in the Revolution, in June 1792 the doorman was decked out in traditional dress of artisans or sans-culottes so called because they wore trousers, not the knee breeches of the rich.

The Legislative Assembly, elected in the autumn of 1791, soon became internally divided between two main factions, the Girondins and Jacobins. At first the Girondins were in the ascendant, but they were constantly attacked for their supposed tepid revolutionary fervour by the more radical Jacobins, who could command popular support in Paris. In April 1792 the Girondin government took France into war with Austria, on the grounds that the emperor, by shielding French émigrés, including the king's brothers, was encouraging counter-revolution in France. The French assumed that they would secure an easy victory in the Netherlands, where a revolution against the empire had already taken place. The French army was, however, in chaos. Almost two thirds of the officers had deserted and many had joined the émigrés. Equipment was lacking and the economy as a whole was badly disrupted by the Revolution. Led by Lafayette, the army attempted to advance into the Netherlands, but was quickly forced to retreat. In a situation of mounting internal anarchy, a popular revolt in Paris in August 1792 unseated the monarchy. In September 1792 a massacre of prisoners in Paris gaols was followed by the election of a new assembly, the Convention, and the increasing ascendency of the Jacobins. The king and queen were put on trial and on 21 January 1793 Louis XVI was guillotined.

In October 1792 the Jacobin Club, of which Curtius was a member, gave him the job of accommodating Austrian and Prussian deserters who had asked the Jacobins for help. They slept in his house, and, when there were too many, on folding camp beds in the actual exhibition halls. This must have been a considerable burden, not least on Madame Tussaud's mother, who did all the cooking. The episode is confirmed by an otherwise inexplicably large number of camp beds listed among Curtius's possessions at

15. The execution of Louis XVI, 21 January 1793.

20 Boulevard du Temple after his death. The episode was relived in the First World War when John Theodore Tussaud declared open house in Marylebone Road, encouraging soldiers on leave, to rest and recuperate in the galleries if not to sleep there.

At the end of 1793 Curtius was sent on a brief mission to General Custine, commander of the army of the Rhine, where presumably his knowledge of German was helpful. Custine was under investigation by the Jacobins and Curtius's task was to assess Custine's loyalty and patriotism, which he did in favourable terms in a report to the Jacobin Club on his return. He also used the opportunity to pursue his claim to his long lost brother's share of a relative's inheritance.[18] While he was away Marie was left to run the Boulevard du Temple waxworks. As a foreigner, and a showman, Curtius was always anxious to show himself a patriotic citizen and national guard officer. Government strategies to finance the war included demands that all luxury items, especially jewellery, gold and silver, should be turned over to the state; or the property owner risked a house search. Curtius complied fully, as the negligible amount of such goods left after his death shows. In addition, the government sought voluntary donations to finance extraordinary war expenditure. This strategy was regularly used to help pay for the war effort during the revolutionary period. Lists of donors and amounts given, in descending order, were published regularly, and were tangible evidence of a citizen's 'patriotism'. Curtius made a number of these 'voluntary' contributions, including 220 *livres* towards the provisioning of the Rhine army in June 1793.[19] He also made a bust which he presented to the Jacobin Club in November 1793.[20]

Because Curtius was frequently involved in national guard business, Marie usually undertook the gruesome labour of modelling the severed heads of enemies of the Revolution for the Convention. She detailed this quite matter-of-factly in her memoirs. When she dictated her memoirs in the 1830s, she might have expressed horror and disgust, and her British readers would have been sympathetic, but her remarks were restrained and guarded. The reader is left guessing whether Marie was unemotional by nature or simply very circumspect. Probably she was both. She was obliged to make models of many individuals she had known at court, including the princesse de Lamballe, Marie-Antoinette's favourite, when she was murdered during the September Massacres. She was asked to produce a head of Curtius's old landlord, the duc d'Orléans, later known as Philippe-Egalité. She made a death mask of King Louis XVI, after his execution in 1793, and later one of the queen. These last two were never exhibited, it seems on the orders of the Convention. Prudhomme, a journalist, criticised Curtius because he made a tableau of the murder of Lepeletier, a deputy who had voted for the king's death, a day before the king's execution. Curtius never showed a model of the execution of Louis XVI.

There was one tableau that Marie made which did much to preserve the exhibition's popularity and credibility. Marat was one of the most famous, and most bloodthirsty, of the revolutionary leaders. He was stabbed to death on 13 July 1793 in his bath, where he habitually worked to ease a painful skin complaint, possibly leprosy, by the idealist Charlotte Corday, who was appalled by his role in the Terror. Marie claimed that she rushed to the scene to take a death mask of the corpse, arriving so quickly that the murderer was just being taken away as Marie arrived. The murder of Marat was also recorded dramatically for posterity by the famous painter, David. Marie always claimed that David used her wax model of Marat when he painted his own version of events. This is one of the claims in Madame Tussaud's memoirs that is probably accurate. The day after the assassination the Convention ordered David to paint the scene of Marat's death as part of the public mourning for a hero of the Revolution. It was a hot July and, although David went to work immediately wrapping most of the body in wet cloth to delay putrefaction, the corpse rotted so fast that it had to be interred on 16 July. The bath-tub murder scene, one of the most famous images of the Revolution, may have been reconstructed by David in the summer and autumn of 1793 from the wax tableau already on display in Curtius's *salon*. Hence it is no coincidence that *Marat Assassiné*, presented by David to the Convention on 14 October 1793, has a strong resemblance to a wax model rather than a cadaver.[21]

Marie's tableau was displayed in the *salon*, first to show Marat as a martyr, an innocent victim of the Revolution; later, when he was disgraced, marking him as the epitome of an enemy of the Revolution. Wax models tell no tales and can be used to suit the mood of the moment. The Marat display was among the models Madame Tussaud shipped to England with her in 1802. Charles Dickens, a great enthusiast of Tussaud's, recalled seeing 'a man eating an underdone pork pie' and 'a young man from the provinces with a red, beefy neck' gazing at Marat transfixed.[22] Marat and his bath are still on display.

Curtius made a second model of Louis XV's last mistress, Madame du Barry, in December 1793, this time taken from death. When the Revolution came, Madame du Barry was living very comfortably in retirement on her country estate at Louveçiennes. In early 1791 her jewellery was stolen when she was away and she spent the next two years trying to locate it. This included a spell in London, where she socialised with émigrés. Her property was sealed in her absence, and when she came back she was arrested, tried and sentenced to death. She did not greet death with the stoical silence of

1. Guillotined heads modelled by Madame Tussaud. Louis XVI and Marie-Antoinette (right) are opposite the revolutionaries Carrier, Fouquier-Tinville, Robespierre and Hébert (left). Before them is Marat, murdered by Charlotte Corday in his bath. (*Madame Tussaud's Archives*)

2. Bernard Tussaud, with his great great grandmother's last self-portrait in wax. (*Madame Tussaud's Archives*)

3. Bernard Tussaud, working on his model of the broadcaster Richard Dimbleby. (*Madame Tussaud's Archives*)

4. The sculptors' studio, at Madame Tussaud's in the Marylebone Road, at work (right) on the head of King Hussain of Jordan. (*Madame Tussaud's Archives*)

5. Joseph Tussaud, Madame Tussaud's elder son. (*Madame Tussaud's Archives*)

6. Francis Tussaud, Madame Tussaud's younger son. (*Madame Tussaud's Archives*)

7. John Theodore Tussaud, great grandson of Madame Tussaud. (*Madame Tussaud's Archives*)

8. John Theodore Tussaud in his studio. (*Madame Tussaud's Archives*)

9. John Theodore Tussaud and his family. (*Madame Tussaud's Archives*)

10. Bernard Tussaud, great great grandson of Madame Tussaud and the staff, 19 April 1959. (*Madame Tussaud's Archives*)

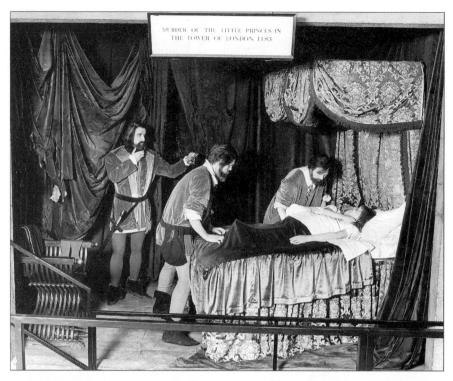

11. The murder of the Princes in the Tower, 1483. (*Madame Tussaud's Archives*)

12. The execution of Mary Queen of Scots at Fotheringhay, 1587. (*Madame Tussaud's Archives*)

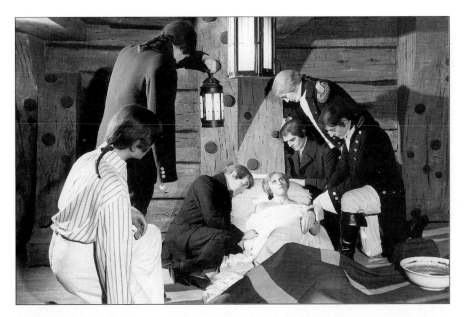

13. The death of Nelson at Trafalgar, 1805. (*Madame Tussaud's Archives*)

14. Napoleon and Wellington at a loss as to what to say to each other. (*Madame Tussaud's Archives*)

15. George VI and Queen Elizabeth's visit, following German bombing that severely damaged Madame Tussaud's on the night of 9/10 September 1940. (*Madame Tussaud's Archives*)

many victims but screamed and struggled. Curtius sorted out her head from the basket of severed heads which were dumped that evening at Madeleine cemetery and made his second effigy of the du Barry. He never displayed it, nor did Madame Tussaud take the model to London, preferring the earlier and more glamorous 'Sleeping Beauty'.

Curtius followed the contemporary trend of moving out of Paris, as far as was compatible with earning a living. In 1793 he began to pay instalments on a small house at Ivry-sur-Seine, not an industrial suburb in those days but a peaceful rural village by the river. The garden produced vegetables, and fruit and chickens could be reared; an invaluable asset in these years of food shortages. Curtius despatched all his property apart from absolute essentials to the new house, echoing the growing sense of unease among Paris residents.

The violence and strident egalitarianism of the Revolution, plus civil and foreign wars, were eventually disastrous to the entertainment industry. The wealthy end of the wax market withered away. Foreign visitors stayed at home. Many French families retired to their country estates, closing down their Paris homes and foregoing the usual winter season in the capital. Some left the country totally and became émigrés. The population of Paris almost halved during the quarter of a century of revolution and war between 1792 and 1815. In June 1792, when Prussia joined Austria in the war, there was real fear that their armies might invade France, following easy and undefended roads to Paris. The government ordered provincial national guardsmen to the capital to strengthen their defences. All the theatres were ordered to close during the crisis, which also presumably hit the wax exhibition.

Because people were enjoined to hand over all but essentials for the war effort, flaunting wealth could be dangerous. Curtius's wax models had to follow the fashion. A wax figure bereft of expensive and elaborate clothes was unimpressive. Before the Revolution a *grande toilette* for a lady included *paniers*, supporting hooped skirts, of which the dress material lay so heavily on her shoulders that she could hardly lift her arms. Dresses were impossibly long and made of thick, rich material, often embroidered in gold. Hoop petticoats were worn. Hair was piled high and decorated with precious stones. Earrings consisted of heavy clusters of diamonds. Men wore richly ornamented embroidered coats with further embroidery on their sashes. Their hair was oiled down and plaited. With the Revolution and the war there was a tendency to uniformity, visual patriotism and ostentatious economy. Anyone who wore obviously expensive and glamorous clothes risked not merely theft but accusations of being a counter-revolutionary, and possibly the guillotine. The rich made a fashion of revolution. Some

Parisian ladies adopted short skirts dubbed *à la circassienne*, with blue, white and red stripes to match the tricoloured flag. Others wore simple short white gowns. Jewellery was simple and might be inscribed with the patriotic messages, 'liberté, égalité, fraternité ou la mort'. Men seem to have escaped the sillier rigours of revolutionary fashion. They retained the traditional culotte or knee breeches and a simple silk stock at the neck. Some fervent revolutionaries ignored the trend to try to look like a member of the *classes populaires*. Robespierre, a short man, was always elegantly dressed. His associate, Saint-Just, liked to wear a sky-blue coat with gold buttons.

16. Maximilien Robespierre.

Conspicuous consumption of luxury goods was no longer either fashionable or politically wise. This had a knock-on effect on Curtius's two *sous* customers. There were simply no orders for the varied luxury consumer goods made in Paris, from gold and silver work, to clothing and furniture. The artisans of the capital therefore faced much-reduced earnings at a time when food prices were high. Many lacked surplus funds for entertainments like the waxworks. Years later in London, Madame Tussaud remembered specifically that by the summer of 1792 they had had to reduce the entrance fee to keep open. In addition, they had great difficulty finding suitable material, even for the austere costumes now required to clothe politicians and military figures. A candle 'famine', still a problem in 1794, was a serious matter for a business so dependent on lighting.

Keeping up with revolutionary events was becoming increasingly tortuous, particularly for someone like Curtius whose exhibition could not fail to indicate clearly where his political sympathies lay. Wax exhibits had to reflect contemporary politics, but the pace of events in the early 1790s made it hard to keep abreast of affairs, even in a material as easy to reconstruct as wax. Perhaps because of Curtius's prolonged absences, perhaps because of the speed and violence of revolutionary changes, the exhibition became dangerously out of date. In August 1792, after his attempt to lead his troops back into France to suppress the revolution of 10 August had failed, Lafayette deserted to the Austrians. Curtius was criticised for leaving his wax effigy on display too long after the event. Eventually he had to apologise to the Convention, and to publicly decapitate the model in the Boulevard outside his *salon*. The war was turned round, partly due to the leadership of General Dumouriez, commander of French troops in the Netherlands. In November 1792 he routed the Austrians at Jemappes and occupied Brussels, to great acclaim in Paris. The Convention now became convinced that French armies could launch wars to liberate the peoples of Europe and by March 1793 it had declared war on most of Europe. Dumouriez, in contrast, expressed disquiet at the way in which the government was running the war and, like Lafayette, tried, in conjunction with the Austrian army commander, to persuade his troops to march on Paris. His aim was to restore a constitutional monarchy in the name of Louis XVI's young son, then a prisoner of the Convention. When his mutiny failed, Dumouriez followed Lafayette into Austrian exile. Unfortunately for Curtius, Dumouriez's statue also lingered too long after his treachery.[23] His support for a third general, Custine, also rebounded. In December 1792, when he had been sent to the Rhine army, Curtius had reported enthusiastically on Custine's patriotism. In August 1793 Custine was guillotined for counter-revolutionary sympathies as well as military failure. No wonder Curtius had to struggle to prove his own revolutionary credentials

As early as its 1792 edition, an almanac which had enthused about Curtius a year earlier was dismissive and curt.

> Curtius has let himself down by publicly insulting worthy men and praising those who have behaved dishonorably. We have nothing whatsoever to say about his exhibition, because it has interested no one since Curtius's patriotism has proved to be false and dangerous.[24]

The almanac also attacked Curtius's artistic skills, curious after the undiluted praise of the previous year. He was criticised for showing substandard models, merely wax heads draped in clothes, but without proper bodies;[25] a strange accusation, since this was the normal way most models, unless for anatomical purposes, were constructed at the time. He was even condemned because all his attractive exhibits had been replaced by drab and transitory models of republican politicians. Yet this was precisely what his critics had demanded. A glimpse of such glamorous royal or aristocratic figures would have meant the guillotine for the proprietor. Apparently the Republican Society of Arts considered closing the exhibition because the models were not good likenesses. David, it is said, criticised the lack of historical accuracy in the costumes, particularly of classical figures such as Brutus.[26]

In 1793–94 the Revolution reached its apogee of uncertainty and violence. Although invasion had been averted and the foreign war was going better, civil war raged in western and southern France and food shortages were acute. By June 1793 the Jacobins, led by Robespierre, had asserted their control. The Jacobin clubs dominated, organising revolutionary festivals and executions. Terror was made the order of the day by the Convention on 5 September 1793. The Jacobin Terror against 'traitors' persisted until July 1794 when Robespierre was overthrown. Over half a million people were arrested. The Revolutionary Tribunal in Paris sentenced 16,594 people to death and up to 40,000 in total were killed, either executed without trial or in prison. The majority perished in Paris, but large numbers were killed in the provinces, particularly in the main centre of counter-revolution, the Vendée, where a total of perhaps 200,000 people died as a direct consequence of civil war during 1793–94.[27]

The processes of the Terror threatened the entertainment industry, not only because the rich shunned Paris, workers lacked funds and people were afraid to be seen having fun; the Terror itself offered a ghastly alternative leisure activity. A highly stylised theatre of injustice was set up, followed by a dramatically staged process of death by the guillotine – and all took place very publicly. The specially-created Revolutionary Tribunal met in the building where the *parlement* had assembled before the Revolution. It was a spacious room, with a high gilded ceiling and a marble floor. The tapestries were stripped from the walls, and the carpet rolled up. The king's throne and Dürer's famous painting of Christ were removed. At the end of the room, behind a long plain table, sat the judges, and in front of them the public prosecutor. The officials did not wear the elegant traditional robes of the pre-revolutionary magistrates, but simple dark clothes with black plumes in their hats. On their left were more tables and chairs for the jury and on their right a stepped platform for the accused. Opposite them was the bar, where witnesses stood to give their evidence. The public always crowded into the room and overflowed into the passageways and staircases. When they made too much noise, the chief judge gave orders for the courtroom to be cleared.

The judges, public prosecutor and the jury were all convinced revolutionaries. From October 1792, a captured émigré returned to France faced a certain death penalty, as did anyone with monarchist leanings, or even those simply suspected of conspiring against the new republic. The public prosecutor, Fouquier-Tinville, drew up regular lists of suspects, and Robespierre ticked those who were to die next day. The jury, nominated by the Convention, and well-paid at 18 *livres* a day, was merely a rubber stamp. Defiance would have meant their own death.

The accused were not told the charge until just before they faced the tribunal and often the same charge was levelled at a whole batch of prisoners. Sometimes a prisoner protested when the charge was being read out, but was shouted down, 'You have no right to speak'. After the charge had been read out and the evidence heard, the jury retired to consider their verdict. When they returned to the court, the judge asked each of the jurymen in turn, 'Was there a conspiracy against the unity and indivisibility of the

17. Antoine Fouquier-Tinville. The public prosecutor during the Terror, he was himself guillotined in May 1795.

republic, against the liberty and safety of the French people?' Each juryman stood to answer, 'On my honour and conscience, the case is proven'. After the judges had passed the death sentence, the jurymen retired to their quarters below the courtroom for a good meal. They were given plenty to drink and sang the night away. Up to sixty people were condemned every day during the Terror and within twenty-four hours all were dead. Important trials took longer. Marie-Antoinette was accused at 8 a.m. and in court until 4 a.m. the next day, without food or water.

The next stage in the theatre of Terror, the daily public and ceremonial execution of an increasing numbers of victims, provided 'entertainment' for far more people than the trial itself. At 8 a.m. on the day after the verdict, the condemned were taken in a cart from the Conciergerie prison, where they had been held during and after their trial. Marie-Antoinette had a cart to herself, but generally substantial numbers were crowded in together, accompanied by a guard of gendarmes. The lieutenant of the gendarmerie who took the queen from her trial to her death made the mistake of doffing his hat to her, giving her some water and helping her down the steps, for which he was denounced to the tribunal. A priest accompanied the prisoners. Behind them in another cart rode Sanson, the executioner, and his assistant. The carts bumped slowly along the route towards the Rue St-Honoré. It would be midday before the condemned reached the Tuileries, leaving plenty of opportunity for onlookers to shout abuse at them. Finally they reached the Place de la Révolution where the guillotine stood, surrounded by a barrier to keep the crowds away. People usually shouted 'Vive la République!' when the blade fell, but when the queen was executed a hush fell on the large crowd.

It is strange to think that death by the guillotine was adopted by the revolutionaries because it seemed a more humane method of execution. In August 1789 the National Assembly decided to find an egalitarian method of execution, so that privileges of birth and wealth did not extend to the way a criminal died. The Penal Code of 25 September 1791 decreed death by public decapitation, but the deputies could not agree on the method and a backlog of condemned criminals built up. Charles-Henri Sanson, who had inherited the job of public executioner, advised the deputies that there were too many condemned for his two swords to execute. Even one execution would blunt a sword, and often it took more than one blow to complete the process. In March 1792 Dr Joseph-Ignace Guillotin (1738–1814), a distinguished reforming doctor, proposed execution by a quicker, more accurate method. He did not, however, invent the machine which soon took his name. It had been used for executions in Europe for centuries and was known as the 'Maiden' in Scotland. It was initially referred to as the

'Louison' or 'Louisette' in France after Dr Guillotin's colleague, Dr Antoine Louis, secretary of the Academy of Surgery, who drew up the plans for the French model. It was used for the first time on 25 April 1792.

Red was the colour of death. The guillotine and the baskets ready to hold the decapitated corpses were painted red. Two ten foot high grooved uprights were placed twelve inches apart and a convex blade, secured by two ropes, was set in a holder that slid up and down in the grooves. The victim was placed face down on a wooden bench with his head beneath the blade. The victim's neck was held firmly in place by a lunette, literally a moon-shaped piece of iron set within a metal crescent. When the ropes were released the knife fell accurately in less than a second. At some stage the convex knife was replaced by the characteristic sloping one. Rumour had it that it was the king who recommended the improvement.

The stage for the guillotine was the Place de la Révolution, the present-day Place de la Concorde. Hawkers sold lists of who were to be executed each day and a restaurant owner included the names on his menu. Seats were arranged to provide a comfortable view; the side next to the Jardin des Tuileries being considered the prime site. People went repeatedly to stare at the scene and families took their children. The guillotine was set up in the centre, next to a huge statue of Liberty, complete with Phrygian cap, spear and shield. Carts, filled with big baskets for the bodies, were lined up on one side. The victims were taken by cart to the base of the guillotine and led one at a time up the steps.

All participants to the mass guillotinings of the Terror were deeply conscious that they were taking part in a public performance. Most of those executed during the Jacobin Terror were accused on political, not criminal, grounds. People compared the ritual and ceremonial to a theatre, with agreed rules on how to die. Next day's victims practised their role in the prison. With few exceptions, people were determined to demonstrate their innocent sacrifice and loyalty to the Republic by dying with stoical dignity. Madame du Barry was scorned because she screamed and resisted. Although the actual moment of death was swift and the final agony was not prolonged, the procession to the Place de la Révolution was slow and long drawn out, and the sight of the death of earlier victims must have tested the courage of those waiting. Female victims tried vainly to stay modest and keep their bodies and legs covered as they arranged themselves on the block. The most dramatic moment was the one the victim missed, when the blade struck and the head bounced away violently to the accompaniment of fountains of spurting blood. The head and body were flung into a basket, the wooden block perhaps wiped down cursorily, and the process repeated. The actual beheading was so swift and mechanical that in the Terror onlookers must have become numbed to the routine, almost forgetting that human life was being sacrificed. They were not entirely desensitised, however, for in hot weather the Place de la Révolution smelled like a knacker's yard. Later the guillotine was moved to a more plebeian district, the Place de Grève, today the Place de l'Hôtel de Ville.

The guillotine quickly came to exert a terrible fascination. The Terror had to be turned to humour of sorts to be bearable. The guillotine became a standard theatrical prop.[28] As well as numerous illustrations, people sang comic songs about the guillotine. Louise Contat, the *Comédie Française* actress who was saved from death by Robespierre's fall, had her own guillotine ditty ready.

> I'm going to climb the scaffold
> 'Tis only a change of theatres.

Toy guillotines were sold for cutting bread and some *salon* hostesses provided additional amusement for their guests with tiny dolls, who looked like the enemy of the day, filled with 'blood' (perfume) to fly out after decapitation. Children chopped off the heads of dolls, birds and mice with two-foot high toy guillotines.[29] People even became bored and attendance at executions fell in the months before Robespierre's fall.

Philippe Curtius showed the first of the toy guillotines, a quarter-size model, in his *salon* as well as a growing display of deaths' heads. Very quickly the victims realised that their wax head would live on, and apparently they regarded this macabre practice with pride rather than revulsion. People about to face the guillotine often asked for their portrait to be painted. One such was Charlotte Corday. Later in the century it became the norm to take a photograph of the severed head,[30] although by then it was usual for the Grévin waxworks to model the victim before death. Although Curtius established the trend of modelling the harvest of the guillotine, the Terror brought him little profit. The ubiquitous atmosphere of suspicion and the unpredictable witch-hunts against individuals seem to have been disastrous for the wax business. The toy guillotine did not work the magic that the Bastille models had wrought for him. Customers were afraid to comment on the rapidly changing exhibits for fear that they might be the next victim. Curtius's problem of a lack of customers may also have been related to competition, not least the daily guillotine performance.

The fashion for ghostly magic lantern shows may have echoed on stage the atmosphere of the real political Terror of 1793–94 more successfully than wax displays. The magic lantern was ideal entertainment for this Romantic age which gloried in newly-built 'ruins', freshly-written medieval literature, horrific fairy tales set in ghastly castles, and Gothic-style novels, such as *The Monk* written by M. Lewis in 1796, followed two years later by *The Castle Spectre*.[31] Audiences were programmed to delight in sitting in total darkness in a magic lantern show, complete with sound effects and mystifying smoke, to enjoy stylised horror. A *phantasmagorie* was first staged in Paris by a Belgian, Etienne Robertson, and quickly became a popular entertainment.[32] Robertson put on his show first in the Palais Royal and then went a series of European tours.

One of Curtius's associates, Paul Philipstal, also staged a *phantasmagorie* in the nearby hôtel de Chartres, rue Richelieu. The climax of his show was a red devil, complete with cloven hooves, whose face successively resembled Marat, Danton and finally Robespierre. Even magic lantern impresarios could step out of line. In 1793 Curtius had to negotiate Philipstal's release from prison, after he had apparently mistakenly shown an image of the recently-guillotined king on his magic lantern screen. When the operator realised his mistake, he had added to his disgrace by withdrawing the picture of the king upwards, which, it was suggested, gave the illusion that that the monarch was ascending to heaven.

Curtius struggled to keep pace with revolutionary politics, despite his apparently successful attempts to cultivate Robespierre. Marie claimed that Robespierre was a frequent guest at dinner. In October 1793 Curtius made another 'patriotic' donation. The *salon*'s problems were also exacerbated by a persistent illness that dogged Curtius after his mission to the Rhine army. In early 1794 business was so slow that Curtius sent twenty of his compromising models of the royal family on a successful two-year tour of India in the care of an Italian showman, Dominick Laurency. Their sumptuous outfits, including the queen's Rose Bertin gown, went with them, being not merely superfluous but dangerous in Paris. Accompanying them were assorted, and presumably also politically inappropriate, foreign dignitaries, together with Voltaire, Rousseau and an optic of Zaler. This last was a charming optical illusion that showed sunrise over the capital cities of Europe. One of the most popular, though less attractive, exhibits mentioned in the newspapers in both Calcutta and Madras, proved to be the head of Foulon, still 'dripping blood'. In Madras the exhibition was held in the house and garden of 'His Highness the Nabob' and was popular with East India Company families, who could visit it for two star pagodas, or tour it privately for an extra pagoda.[33]

In March 1794, as the number of executions in the Terror escalated, Marie modelled a decapitated extreme revolutionary, Hébert, on the orders of the Convention. In her memoirs Marie claimed that just before the Terror and Robespierre both came to an end on 9 Thermidor, 27 July, when Curtius was on a mission to the Rhine army, she and her mother were imprisoned briefly, first in La Force prison, then in the Carmes. She claimed that there she met Josephine Beauharnais, wife of General Beauharnais and the future empress, who was also a prisoner.[34] General Beauharnais had been in the same gaol since he was arrested after the Prussians had recaptured Mainz in July 1792 and was guillotined in July 1793. Josephine was held because of her efforts to secure his release.

If they were imprisoned, they were free by mid July. Neither Marie nor her mother appear on the lists of detainees of any of the main prisons in Paris. Why did Marie say they were arrested? Her explanation was ambiguous. She suggested much later that perhaps she had been denounced by Jacques Dutruy, a *grimaçier* or girner, a clown who entertained the audience between acts, literally by grimacing or pulling funny faces. He worked at a neighbouring theatre.[35] Dutruy had a second job, as assistant to the executioner, Sanson, so he may have been the informer. Marie had an equally convenient explanation for her release. She claimed David intervened because he found her models useful for his own paintings.

Madame Tussaud liked to associate herself with the famous, in life as well as in wax, but who can tell if this or any other of her tales were true? Ironically, in May 1795 the last guillotined head Marie modelled was that of Fouquier-Tinville, the public prosecutor in Paris during the Terror, who may well have signed the warrant for her arrest. Was Marie in fact ever arrested? It was as convenient a tale to tell in post-war London as the story about living in Versailles. It was a claim that many people made after the event if they wanted to disassociate themselves from the Revolution. The claim that she had been imprisoned, which no one in Britain could challenge in the 1830s, became an important part of her image and one that obituarists invariably mentioned.

On 26 September 1794 Curtius died, aged fifty-seven, after a short illness in his house in Ivry. The doctor confirmed that he died of natural causes. Marie arrived the next morning from Paris. Waxworks need drama. She later alleged that Curtius had been poisoned, perhaps initially on the orders of General Custine. In her memoirs Marie constantly drops the names of people she claimed were Curtius's influential friends, but only neighbours and show business associates attended his civic funeral. (Religious funerals were still banned by the revolutionary government.) A detailed inventory had to be drawn up of all Curtius's possessions, room by room, in both houses. The exhibition must have been extensive because there were a total of 150 oil paintings. There were thirty life size wax models and seven part bodies. There were three ladies lounging on beds, the du Barry, the princesse de Lamballe and Madame de St-Amaranthe, none of whom were suitable for display during the Revolution. There were also cases of busts and objects protected by glass covers, and the list of lighting equipment was extensive.

Curtius left the proceeds of the sale of his silver and jewellery to the poor of the Temple district of Paris where he had lived and worked. He had, in fact, already donated all but half a dozen silver spoons and knives to the Convention's war effort. Marie, 'my pupil in my art', inherited his business and property.[36] She had to fight to secure her inheritance, as she was not accredited as a blood relative. She even had a battle to keep his few remaining possessions, including an ivory snuff box, decorated with a silver medallion, which Curtius had given her some years earlier when she began to take snuff. An indication of the run-down state of the entertainment industry was that afterwards she had to take out a substantial mortgage to keep the Ivry house and run the exhibition.

With the death of Robespierre, the radical Revolution was over. The Jacobin Club closed in November. Carrier, who had been instrumental in organising large-scale drownings in the Loire a year before, was guillotined, and mass executions stopped. The wax *salon* packed away Robespierre and the violent revolutionaries, and concentrated on showing the victims of the Revolution, Charlotte Corday, Camille Desmoulins, Madame Elizabeth and so on. The sans-culotte doorman at the waxworks was replaced by a young man dressed in the new fashion of 'jeunesse dorée' adopted by actors and singers, with long hair, close-fitting tail coats and boots with pointed toes.

Meanwhile in October 1795, Marie Grosholz aged thirty-four, married a man some eight years younger than herself, François Tussaud, a civil engineer from Mâcon, who also lived in the Temple district. In her marriage agreement Marie retained control over her own property. This was unusual in France, where customarily a husband had complete control of all his wife's property. Within a short time they had three children, the eldest a girl. Marie made a wax model of the baby, who died in early infancy. Next came Joseph (1798–1865) and François, later known in England as Francis (1800–1873). The marriage was not successful. François senior liked to speculate, quite wildly, in theatre property. He spent money faster than his wife could earn it. Although he was an engineer, he does not seem to have checked his purchases carefully. In 1801 an injunction was served on him to demolish part of one of his establishments because its poor construction meant it was in such a 'dangerous condition as to threaten the safety of the public'.[37]

The wax business remained in Marie's hands, but it had become so run down that she needed to raise a loan to keep going. She continued to make models of leading political figures, including Talleyrand, who, on his return from exile, became Foreign Minister in the government of the Directory.

Marie also made a model of Josephine after her marriage to Napoleon in 1797. In 1801 Josephine commissioned her to model her husband. He agreed to a sitting in the Tuileries palace at 6 o'clock in the morning; Napoleon slept very short nights. He was so satisfied with the likeness that he sent two of his generals to the Boulevard du Temple to have their own portraits made.

Napoleon appreciated the usefulness of anatomical waxes in the training of his army surgeons, large numbers of whom were kept extremely busy through nearly a quarter of a century of constant warfare. In Italy in 1796 he visited the workshop of a famous wax anatomical sculptor, Felice Fontana, and ordered a number of models. Some were shipped to Paris by boat, but arguments about the price meant that most were sold to Russia instead.[38] Napoleon's interest in the use of wax for medical education grew and in 1806 he even set up a school in Rouen to train sculptors in the art of making anatomical waxes.[39] If Napoleon saw value in wax models, why did not the Curtius business pick up? The Directory (1795–99) was perhaps a tricky period for wax figures. There was no chance of displaying any of the royal family and the Terror was too close for either its perpetrators or its victims to be marketable. No one knew if and when the Revolution might swing again into a violent phase. Delecluze, a pupil of the artist David, described a visit he and David paid to the waxworks in 1801. Realising that they were knowledgeable about things artistic, their guide offered to show them items not on display. Although David at first refused, thinking that they were being offered erotica, a chest was opened to reveal the heads of revolutionaries, including Robespierre's death's head. The marks where Robespierre's head had been bandaged, after his attempted suicide just before his execution, were clearly visible.[40]

Personal factors may also have played a part in the failure of the *salon* to recover. The death of Curtius must have involved Marie in a great deal of bureaucracy and legal business. Curtius made her his heir, but the lack of any proven blood relationship must have tested Marie's considerable determination and persistence. Even today, with better medical care, three babies in less than five years would be exhausting for a woman in her late thirties; then it was likely to have been shattering. The death of her first child must also have been devastating. Marie presumably had expected that her husband would help run the business while she was preoccupied with the babies. On the other hand, Marie had her mother and aunt at home to help with the children and it was normal at the time to send babies away to a wet-nurse at least until they were weaned. It is unclear why she did not exert more effort to rebuild the wax business in Paris, when later she showed stupendous drive and determination to make her fortune in

Britain. That Marie had excluded her husband from control over her property in her marriage agreement suggests that she never expected much from him even at the outset. It seems clear from their later correspondence that Marie's decision to leave France was motivated more by a ruthless determination to escape from an unsuitable husband than because she doubted her own abilities as a businesswoman.

In 1802, just turned forty, Madame Tussaud agreed to join Philipstal, the old friend Curtius had saved from prison, on a tour of Britain. Philipstal had held a successful magic lantern season in the Lyceum Theatre in the Strand a year earlier and was granted a royal patent and asked to return. The signing of the treaty of Amiens in March 1802 marked a temporary break in the war between Britain and France, so Marie was free to leave.

Marie gave her husband total control to run the Boulevard du Temple waxworks. Once she had gone, she never asked for any income from it. She left her mother and aunt in charge of her baby son, taking her elder child, Joseph, aged four with her. Marie never returned to France.

4

The Travelling Wax Exhibition

Marie Tussaud crossed to England in 1802, taking advantage of the peace of Amiens signed between Britain and France in March. She travelled as the junior partner of Philipstal and his Phantasmagoria magic lantern show. Philipstal had performed at the Lyceum Theatre on the corner of the Strand the previous year and had taken a lease for a second season. He offered Marie the lower floor. The terms were poor: their agreement guaranteed that 50 per cent of Marie's profits would go to Philipstal; in return he would cover advertising and transport costs. Presumably Marie, calculating that he had valuable experience and a reputation in England, took the gamble that, even on disadvantageous terms, she was likely to do better business in England than in Paris. England was a prosperous country, with no first-hand experience of war. Philip Astley's circus did better in London than in Paris, a particular triumph being the deaths' heads he had bought from Curtius.

It was Marie's first visit to Britain, but from the second half of 1795 'Curtius's Grand Cabinet of Curiosities' had been shown in London in Bond Street and had then set off on a tour of Britain, starting with Norwich in January 1796 and then Cambridge. In May the tour arrived in Chester assembly rooms while the annual races were in progress. Afterwards they moved to Manchester, then to the Neptune coffee house in Liverpool, to arrive in Birmingham in September. In February 1797 the (unnamed) organiser fell sick and advertised for partners to take over Curtius's share in the show.[1]

From the start the Curtius exhibition had also included some British material, including miniatures made by the Irish artist Eley George Mountstephen, who did work for Josiah Wedgwood.[2] Marie's husband may have accompanied this exhibition for part of the time.[3] The show then moved to Baden. In December 1797 with the main revolutionary leaders prominently displayed, the 'Cabinet de Curtius' was running in Baden during the meeting of the Congress of Rastatt. Napoleon Bonaparte himself visited the exhibition on its opening day. The 'Cabinet' stayed until the congress ended in 1799. Marie hoped that this exhibition would be remembered and that she could build on its success.

The Lyceum Theatre (not the present building) had been constructed in 1765 as an exhibition centre. It was converted to be a theatre in 1790, but had no licence to perform drama. Although the state did not directly intervene in the theatre, as in Paris, it did issue licences to theatres for dramatic performances and only three London theatres had such a licence: Covent Garden, Drury Lane and, in the summer, the Haymarket.[4] Other theatres, including Astley's Amphitheatre, limped along on annual licences which dictated what they could perform, rather like the theatres in the Boulevard du Temple in Paris. The Lyceum came into this category.

Marie took lodgings near the Lyceum in Surrey Street. She found, however, that her exhibition was not mentioned on Philipstal's posters and she had to pay a disproportionate share of the travelling costs. The sea journey had also damaged both figures and costumes, which she had to set to work to repair without any help, and she had to cope with Joseph without her mother and aunt to help. At first her show focused on France. The English were fascinated by the fate of the French monarchy and the horrors of the Revolution. Marie took her best models to Britain and the original moulds in case of accidents. In addition to the whole royal family, including the princesse de Lamballe, Marie packed Napoleon and Josephine. She took all the deaths' heads, although those of the king and queen were not shown, out of respect for the large number of émigrés in London. Indeed they did not go on display until after Joseph Tussaud's death in 1865.[5] Marat, martyr then villain of the Revolution, and his bath had pride of place.[6] There was also the comte de Lorge, one of the prisoners released from the Bastille, plus a model of the Bastille made in 1786, Hébert, Mirabeau, Fouquier-Tinville, Rousseau, Voltaire, a national guardsman, Madame St-Amaranthe, Madame du Barry, and Robespierre's death's head. The model guillotine displayed at this time was actually not French but a version of the much earlier Scottish 'maiden'. Marie left her visitors in no doubt that these models illustrated the destructive and evil force of revolution. Her first catalogue, published when she reached Edinburgh, observed:

> The French Revolution, ever changing, ever new, has at length not only returned to her ancient start of absolute sovereignty, but even degenerated to despotism itself, for whether the ruler be called a monarch or a consul, it is of little consequence to the people, if their liberties must be sacrificed for his aggrandisement.[7]

Napoleon earned a thirteen-page commentary and Robespierre ten out of a seventy-page brochure, 'vested with supreme authority ... he threw off the character of humanity and became a demon'.[8] In this first catalogue there were few details about the royal family, perhaps it was assumed that

Patronized by THE DUKE AND THE COUNT

DUCHESS OF YORK, MONSIEUR D'ARTOIS.

MADAME TUSSAUD,

Lately arrived from the Continent,

Artist to Her late Royal Highness Madame Elizabeth, Sister to Louis XVIII.

Most respectfully informs the Nobility, Gentry, and the Public, that her

UNRIVALLED COLLECTION

Of Whole-Length

FIGURES,

AS LARGE AS LIFE,

CONSISTING OF

83 *Public Characters,*

Which have lately been exhibited in Paris, Dublin, Edinburgh, &c.

IS NOW OPEN FOR INSPECTION, AT THE

MAGNIFICENT MERCATURA,

No. 29, St. James's Street.

CHARACTERS AS FOLLOW:

THE FULL-LENGTH PORTRAIT MODELS

OF

THEIR MOST GRACIOUS MAJESTIES GEORGE III. AND QUEEN CHARLOTTE,

18. Advertisement for Madame Tussaud's collection of figures.

the tragedies of the king and queen were well-known, although the sad tale of Madame de Lamballe was told at length. The violence of politics was underlined by the presence of Henry IV's shirt and lightened by the chance to see a mummy, part of Philipstal's collection, but apparently on permanent loan to Marie.

Exhibitions illustrating the iniquities of the Revolution were popular in Britain. What made Marie's unique was that she and Curtius had made the figures from the living, or dead, bodies of their subjects. For the first time

English audiences could really see the features of the guillotined king and queen, whose deaths they had publicly mourned. Less congenial to the British, but fascinating, was their first sight of the actual features, modelled from death, of the leading revolutionaries. People were eager to gaze on their great enemy, Napoleon. Like all waxworks, the tenor of the Tussaud show in Britain was distinctly monarchist. It was also emphatically anti-revolutionary, which appealed to English audiences. That Madame Tussaud, a Frenchwoman, condemned the Revolution, added a delightful piquancy for the British. It was nearly as appealing as if she were actually anti-French.

In France, Marie had been Curtius's faithful pupil and had lived on his reputation. In England, she continued to present her show as 'Curtius's Cabinet of Curiosities' until 1808, while she developed her own reputation as a sculptor and a businesswoman. The decision had nothing to do with modesty or gender, because some of the most famous wax sculptors and entrepreneurs in eighteenth-century England were women. She referred to the show as a 'cabinet', later as an exhibition; the term *salon* was no longer used. The presence of a large number of aristocratic French émigrés in Britain in these years meant there was a French community in cities like London and Edinburgh. Marie's letters record her attempts to attach herself to the fringes of their society, but she would not have been considered a social equal by the mainly aristocratic exiles.[9] The French émigrés living in London enjoyed visiting the exhibition out of nostalgia to shudder at the Terror they had escaped,[10] but they did not have the spare cash to buy models.

Madame Tussaud consciously reinvented herself in an environment where she was totally unknown. She presented herself to the British as an artist who had moved in high society and politics in France. The final seal to her new persona culminated in 1838 in a volume of published memoirs, appropriately ghosted by a former émigré, Francis Hervé.[11] In these memoirs, and in all her publicity, catalogues, posters and press announcements, she repeated her claim that before the 1789 Revolution she had spent eight years at Versailles.

Her alleged royal links gave Tussaud a stature and reputation in Britain. They enabled her to present her show as an upmarket entertainment for the prosperous – rather than as a fairground item. They also made it easier for her to approach the wealthy and titled to solicit commissions. It was not enough to make models and show them, a sculptor needed private orders. Marie, well-coached by Curtius, courted both high and low society. One of her first clients was Sir Francis Burdett, the radical MP and prison reformer. Burdett had spent time in France in the early period of the Revolution and opposed Britain being at war with France. Plugging her own French royal models and connections, Marie worked hard to secure royal backing and was delighted when the duchess of York, the wife of George III's second son, agreed to purchase a wax model. The duchess had been abandoned by her husband for another woman and had no children, only a house full of dogs. She also asked for a model of a little boy. Marie made a second boy model for her own exhibition, probably using Joseph as the template. The duchess allowed her name to appear on Marie's posters and press advertisements when the model was shown.

The war and the Revolution gave Marie's show the edge on other exhibitions, particularly by the deaths' heads of the revolutionaries. The exploitation of 'Horrors' material was as crucial to Marie as her attempts to hob-nob with the elite. At the outset pure luck offered her the first English severed head, with a suitably modest French side-dressing. In 1802 there was a most unpromising and abortive conspiracy to murder George III hatched by Colonel Edward Despard. Despard was an Irishman with personal as well as political grievances against the British. He had joined the British army at fifteen and had served in the West Indies. He was recalled in 1790 on charges from which he was cleared, but spent two years in gaol after unsuccessful attempts to secure compensation. He joined Wolfe Tone's United Irishmen, formed in 1791, initially as a legal organisation to press for rights for the Irish. When Britain engaged revolutionary France in war the organisation went underground, conspiring with English Radicals and with the French. In August 1798 the United Irishmen backed a French invasion of Ireland, but it had collapsed by October and Wolfe Tone was captured and committed suicide just before his execution. As a consequence of the rebellion in 1800 the Irish parliament was abolished and Ireland was merged into Great Britain. Despard's plot was a last-ditch attempt by the United Irishmen. Together with six fellow conspirators, he plotted to murder George III and seize the Tower of London and the Bank of England, but the scheme was discovered before it began. The seven were hanged, beheaded, drawn and quartered. To the amazement of Despard's friends, after they had been sent his remains, Marie asked for permission to make a cast of the head. The exhibition was cleverly lit by a blue-tinged light to indicate hugger-mugger goings on. The fact that Marie was French and the United Irishmen had French support added piquancy to the display. Attendances at the Lyceum immediately rose.

Philipstal's own show at the Lyceum, a Phantasmagoria, a 'Grand Cabinet of Optical and Mechanical Curiosities', offered both popular science and a magic lantern performance. A scientific show might seem odd, but Philipstal's mechanical and automatic items appealed to a lively contemporary interest in science. The Royal Institution had been founded in 1799 by

19. Advertisement for Madame Tussaud's Exhibition at the Reindeer Inn, Hull, February 1812.

Count Rumford. It focused on interpreting physics, chemistry and geology to non-specialists. In 1801 Humphrey Davy lectured to enthusiastic audiences. There were more dramatic displays, such as the National Gallery of Practical Science in the Lowther Arcade, where Madame Tussaud had an exhibition in 1834. This establishment included a six thousand gallon mini-canal to illustrate the technology of contemporary canal construction.[12]

There were also more elaborate mechanical illusions such as the mechanised 'Turk', a life-size wooden model which successfully challenged all comers to a game of chess, until it was realised that a real chess-player was concealed within the cabinet.[13] Tippoo Sahib's man-eating tiger was the biggest attraction. Tippoo had a passion for tigers and a hatred of the English. A life-size clockwork tiger prepares to eat its prey – a terrified Englishman, dressed in green breeches and yellow stockings with a round black hat. To add to the drama, the son of Sir Hector Munro, the general who had defeated Tippoo Sahib, had been mauled to death by a tiger, dying in agony twenty-four hours later. Tippoo's tiger was captured when his stronghold of Seringapatam, the capital of Mysore, fell to the British in 1799. It became the star exhibit in the museum of the East India Company. Within the tiger was a barrel-organ, operated initially by a slave, later by ecstatic visitors to the museum. When the handle was turned the tiger roared, and the man died with heart-rending groans.[14]

Philipstal provided more modest, but innovative, mechanical science. There were life-size automatic figures, a rope dancer, a miniature dancing Cossack, a self-propelled windmill, a mechanical peacock which 'eats, drinks, cries and unfolds its tail', mechanical fireworks and a most entertaining and potentially rather useful device, a self-defending money chest which fired on anyone who tried to force it open.[15] Then there was a 'spectral' magic lantern show, something that was experiencing a real vogue at this time when people were fascinated by 'Gothic' culture. Philipstal erected a magic lantern some distance behind a semi-transparent screen. The audience was plunged into total darkness. A moveable carriage and adjustable lens allowed images to be projected onto the screen, and enlarged or shrunk at will. Figures painted on a glass slider were manipulated to simulate a graveyard, or similar ghostly illusions, 'with more certainty and facility than has been known or done'.[16]

Marie was dismissive of Philipstal's show, but this must have been just sour grapes. Cartoonists such as Gillray illustrated this popular vogue with his *Philipstal: A Phantasmagoria, 5 January 1803*. Philipstal's show sparked off other cartoons, *A New Phantasmagoria for John Bull* and *The Flushing Phantasmagoria: The King's Conjuror's Amusing John Bull*. Magic lantern artists themselves responded by copying the caricaturists well into the second half of the nineteenth century.[17] The 'German Baron', an associate of Philipstal, put on magic lantern shows for the Prince Regent in the Brighton Pavilion.[18] Later Madame Tussaud's son, Joseph, used a machine similar to Philipstal's to make silhouettes for sale.

When the Lyceum season finished in April 1803, Marie moved to Edinburgh. She did not have another exhibition in London until 1816. She may have been glad to quit London in the spring of 1803, because England was again at war with France. On a more personal level, London may have seemed uncomfortably close to Paris. Marie had received a letter from her husband complaining that the Paris waxworks were still not making money and that his debts were rising. Before leaving London, Marie agreed to instruct her solicitor to make over her French properties entirely to her husband, so that he could raise yet another mortgage. Her decision to renounce all control may, however, have owed less to concern for the welfare of her family than to French marriage law, which at that time was being rationalised and set out in the new *Code Civil.* A wife gave up all control over the property she brought into a marriage. Marie's departure would also have made it more difficult for her to enforce her original marriage agreement. In addition the new code stated that anything a wife earned automatically belonged to her husband. A working wife's wages were simply paid to her spouse. Marie, however, steadfastly refused to send any of her earnings in England to her husband. At this stage, indeed, she and Joseph seem to have been barely surviving. Marie had to fight to persuade Philipstal to release funds to transport her models, herself and Joseph. Marie complained to her husband, 'M. Philipstal treats me as you do. He has left me all alone. He is angry.'[19] She had exchanged one poor relationship for another.

Marie again packed the models in crates to be shipped by sea up the east coast to Scotland. In these early years even a rough sea was gentler with wax models than road transport. The journey took them from 27 April to 10 May through raging seas. When they arrived in Edinburgh Marie found that Philipstal had failed to pay the cost of transport, which she had to cover with a loan, negotiated for her by Mr Charles, an English ventriloquist she had known in Paris and at the Lyceum. (This may have been the man who had performed with Curtius in the Palais Royal.) Marie must have been very relieved to find lodgings with a woman who spoke French. She at this point had barely learned English, but now had to cope with the Scottish accent. When the crates were unpacked, there were thirty-six breakages to make good, but the tone of Marie's next letter home was upbeat and confident. She had met French people at the castle, Nini (Joseph) was adored by everyone, and she expected to be ready to open within a week.

She was soon boasting of her friendship with the governor of Edinburgh Castle and his French wife; but, as the governor was a bachelor, Marie must in fact have made the acquaintance of a lesser official. She was always anxious to be accepted as a royalist lady. She assured her family, 'I am taken for a great lady', and never stopped mentioning her personal connections with the French royal family.[20] Edinburgh was a mecca for émigrés, a number of whom had moved from England since the outbreak of war between England and France. Louis XVI's younger brother, the comte d'Artois, was living with his retinue in Holyrood Palace. Marie was quick to slough off all her revolutionary antecedents, remembering and embroidering only her tenuous pre-1789 links with the royal family. Her elegant portraits of the royal family and the hostile manner in which she presented the French revolutionaries must have been appealing to the émigrés. Marie did her best to ingratiate herself into their society. She did not get far at this time, when émigrés were confident that they would one day return to France, although she obviously established links with some of them and exploited the expatriate community as much as possible.[21] Her main customers were Scots, however, who were more inclined to interpret the exhibition's tone as simply anti-French.[22]

Marie's Edinburgh exhibition opened on 18 May 1803, timed to coincide with the start of the Edinburgh horse show, when the maximum number of visitors was crowding into the city. Her show was open from 11 a.m. to 4 p.m. and from 6 p.m. to 8 p.m. She was pleased with her takings, full details of which she sent to her husband: £3 14s. on the first day, but £13 6s. by the eighth. By the eighteenth day she had taken £190 in all and was delighted.[23] As the entry fee was a substantial two shillings per person, she must have had thirty-seven customers on the first day and 133 on the eighth. In less than a fortnight she wrote to her husband that the exhibition was always full. When the horse show finished, Marie reduced the entry fee to one shilling, which was to be Tussaud's standard charge throughout the century and which was the norm for all similar entertainment. By 23 July 1803 she had taken £420 10s. at the door in Edinburgh. Allowing for the cost of shipping the models from London, rent, posters and newspaper advertisements, which amounted to £118 18s. she had a profit of £301 12s. She also published a catalogue which she sold at the door for 6d. This was a complete innovation. There is no evidence that Curtius had produced a written catalogue, but the idea of a catalogue was catching on as public exhibitions began to proliferate.

Marie's letters home were full of details of her accounts, but she never considered trying to send money to France. She reminded her husband that she had been forced to hand over half her profits to Philipstal. 'I have been

20. Waterloo Place, Edinburgh, engraving by Thomas Shepherd.

forced to accept his accounts as he placed them before me ... He treats me like a slave.'[24] Marie always kept her own scrupulous daily cash flow accounts, listing what she took and what she paid out in rent, for candles and materials.

Although Marie was to become one of the leading women entrepreneurs in nineteenth-century Britain, in 1803 she was a beginner. Until his death Curtius had run the business and done the lion's share of hustling for customers. Marie's letters to her husband indicate that she had hoped that he would inherit Curtius's mantle, but she must have been increasingly aware that she had judged ill in accepting him as a husband. Her decision to accept an unequal partnership with Philipstal was no wiser. In Edinburgh it came home to Marie that her agreement to share her own profits with Philipstal, with no return from him except his name, was binding until she was able to buy her way out. On 26 May she wrote to her husband of Philipstal: 'I know him as my enemy wishing me harm. But I hope in six months to have done with him. His business is in a bad way and he has only my Cabinet on which to rely.'[25] The next stop for the touring wax exhibition in October 1803 was Glasgow, less sophisticated and elegant than Edinburgh, but full of monied potential customers with time on their hands and a desire to appear cultured and informed. Marie then followed Philipstal to Dublin, perhaps a diplomatic departure, given Napoleon's plans to invade England. Marie toured Ireland, following the route of touring theatre companies, until 1808, when she returned to Scotland.

Marie's long absence from England may have been in response to the wartime Alien's Act. Any foreigners who arrived in Britain after October 1801 had to remain within thirteen miles of an agreed residence and not live within ten miles of the coast. There was a three month limit on their visits. Marie stayed away from England from 1803 to 1808, years when the threat to England from Napoleon was taken seriously and anti-French feeling was at its height. When she returned to England in 1808 the threat of invasion had faded and Wellington was beginning to put pressure on French troops in Portugal. Marie toured Scotland just as the war between England and France flared up again. French émigrés regarded Scotland as a safe haven and in 1803 Marie may have shared their sentiments, although at no point does she mention fearing a hostile reception. In Ireland it is conceivable that Marie also hoped that the strong anti-revolutionary bias of her French material would arouse the curiosity of customers just five years after the abortive French invasion.

In the years of greatest wartime tension, Marie may have feared hostility in England, but she never had any such setbacks and probably her touring venues were dictated purely by the quest for large audiences and profit. The only time the exhibition encountered unrest was in 1831 when, by pure coincidence and mischance, Marie had a show in Bristol at the time of the Reform Bill riots. The riots there were a product of frustration that the House of Lords had thrown out the Reform Bill, designed to improve parliamentary representation, and the repercussions of harvest failures and the economic crisis. The buildings in the square in which she was staying and holding the exhibition were set alight, but Marie was warned in advance. Her employees formed a protective cordon while the models were removed, but the house opposite, where the Tussauds were staying, was set on fire. Ironically a water colour painted to show the hasty removal of models as the surrounding houses burned was itself destroyed in the 1925 fire that devastated the whole Tussaud exhibition.

In these early touring years insight into both the personal and business side of Marie Tussaud is provided by the letters she wrote home. The letters are a strange mixture of precise accounts of exactly what she took in each show combined with loving references to her family and rather boastful statements about her success. She seems to have felt the need to explain and prove herself to François. She had defied her husband in going on tour and staying away, and was keen to prove that she had made the right decision. On average she wrote about twice a week, in affectionate if ungrammatical and sometimes almost unreadable French, interspersed with

21. The Bristol Riots of 1831.

odd German words such as *lieber* and *nicht*. Some of her grammatical constructions are German. Presumably, although she had moved to Paris when she was a small child, German had remained the family language. Her husband, who was French, complained that he could not read her letters, which were written in a firm, large script, not typical of the time, so sometimes she dictated them to the assistant who translated the labels she wrote to describe her models. The assistant seems to have corrected her French.

Marie wrote to her whole family. Her younger son, her mother and an aunt were still with her husband in Paris, and Marie always wrote lovingly to them all, frequently referring to her eventual return home. She was full of her success and of how well she was received among the elite. She was always keen to ensure that Nini (Joseph) was not forgotten by his family in France. She assured them constantly that everyone adored him wherever they travelled. In Scotland they took his French accent for English, which must indicate that the young boy was already far more fluent in English than his mother was ever to be. On 26 May 1803, six days after her Edinburgh show opened, Marie wrote critically to her husband for the first time. Perhaps she felt that her argument that she was on tour to improve their finances was being borne out by her success. She complained that she had written a hundred letters, without a single reply: 'I pray you remember that I am your wife and that you are the father of my children.'

François was finally stung to answer. He demanded that she return home. Marie firmly and rapidly replied that she had told him she would not come back until she had a full purse. Additionally, the war between Britain and France meant that the ports were closed and journeys between the two countries were difficult; letters could take several months to arrive. Marie tried to pin her husband down. Was he helping with the cooking, was he working hard, was he taking care of their son François, her mother and aunt, and had he made any changes to the *salon*? A woman of firm purpose and sharp tongue and pen, she pointed out that her husband could change the *salon* around while she was away.[26] A few month later, assuring her husband that her receipts were more than covering her expenses, she wrote, 'I hope, my friend, that it is possible for you to take on the duty of being the head of the family. Look after my mother and my aunt'.[27] Such peremptory orders, when it was Marie who had left, seem somewhat unreasonable. It is easy to infer, however, that François Tussaud was disinclined to shift for himself. Clearly he had married a woman older than himself in the hope of a life of leisure and was far from pleased that the means to this easy existence had disappeared across the Channel.

Marie kept in contact with her husband until she had bought herself out of her agreement with Philipstal. In March 1804 she wrote her usual sort of boasting, nagging letter to her husband, in reply to one which had taken five months to reach her. Tenderly embracing young 'Françison' (François) and the rest of the family, as she always did, informing them that Joseph had entirely forgotten French, Marie remarked that her hard work would ensure that she could now promise their children a start in life that would make them proud of their parents. This was the first time she had claimed that her tour to Britain was designed to provide for their children's long term future. She told her husband firmly, 'We shall not write to you about our plans', but she urged him, 'Write a little, when you can'. She ended, as never before, 'Adieu, adieu, we can each go our own way', although she still signed off as usual, 'Je suis pour la vie ta femme Tussaud'.[28] Perhaps, now that she was beginning to make real money, Marie wanted to assert that her spendthrift husband would have no call on it. They both knew that, if she went back home, under the new French *Code Civil* her husband would be able to get his hands on every penny she had made. Despite the *adieu*, she wrote twice more. In her next letter, of 20 June 1804, Marie hoped wistfully that Joseph would quickly relearn his French when he returned to Paris, and wished that her beloved Françison was with her 'so that he could have the same chances as his brother. I would be so happy if he could travel to me by land or sea'.[29] Given the fact that her younger son was four at the time and that the only person likely to travel with him, his father, would not have been welcome, this was an untypically sentimental declaration. On 27 June Marie wrote what turned out to be her last letter to her husband, although there was no clue that she would never contact him again. Indeed she wrote, 'when I return let there be no reproaches', and she was careful to give him her new Dublin address.

Her letters give no exact indication why she cut free of her husband at this point. Nor do they explain how she could write so lovingly about both sons, yet have no contact with the younger until he was an adult. There seems no doubt that she embarked on her British tour in defiance of her husband. Either she left because divorce was impossible and marriage unbearable, or because her business was in insuperable difficulties in 1802 and she genuinely believed that her stay in Britain would be limited to a season or so. It seems unlikely that she deliberately cut herself off from her younger son and mother for life. It seems more likely that she intended the tour to be a money-spinner of limited duration and that the war made it impossible for her to return. Europe had been at war for ten years when she left and no one could have predicted that it would last another thirteen years.

Marie was later very shocked to be told in September 1808 that her husband had handed over the entire Paris exhibition and the house in the

Boulevard du Temple to Madame Salomé Reiss, to redeem the mortgage that Marie had taken out with her to keep the houses and business intact when Curtius died. François was ever eager for the business speculation that would make his fortune. He spent the money he raised to buy the lease of the Théâtre des Troubadours and the land on which it was built.[30] He moved the family into the smaller house in Rue des Fossés du Temple which Curtius had bought and which had always been let to a tenant. After that her husband had no rental income and there was no suitable property in which Marie could have re-established her exhibition.

From 1808, when Marie returned to Scotland, she toured Scottish and English towns until 1816. She had an acute perception of what would attract customers. In both Ireland and Scotland a small wax Joseph Tussaud welcomed visitors to the show, stressing the family character of the entertainment. The exhibition gradually became more elaborate and predictably there was an increasing emphasis on British characters. There were two rooms, the first being devoted to history and current affairs, political and cultural. An extra 6d. allowed the customer into the other room, which contained the revolutionaries, including Marat in his bath and the deaths' heads of Robespierre, Carrier and Fouquier-Tinville. Alongside them were the other items brought from Paris, including the models of the Bastille and of a guillotine. In addition Marie constantly advertised for private commissions, alive or dead, assuring people that a dead subject would be given 'the most correct appearance of Animation'.[31]

Customers liked to see exceptional individuals whom they would never encounter in the flesh, as fabulously dressed as was appropriate. They enjoyed the sensation that they were learning something new, were fond of a few shocks and thrills, and were fascinated by a topical display. The Edinburgh show in 1810 was a typically successful recipe. It highlighted the good-looking Mrs Mary Ann Clarke, the duke of York's mistress. She had spoken up jauntily in her own defence when the duke was charged with selling army commissions illegally at her suggestion. People were talking about her and curious to see what this woman actually looked like.

By 1810 Marie was well on her way to developing the British royal family as a special feature of her exhibition. She modelled George III from life in 1807 and Queen Charlotte and the Prince of Wales shortly afterwards. At this point, when his mental health declined, his British subjects were just beginning to warm to George III (king from 1760 to 1820). Before that the gentry had liked his love of country life and sports and were comfortable with his disregard of things intellectual and artistic. The middle classes empathised with his morality, his strict Protestantism, his prejudices against Roman Catholics and his enthusiasm for the war against the French.

He had less engaging personal qualities, however, and the court was run with rigid pedantry in a very Germanic style. There had been several attempts on his life and he was a favourite butt of the scorn of many members of parliament, journalists and especially the London mob. An 1819 sonnet written by the poet Shelley expressed a quite widely-held distaste for monarchy:

> An old, mad, blind, despised, and dying king,
> Princes, the dregs of their dull race, who flow
> Through public scorn, mud from a muddy spring,
> Rulers who neither see, nor feel, nor know,
> But leechlike to their fainting country cling.

When his eldest son was appointed Prince Regent in 1810, however, George III had become exactly the model of a puppet king the Whigs had always wanted: blind, deaf and insane. The Tussaud's catalogue of 1818 commented in the first of its biographical sketches, 'Of all the monarchs that have reigned over this happy and highly-favoured nation, none has been more beloved by their subjects than his Gracious Majesty'.

George III's wife, Charlotte, earned a page biography that did little more than compliment her fecundity with the comment: 'As a wife and mother, the conduct of this illustrious woman has been a pattern to her subjects.' Opinion never faltered in its condemnation of her eldest son, the Prince of Wales. The 1818 catalogue, unusually, was more than economical with the truth when it said that the Prince Regent had 'the love and respect of a free and happy people'.

> His Royal Highness, to a fine person and handsome features, possesses mental qualities which seldom fall to the lot of princes. His affability and generosity are universally known. As a patron and admirer of the fine arts he is surpassed by no prince of the present time. [32]

No sophisticated reading between the lines was needed to interpret these words, and most British people would have had no trouble deciphering them. Prinny was universally hated; perpetually quarrelling publicly with his father and demanding that Parliament pay his huge debts or urging his ministers to make unjustified decisions because he was in debt to some notable or other. He lived in conspicuous luxury at Carlton House. His arguments were as incessant as his drunkenness, vanity and immorality.

As part of a deal to get Parliament to pay his debts, he had agreed to marry a German princess, Princess Caroline of Brunswick. Repelled by her at first sight, they almost immediately parted. (He had previously contracted a morganatic marriage with the Roman Catholic Mrs Fitzherbert.) Caroline was as popular with the English people as her husband was detested. People found the scandals about her extra-marital affairs, rumoured and real, colourful and entertaining. First modelled from life by Marie in 1808, the Tussaud's catalogue for 1818 commented discretely.

> The subsequent separation of the royal pair – an event greatly to be deplored – is too delicate a subject to be here entered into. On the 9 August 1814, her Royal Highness went to the Continent, where she has ever since continued, passing the greater part of her time in travelling.

In addition to the current royal family, Marie offered the Scots new models of old favourites, including Mary Queen of Scots and Bonnie Prince Charlie. Nelson and Sir John Moore, both dead heroes, the latter killed at Corunna in the British withdrawal from Spain in 1809, stood with a mixture of English and Irish politicians. Napoleon appeared, bigamously content, with both Josephine and his new empress Marie-Louise. While television and film personalities may glisten in wax in Marylebone Road today, many media giants of the early decades of the early nineteenth century were novelists and clergymen. Madame Tussaud added Sir Walter Scott, the most popular novelist in Britain and in France at the time. She modelled him from life in Edinburgh in 1828. A troop of nine Anglican clergymen joined the ranks.[33] Today they are forgotten names, but in this period doctrinal arguments attracted attention, as did their wax models.

The qualities that turned Madame Tussaud's touring career from a transient entertainment into a permanent success can be seen emerging. In developing her exhibition, and adapting it to appeal to a well-heeled British audience, Marie learned from other touring companies, particularly the theatre groups. Crucial to success was where and how the exhibition was displayed. Marie always tried to set up shop in a town's assembly rooms, otherwise settling for a town hall or a theatre (seats at the time were removable). In 1824 the theatre pit in Northampton was boarded over level with the stage for the exhibition, to make 'one of the largest rooms in Northampton'.[34] Assembly rooms were designed for display, the relatively new playground where the wealthy, respectable middle class lived their indoor public existence, when they were not in church, chapel, shops or earning a living. Many towns were busy erecting assembly rooms in this period. Inside the inevitably imposing exterior the rooms were often high-ceilinged and long, with rows of pillars down each, larger, but similar in design, to the *salon de cire* in the Palais Royal. This was an impressive backdrop for Tussaud's' ninety or so wax figures and offered opportunities for the prolific displays of candle-lighting which became Marie's trademark, as it had been Curtius's.

The Tussaud exhibition invariably announced its arrival in a carefully planned series of advertisements in the local newspaper, with tours mostly confined to large towns with a local press. These advertisements were supplemented by posters and handbills, which were printed to a high standard. In the main this advertising was verbal. Wood cut or lithograph illustrations were sometimes used, but the quality was variable and the cost still high. Hence hyperbole and colourful descriptions were the norm. Until cheap good quality lithograph illustrations began to be used in new journals such as *Illustrated London News* and *Punch* in the early 1840s, people relied on wax models to know what the famous (and infamous) people they had heard about actually looked like. This must have been a significant element in the appeal of the exhibition, not just until the illustrated papers appeared, but effectively until photography was more fully established. One can usually follow Tussaud's tours in local newspapers, which charged a fee to reproduce the posters. Marie personalised her publicity for each town.[35]

Catalogues were important. From 1818 substantial catalogues of each exhibition were published for each town visited. They providing a numbered list of the models and the lay-out of each room, followed by highly dramatic biographies of each figure, sometimes several pages in length. Marat 'evinced the most barbarous intentions' while Charlotte Corday, who assassinated him was 'zealous for freedom ... republican ... an enthusiast, but not a fanatic'.[36] The catalogue was an integral part of the visit, as there were no guided tours (as there were at the British Museum) and visitors wandered around freely. At 6*d.* catalogues were competitively priced. A generation later the new National Gallery charged 1*s.* for a catalogue which was a mere list of titles and painters. The 1819 edition of the Tussaud's catalogue stressed, as it always would, both the historical authenticity of clothing and other artefacts, and the educational experience to be gained by young visitors:

> Madame Tussaud, in offering this little Work to the Public, has endeavoured to blend utility and amusement. The following pages contain a general outline of the history of each character represented in the exhibition; which will not only increase the pleasure to be derived from a mere view of the figures, but will also convey to the minds of young persons much biographical knowledge – a branch of education universally allowed to be of the highest importance.

Marie always claimed that one of her first duties was pedagogic, to recreate the past for adults, but especially for children. To prove its cultural content, the front cover always included a short quotation from Shakespeare's *A Winter's Tale.*

> Eye, nose, lip
> The trick of his frown, his forehead; nay the valley
> The pretty dimples of his chin and cheek; his smiles,

The very mould and frame of hand, nail, finger:
Would you not deem it breath'd and that those veins
Did verily bear blood ...
The very life seemed warm upon her lips
The fixture of her eye has motion in't. [37]

Rational recreation, where some education was laced with entertainment, was very much the vogue. The British Museum was criticised for failing to present its huge mass of exhibits in a systematic way or to provide a catalogue. Tussaud's never forgot to claim that it was providing educational information, but took care to keep its contribution light and undemanding, though not unobtrusive.

Catalogues and posters were invariably interlaced with lists of royal patrons. In 1830 the catalogue for the Duffield show identified Madame Tussaud as

artist to her late Royal Highness Madame Elizabeth, sister to Louis XVIII. Patronised by his most Christian Majesty, Charles X, Louis XVIII and the late royal family of France; their late royal highnesses the Duke and Duchess of York.[38]

Most of this was pure hyperbole. Madame Tussaud never met either Louis XVIII or Charles X when they were kings of France between 1814 and 1830, but it all sounded impressive.

The Tussaud family enterprise developed encompassing both sons and, eventually, their families. François (Francis in England) eventually joined his mother and brother in England. His grandson Victor told the tale of his grandfather's early life to his own nephew, John Theodore, many years later. The details may or may not be true, but it is all we have. Marie's husband, who raised François in Marie's absence, was a gambler and later a miser. François junior's dreams of training as an architect were apparently dashed when his father apprenticed him to a grocer, until he found that the apprenticeship would be costly. He was then put to work with a man who made billiard tables. At seventeen he tried to join his mother, with very little financial help from his father. When he reached Dover his money had run out, so he walked to London carrying an old military knapsack full of stale ship's biscuits. He slept under haystacks and was arrested as a military deserter. Fortunately, his total lack of English was deemed to be adequate proof that he could not be an English soldier, so he was set free. When he reached London he was told that his mother's ship and all her models had been lost at sea returning from Ireland. (In fact Marie survived the disaster, but the fate of the models is unclear.) François returned to Paris and finally in 1822, when he was twenty-one, joined his mother and brother in the exhibition.[39]

From 1814 Joseph had taken a full part in the business, playing the piano and leading a small orchestra, which performed during opening hours. Francis played the harp in the orchestra, now named 'Messrs Tussaud and the Fishers'. There is no clue how the name originated. That Francis knew how to play a harp indicates that his father had been less of a miser than his grandson later alleged. The orchestra, although small, was the epitome of the snobbish and monarchist aura in which Marie delighted. It included a Frenchman who claimed to be the younger of Louis XVI's sons who had miraculously survived imprisonment. In 1815 Joseph was taught to make silhouettes by a relative of the Marie's memoralist, Hervé, who himself made a silhouette of Marie. Silhouettes were made by an adaptation of the popular magic lantern machinery. The subject of the silhouette sat very still while a life-size profile was thrown onto a sheet of glass, on the far side of which was a sheet of paper. The artist then outlined the sitter's shadow, which could be later reduced with a pantograph to the required size and completed with black ink. The silhouettes were popular and sold well for several years at 1s. 6d. for a black profile and 3s. for one in bronze. They were a neat marketing opportunity, designed for families with some spare cash, but who could not afford a wax model or an oil painting of a favourite relative. They were advertised to good effect in the exhibition's catalogue.

In her efforts to be recognised and accepted in society, Madame Tussaud was careful to be seen supporting good causes, including local and national charities, as long as her contribution was acknowledged. In October 1824 a whole day's takings in Cambridge was donated for the benefit of Addenbrookes hospital. In 1826, when the exhibition was in York, a pre-Christmas ball was held in the same room, separated by canvas screens. When the guests had finished dinner, Joseph Tussaud removed the screens and guests could mingle with the models. The £15s. 10d. raised was given to 'the distressed Manufacturers of York'. Visiting Coventry in 1831, Tussaud's made a donation to the local lying-in charity. In publicising this generosity, the local newspaper commented, 'a desire seems to be manifested by all classes to view this charming collection … everyone is surprised at the perfect state of cleanliness in which the figures are kept … we recommend a visit to the lovers of the Arts'.[40]

Because the exhibition paid return visits to towns, Marie was careful to keep her winning formula of coronations and horror up to date. The royalism of the exhibition became increasingly accentuated. The biographies of the numerous royals always had prime positions in the catalogue. In 1818 the brief and happy marriage of Princess Charlotte, the Prince Regent's daughter, to Prince Leopold of Saxe-Cobourg was applauded, and her subsequent death in childbirth regretted. Coronations were the key to the new, very visible royalism. The Romantic movement and Sir Walter Scott had a lot to answer for. In France, where Scott was everyone's favourite novelist, Charles X staged an elaborate pseudo-medieval coronation in Reims Cathedral in 1825, unlike his brother a decade earlier, who had contented himself with a simple oath in Notre-Dame. In 1820 George IV set a new standard for showy coronations, spending £250,000 on an elaborate, fantastic display of peacockery. The cost and vulgarity of the event itself drew much criticism, but memory was a different matter. People rushed to Westminster Abbey to gaze at the special coronation decorations. A panorama, a huge, wide reproduction of the scene in the abbey containing 30,000 figures, drew large crowds.[41] In her Manchester show in 1820 Marie staged a tableau of the event complete with mock up of both the throne room and the throne itself. Tussaud's played their part in making those unlovable brothers, George IV and William IV, tolerable.

What made the coronation of George IV particularly memorable and worthy of rendering in wax was the ludicrous side-show staged by his excluded consort. During the ceremony the popular, but rejected, Queen Caroline bustled around Whitehall, trying abortively to enter the abbey and claim her crown. In August 1820 the House of Lords had debated a Bill to annul her rights as queen and dissolve her marriage to George IV. Caroline was defended brilliantly by Henry, Lord Brougham, who thus earned the hatred of the king and public acclaim. In August 1821 two people were killed at riots during her funeral. Her effigy in Tussaud's was well worth the investment.

In Liverpool a year later Marie took the opportunity of Napoleon's death to present an even more glamorous tableau of his coronation as emperor, modelled on David's painting. Characters were increasingly grouped in set-piece dramatic situations as if on stage. In this scene Napoleon was crowning himself, watched by Josephine, the pope, Napoleon's uncle Cardinal Fesch, and two Egyptian mamelukes, to remind everyone that Napoleon had fought and defeated them. Journalists were fascinated by the mamelukes. When the opportunity arose later, Marie bought the actual robes that had been worn at the coronations of both George IV and Napoleon, to add an even more authentic touch.

Madame Tussaud instantly set a fashion for tableaux, placing a group of individuals in dramatic scenes that told a story without movement. Theatres imitated the idea and there were a number of shows dedicated to stationary *tableaux vivants* in London and through Europe. In 1840 George Catlin, who had lived for eight years among the Crow Indians in the far west of North America, recording their lives in a series of drawings, put on an unintentionally amusing version. By day he ran an educational show in the

Egyptian Hall, a venue made popular earlier in the century by William Bullock. A twenty-five foot Crow wigwam was surrounded by artefacts and Catlin's numerous drawings. At night Catlin showed *Tableaux Vivants Indiens*. Catlin's version was somewhat different from the usual tableau because only the *vivant* aspect turned out to be true. Not having had the foresight to import any genuine Indians, he hired twenty assorted local men and boys, who were suitably dark-skinned, to undress and pose in war paint and feathers. Instead of standing like wax models, however, his band got into the swing, imitated war dances and whooped and sang in Cockney accents.[42]

While theatres were imitating waxworks, Marie no longer needed to model directly from life. Personal observation, combined where possible with a famous painting of the subject, was all that was required. Sometimes a wax head could be taken from a statue in another material, although this was as laborious as starting afresh. Heads, hands and any other visible parts of a subject were rendered in wax, the rest of the body still being a wood or leather frame. The accuracy of Tussaud models was constantly remarked on and not only in advertisements written or paid for by Marie. She was prepared to include appropriate wrinkles and imperfections.

In 1830, on the accession of William IV, Marie's sons, now the chief model makers, constructed a new coronation assemblage. Marie continued to claimed royal patronage, now British. William IV's sister, Princess Augusta had written to Marie of their 'amusement and gratification' after a visit with her nephew to the exhibition in Brighton in 1833.

Tussaud's linked the concept of patriotism with an exploitation of royalist sentiment. Traditionally governments tried to whip up patriotic feelings when there were wars to be fought and financed. The French Revolution, in contrast, embodied notions of nationalism which were taken up throughout Europe, being later embroidered with imperialist ambitions. Tussaud's successively illustrated all of these ways in which governments tried to persuade people that their strategies were noble and progressive. From 1835 the coronation tableau of Napoleon was eliminated, presumably as tension began to build up between Britain and France. It was replaced as the leading tableau by the Holy Alliance of the rulers of Britain, Russia, Prussia and Austria, which had finally defeated Napoleon in 1815. Britain's dominant role in the defeat was already stressed of course by the models of Wellington and Nelson. The Holy Alliance tableau emphasised the magnanimity of the Allies and the bellicosity of Napoleon.

> The intention of this group is to show, at one view, the principal actor in a war which can never have a parallel; to give effect to which, the Allied Monarchs

are supposed to be offering to Napoleon, the kingdom of France, as it was under Louis XIV (an historical fact) which he refuses, preferring to risk the chance of war.

This tableau retained its prime place until 1843 when the Napoleon shrine was inaugurated. It was a useful way of taking a dig at the French, asserting the altruism of her former enemies – and making good use of models which otherwise would have become redundant.

To appreciate the success of Madame Tussaud, one has also to glance at her competitors. This was an age when it was assumed that leisure ought to involve a measure of education. In addition to the British Museum and embryonic National Gallery, numerous private establishments saw them-selves as purveyors of popular education, particularly of natural history, anthropology and technology. The most successful of these in London was the Polytechnic in Regent Street, which combined lectures on popular science, a course for engine drivers and magic and variety turns. Although the Polytechnic was the most robust of such enterprises, in time magic and variety came to overwhelm its educational aims. Later in the century it was only saved from the ignominious failure which its rivals had met when Quentin Hogg, a wealthy lawyer, converted it into a college devoted to technical education.

Since the market for entertainment, educational or otherwise, in the early decades of the century was limited to a minority with both money and leisure, leading entrepreneurs only survived by responding rapidly to the tastes of their customers. One of the most successful was William Bullock, the dynamic son of a family of touring waxworkers. In 1807 he stopped touring and settled in London. In 1810 his show included life-size wax figures of the French royal family made by a Parisian, Oudon. Bullock was not only a showman, he was a naturalist and a traveller. A serious scientist, he was elected to the Linnaean Society. In 1812 he established himself in a new building in Piccadilly, whose architecture quickly earned it a name that stuck, the Egyptian Hall. Bullock opened with one of the first scientifically arranged exhibitions of natural history. There were three large exhibition rooms, which were let out to a huge variety of shows. Eventually Bullock sold out, but the Egyptian Hall was one of the longest surviving entertainment centres next to Tussaud's.

There was a wide range of ways of spending at least 1s. on entertainment. In the 1780s one of the most expensive was the Temple of Health in Adelphi Terrace. A self-styled doctor, James Graham, gave lectures, exclusively on sex, with lovely girls, including the future Lady Hamilton, striking poses in

22. The Polytechnic, Regent's Street.

white robes or less. Graduates could hire the Celestial Bed, with a private entrance from the street, at £50 a night. This twelve foot by nine foot monster, reputed to have cost £10,000 was surmounted by a dome that dispensed a variety of perfumes. It was advertised as a cure for sterility. The mattress tilted after use to encourage conception. Music, silk sheets and a series of magnets all played their part. Despite the staggering price, the venture did not make money. Graham moved on to laud the praises of mud baths, lecturing naked covered in mud.

Watching pictures that seem to move and were accompanied by dramatic sound effects became very popular in the years before photography.

They were given different names, mostly ending in 'rama'. Panoramas were massive representations, often of urban landscapes, erected as cylindrical pictures.[43] They were sometimes put at the end of walks in places of entertainment such as the Vauxhall Gardens to give an illusion of greater space. The first person to erect a circular building to house one was Henry Barker in Leicester Square, the heart of London tourism, in 1794. The fashion spread through Europe. In Paris in 1800 an American was responsible for the Passage and Rue des Panoramas near to the Palais Royal. On display was a vista of Paris from the centre of the dome of the Tuileries. Panoramas reflected the contemporary passion for enormous historical paintings, such as those commissioned by Louis-Philippe when he had the palace of Versailles renovated in the 1830s.[44]

At the peak of panorama popularity the Colosseum, conceived as a palace of popular science, was built on the northern edge of London in the recently laid out Regent's Park. The purpose-built panorama polygon was constructed to a Decimus Burton design. The apex was a 112 foot dome, wider than St Paul's. A perfect panorama to display within had been made by a Yorkshireman, Thomas Hornor. He took the opportunity in 1821, when the dome of St Paul's was being repaired, to add more scaffolding so that he was able to make two thousand drawings of the whole of London, checking the detail later on the ground. This was copied by a small army of painters onto the inside of the Colosseum. As they worked the painters were sometimes suspended from the roof in baskets, sometimes balanced on a little stage on stilts that rocked about even when it was not windy.

Unfortunately the main financial backer, Rowland Stephenson, absconded with the funds of his bank. The Colosseum opened, unfinished, in 1829, when four hundred people a day paid 5s. each just to watch the painters and to ride up to the dome in the 'ascending room', one of the earliest hydraulic lifts. Although at its height 150,000 people a year visited the Colosseum, it never paid its way. When the building was started, in 1824, Britain was in boom. From 1825 came nearly eight years of economic uncertainty, involving numerous bankruptcies and industrial setbacks. When the Colosseum was finally complete all entertainment prices were being slashed and in 1832 it had to cut its entry fee to 2s. It also suffered from the competition of the nearby Polytechnic in Upper Regent Street, the most successful exponent of popular science. As the economy recovered the Colosseum's new owner added mechanical pictures, stuffed animals and a grand banqueting hall. Princess Victoria and other notables paid 25s. a ticket for the relaunch in 1835.

Following a trend that Tussaud's had set, the Colosseum tried promenade concerts three years later, but soon descended to become the Colosseum

23. The Colosseum. The panorama seen from the painter's platform. Lithograph
1829.

Saloon, with variety turns. In 1841 it was reborn as the Glacarium, a skating rink using artificial ice made from soda. By 1845 it had been made over again by a firm of cement merchants and dubbed the Glypotheka, exhibiting and selling huge paintings. A new panorama of 'London by Night' was laid over the original one in the dome at night-time. Lamps illuminated the scene and a magic lantern in the top of the dome projected clouds floating past a lighted canvas moon: all for 2s. 6d. The 1848 Revolution inspired a rapidly prepared 'Paris by Night' in which the vestiges of a basket and ropes created the illusion that spectators were actually hovering over the Tuileries in a balloon. The Leicester Square Panorama riposted with 'Paris by Day', so people could follow the events of the revolutionary year as it unfolded.

As well as panoramas there were dioramas, flat pictures with an illusion of 3-D, using lighting to create the illusion of dramatic change. Daguerre had put on the first in Paris in 1822, followed by one in London in 1823. This was in the new Nash Terraces, close to the site of its rival, the Colosseum. The amphitheatre was kept in total darkness for the performance and the sense of depth was created by a series of pivoting screens and shutters. It was instantly popular and took £200 on its first Easter Monday. Unlike the panorama, which was stuck with the same massive picture long after all the curious had seen it, new diorama pictures arrived frequently from Paris. They were mostly sentimental, rather antiquarian, landscapes. Their appeal broadened in succeeding years as audiences soaked up scenes of foreign parts, at a time when most of them were unlikely to have been able to afford to travel. Panoramas and dioramas were quickly adapted for use in theatrical performances, including in pantomimes and fairs. They were serious competitors to the Tussaud travelling show.

Finally there were cosmoramas. They began in Paris in 1808. This was an indoor version of the peep show, though usually involving more re- spectable pictures. A row of paintings would be set up on each side of a room, with a convex lens behind each. Mirrors and dramatic lighting gave an illusion of perspective. Like dioramas, the pictures could be changed easily and the premises were elegantly appointed, leaving plenty of room for people to sit or stand and chat. There were some complaints, however, that at 1s. for each side of the room the cosmorama charged panorama prices for what was essentially a 1d. fairground peep show performance.[45]

Marie Tussaud was careful to emphasise that her exhibition offered value for money – and she was always in a position to judge. Until a few weeks before her death she had total control of the finances of her business. She always had charge of every penny, sitting in a special cubicle throughout opening hours, taking the money. One of her biggest expenditure was wages.

She needed semi-skilled employees, so presumably they travelled with her. Following the fashion of the day, one of her servants was black. Marie eventually established a tight-knit family business, but at the outset she was alone.

Another factor was transport. Travelling became somewhat easier during her touring years with macadamised roads to smooth the journey. As a result coaches eventually reached the speed of ten miles per hour and Marie could be sure of arriving in the next town in advance of the caravans transporting the models. Marie shipped everything in Pickfords caravans. Hiring vehicles was no small expense; she paid £1 4s. for a coach from Leeds to Manchester. Later she bought her own vehicles and transported and advertised at the same time. Her caravans were decorated with gilding and her own name.

Each time she packed up the caravans in the travelling decades it was because her account books told her that in the last weeks fewer people were coming to the exhibition. She would often postpone a move if numbers picked up. Indeed a press notice that a move had been delayed because the exhibition was attracting large numbers was a standard routine to bring in more customers. It seems clear that she planned her touring route but left the date when she moved open. Each destination was calculated on a careful assessment of the potential market. She always ensured that her visit coincided with a significant date for each town, perhaps a race meeting or the arrival of a theatre group, or simply the high point in the town season. She only toured towns with good numbers of well-off middle-class families. She also developed a travelling itinerary to take best advantage of the seasonal mobility of the prosperous middle and upper classes in Britain. Bath was a favourite winter haunt for the rich and idle, and she made repeat visits there and to a number of other towns and cities, including Brighton and Bristol. Bath was such a magnet for those with money to spare that Josiah Wedgwood set up a showroom there.[46] The Tussaud exhibition also paid repeat visits to large cities, notably Manchester and Liverpool, and medium-sized market towns. The travelling years were successful because in Britain there were enough substantial towns, with suitably impressive public spaces, within easy reach of each other along improving roads.

Marie studied her market assiduously. Her target were families with leisure, cash, curiosity and a willingness to accept a smattering of information with their fun. In these years in Britain there were in excess of half a million middle-class families with money to spend on enjoying themselves. The *Liverpool Courier* remarked on the presence at the exhibition of 'some of our first families, who find in this agreeable amusement a most pleasing recreation'. Marie developed her exhibition to be part of the 'public parade' culture of the pre-railway age.

In the early decades of the nineteenth century the British, the French and probably most Europeans, as we know from the novels of Stendhal, Dickens and others, liked to spend weekends and evenings, and the season if they could afford it, strolling in carefully designated parts of the heart of their town. They constructed safe, salubrious centres to their cities for this purpose, with churches, public gardens, assembly halls, museums and, later in the century, department stores. Street lighting and modern drains became the norm. Until the railways were constructed, when they built and moved to suburban villas, middle-class business and professional families lived close to this parade ground and would perform the public circuits on foot or in their own carriage.

Marie ruthlessly exploited and refined this 'promenade' market. She offered more variety than a theatrical performance which would be almost unchanged through its run. She made new models to catch each topical issue, exploring the snobbish glamour of royalty as well as the thrill of being *au fait* with the latest gruesome murder or assassination. Unlike a museum, a waxworks was an active cultural experience. Customers could touch the models, study them in detail, discuss them out loud, imagine themselves in relation to the figures, and, if they were rich enough, consider the purchase of a model of themselves. Unlike a theatre, Tussaud clients were not limited to a short interval for mingling and looking around. Customarily the show opened from 11 to 6 and then from 7 to 10. The models were far more brightly illuminated than was a theatre. This created an excellent medium in which customers could study each other, without appearing intrusive. The promenade was enhanced by the orchestra. The music made a backdrop of sound, under which discreet conversations could be conducted with less restraint than in a theatre or concert hall. A Tussaud's orchestra was first mentioned in 1819. 'The attendance of a band of music renders it a very gay and interesting promenade.'[47] Later in the century programmes of the daily performances of their excerpts of popular classics were printed. Although their orchestra was quite small, Tussaud's seem to have invented the promenade concert.[48] Visitors could spend the entire evening 'promenading', strolling around the assembly room, without it being thought odd. As the *Liverpool Observer* noted, 'The promenade among the illustrious dead and illustrious living is truly delightful'.

The exhibition provided an interactive experience, offering a vaguely educational reason to wander around, apparently purposefully, being inquisitive about models and fellow guests, socialising and perhaps making preliminary sallies in the direction of business, social engagements, even marriage or less respectable liaisons among families. It was an informal, yet formal, location for public social contact. You could chat distantly, or more intimately, and the public setting offered the opportunity to walk away without seeming rude, or to establish closer links.

Marie Tussaud was always keen to stress that the exhibition was designed for the middle and upper classes and it was for these that she emphatically structured her marketing policy. On the other hand, from time to time she made a great fuss of admitting 'the working classes'. Special sessions were designated at unpopular times, for instance part of the last hour, up to 10 p.m., and at half price. 'By this arrangement sufficient time will be given for the classes to view the collection without interfering with each other, and they hope that none but those thus situated will take advantage of it.' There are no clues to how many working-class families could afford the money or were even free to turn up at 9 p.m. A working day might easily run from 6 a.m. to 10 p.m. In common with most other amusements, the exhibition did not open on Sunday, the only free day for working families, nor did it do well on Saturdays, the other day some worker families might have been able to visit. Saturday invariably produced the smallest take of the week, suggesting that at this stage there were few worker customers.[49]

In her pricing strategy, Marie followed the norm for the age. Entertainment was class segregated, mainly by price, although the totally free British Museum sorted out its preferred clientele by giving tickets in response to written requests and refusing entry on demand at the door. A 'rational recreation' cost a minimum of 1s. Only the comfortably off were willing or able to pay more per person for a show. There was plenty to be seen, however, at the cheaper end of the market, although less trace remains of what was available. There were 1d. wax and other shows at fairs and in towns, 3d. seats at variety theatres, and there was entertainment on the streets themselves. Cages of 'families' of animals, monkeys and others, were hawked around for public inspection. There were jugglers and other street performers. The advertisements for shows were often entertainment in themselves. Sandwich-boarded individuals might walk, or a cart displaying an advertisement or a mini-representation of a show might be wheeled, around the streets. In major towns, especially capital cities, upmarket shops in streets like Oxford Street gave ever more enticing free window displays, although they were still restricted to tiny panes of glass and there were no department stores until later in the century.

Until 1834 Tussaud's prospered by touring. Yet London offered far and away the biggest catchment area in Britain, with a population of one million in 1801, rising to a much less densely packed three million by 1861. No other town could rival the size of the capital and in the early decades of the century there was no really large city north of London. Except for the annual fairs, London entertainment of all kinds was concentrated in the centre, with Leicester Square as the focus. Many of their customers were Londoners, although trade from 'country cousins' and foreign tourists was not insignificant. Theatres, exhibitions and other shows were within walking distance, although the rich might well use a carriage. Shillibeer's omnibuses provided the first public transport in London in 1829, but only the rich could ride at 6d. for a short and 1s. for a longer journey in town.

Madame Tussaud and many other entertainers calculated that they were better off travelling to perform. Most customers came for a single visit, although Tussaud made considerable efforts to update her show so that she would have plenty of repeat customers when she visited towns for a second time. Running a touring company was extremely arduous. Madame Tussaud's odyssey was extraordinary at the time, when almost no middle-class married women worked, and when travelling even a short distance was exhausting. Marie remained on the road for thirty-three years in total, visiting seventy-five different main towns and many smaller places. The packing and unpacking alone, without the travelling, model and costume making, would have been herculean tasks for a young person, but Marie set out when she was already middle-aged, with a tiny child, knowing no one and (when she began) speaking not a word of English. She was in her seventies when her touring days ended in 1835. This tiny woman possessed self-reliance, courage and determination to an unusual degree. She was tough, exceptionally well organised and paid fanatical attention to detail, particularly in matters financial. The *Edinburgh Observer* applauded Marie as an example to other women:

> To the ladies this collection must be highly interesting, from its being the work of one of their own sex: who, in the formation of the numerous groups, has proved what may be done when talent is united with industry.

5

The Baker Street Bazaar

In the first half of the nineteenth century public museums sprang up all over Britain; but while claiming to satisfy demand they often frustrated it. In earlier times individuals had amassed collections of natural objects, paintings, books, or whatever took their fancy, and shared them with friends. In the eighteenth century there was a mania for natural history, including animals, plants and rocks. It was part of the eighteenth-century scientific creed that life on earth was progressive and that everything could be rationalised and categorised. Enlightened writers demanded that education itself should be more widely available in the name of the general improvement of society. Turning private collections into public museums became part of that pedagogic process. It was also an apparently worthy and economical solution to the problem of how heirs could dispose of a collector's mania without seeming ungrateful.

The first public museum in Europe was the British Museum, which began with Sir Hans Sloane's very varied collection, including a great deal of natural history. It was purchased for the nation by a public lottery after his death. It went on show in 1759 at Montague House, Bloomsbury, a former private mansion. The term 'public' was a misnomer. The trustees were terrified of the masses: 'a great concourse of ordinary people will never be kept in order'.[1] There was no charge, but admission was by ticket. A labyrinthine process of application excluded all but the most determined, educated and leisured. First you applied at the door and the porter wrote your name, address and social position in his book. That would have kept away all but the most assertive and those desperate to see what a polar bear looked like. Several months later you were invited to return for your ticket. To make doubly sure that the labouring classes did not bring their sweat and bad language, the new British Museum was firmly shut on those days when working people might have attended, Saturdays, Sundays and the weeks after Christmas, Easter and Whitsun. Summer was likely to be the most popular season, so the museum was open only from 4 to 8 p.m. As the working day might well last until up to 10 p.m., few members of the 'popular classes' were likely to penetrate. A tourist in a hurry could obtain a black market ticket, usually paying 2s. Nor could visitors wander at will. They were hustled around by officials at top speed in groups of five and were provided with little enlightenment on the contents of each room. Small wonder that a maximum of sixty a day ever managed to get past the huge front doors until well into the nineteenth century. Excluding the masses from museums seemed totally justified to the trustees when in 1780 the Gordon rioters surged through neighbouring streets and set fire to Lord Mansfield's house, manuscripts and library. The British Museum was untouched, but a military detachment guarded it until the 1860s.

Other specialised collections were established towards the end of the eighteenth century. They limited entry to a tiny, educated elite. These included the anatomical museums of surgeons, such as Brooke and the Hunter brothers in Leicester Square. The Holophusikon was in Leicester Square too, a collection of fossils and stuffed animals made by Sir Ashton Lever. Lever made an admission charge and restricted entry on social grounds. Unable to cover costs, he asked the government to buy his collection. The subsequent lottery failed to raise enough cash, but the winning ticket holder claimed the prize. The 'Museum Leveriarum' then moved to Blackfriars Road and was eventually auctioned off, some specimens ending their days in fairgrounds.[2]

In France the vogue for museums got off to a later but even cheaper start when, during their conquest of most of Europe, Napoleon and his generals stole a huge range of paintings, sculptures and other objects, often from the dispossessed church, and shipped them home. The total of foreign booty has been estimated at one thousand important artistic items from the German states and five hundred items each from Italy and the Low Countries.[3] The most obviously valuable and portable objects were retained by the generals for their own pleasure, but the largest were delivered to the Louvre, previously a royal palace, which, by default, found itself converted into a public museum. The Musée Napoléon thus equipped opened in 1810. Despite the size of the palace and its commodious accommodation, the speed of imperial theft exceeded display and storage capacity. Napoleon made generous 'gifts' of over eight hundred of the largest, least appealing canvases and objects to different cities and towns in France, with instructions to set up public museums in the provinces. In many cases purpose-built buildings had to be constructed. Thus, although the French entered the museum stakes later than the British, they overtook them and municipal museums opened in France faster than in England. It should be noted that the French municipal museums operated the same standards as national ones, rigorously excluding working people, and searching anyone who looked undesirable.[4] Umbrella carriers were welcome, because umbrellas were a sign of bourgeois respectability, but umbrellas were considered potentially dangerous and not allowed in the galleries, which mostly had brand new roofs.

Art galleries were also increasingly in demand. Vienna had a state-owned exhibition by 1781, Paris in 1793. The National Gallery did not open until 1823, using the proceeds of a war loan repaid by the Austrians. In 1838 it acquired a permanent site in Trafalgar Square. Free admission brought half a million visitors in the second year. The Royal Academy already held an annual show. In 1822 there was a big fuss that the 1s. entry fee failed to keep out ordinary 'cockneys' when a picture relating to Waterloo, commissioned by the much admired duke of Wellington, was shown. By the 1830s a number of London aristocrats allowed the public into their collections on certain days. There were private showings, sometimes of individual pictures, in venues such as the Egyptian Hall. Géricault displayed the *Raft of the Medusa* there very successfully, but when it went on tour and arrived in Dublin the admission price had to be reduced from 1s. 8d. to 10d. because of the competition of a much bigger, though eminently forgettable, rival canvas. It is fascinating to realise how much could be charged for the privilege of looking at one painting. By mid century sightseers were spending £4,000,000 a year to visit a variety of exhibitions in London alone.

Madame Tussaud, with her acute business sense, was aware that museums and art galleries were becoming increasingly fashionable after the Napoleonic wars, but that the potential customers, particularly the middle classes, were frustrated rather than satisfied by existing establishments. Around 1820 the Tussaud travelling wax exhibition responded by starting to adopt a combination of the characteristics of an art gallery and museum. Marie acquired copies of Rembrandt's *Belshazzar's Feast* and a Titian. She also bought Le Febvre's portrait of Napoleon in his imperial robes. Marie-Louise had commissioned it and it was the last painting made of him whilst emperor. Gradually the collection acquired so many paintings and other objects that it must have become less and less mobile and the cost of shipping must have increased considerably. It is noticeable that the last few journeys before the arrival in Baker Street were relatively short. Joseph and Francis also devised increasingly elaborate gilded displays, such as the Corinthian Saloon in the Gray's Inn Road, constructed at a cost of over £1000. They used enormous gilded mirrors, which showed off the models to perfection, a trick Marie had learned from Curtius. Also, following Curtius's example, they haunted auctions and bought precious objects to give authenticity and a museum-like quality with which to surround their models. They satisfied the demand for family entertainment with a dash of education – which rivals like the British Museum were very obviously failing to satisfy.

That the exhibition finally put down roots in 1835 had nothing to do with human considerations. The fact that at seventy-four Marie was way past retiring age, or that her sons had eleven young children between them, was ignored. There was no intention to settle in London when the whole caravanserai came to a halt after a tour of Kent in the later months of 1833. In November the exhibition arrived at the Blackheath Assembly Rooms, which were located at the 'Green Man'. Subsequently they spent five months in the assembly room at the Old London Bazaar in Gray's Inn Road. The terminus of the London and Birmingham line was not far away, and even closer was the London and Grand Junction line, in process of construction. It must have occurred to the Tussaud's that the railway terminals being built close by would revolutionise their trade.

The press commended the luxury, elegance and artistry of the Gray's Inn Road show, as well as its educational value:

> We recommend that those that have young persons to take them to see this exhibition, as the view of so many characters famous in history must make them desirous to open the pages of history ... an exhibition ... which will repay the curiosity of those who may be induced to pay ... a visit.[5]

The Old London Bazaar had been a horse and carriage repository and in 1832 briefly Robert Owen's National Equitable Labour Exchange for bartering, rather than selling, goods. There was an impressive room, seventy feet by forty-five, which provided enough space to arrange Napoleon's coronation display at one end and the coronation of William IV at the other. In the middle was a new model of Madame Tussaud herself, which, as always, confused some customers. The orchestra continued to provide a novel background to the promenade.[6] In the second room, then called the blue-beard chamber, revolutionary deaths' heads were still prominent. A star attraction was an ivory model of a gullotine. The exhibition catalogue explained: 'So great is the rapidity with which this machine performs the work of death, that the executioner of Paris (including the preparations) cuts off fifteen heads with it in fifteen minutes'. The Manchester Courier gushed 'the exhibition is one which even a man of business may devote a couple of hours not only with pleasure but with profit'.

In Britain hangings were a major source of free entertainment and were plentiful since a minor thief was as liable to be hanged as a murderer. London had the reputation for offering the best hangings. In the 1770s the place of execution was moved from Tyburn, on the edge of Hyde Park, to Newgate. Another change was that instead of the victim being placed in a cart with the noose round his neck and the cart being driven away, a scaffold with a drop was constructed. The drop was not a long one, so that

24. Old Gray's Inn Road, 1828. For a time the London base of Madame Tussaud's.

the hanging man still died in full view of the excited crowd slowly and horrifically by choking, rather than of a broken neck, as became the method late in the nineteenth century when a long drop was adopted. A white hood was put over the victim's head, but the twitching and writhing of his (or her) body was visible. To add to the entertainment everyone knew that, although breathing might stop, the heart would keep beating for twenty minutes – and presumably part of the thrill of watching an execution was imagining what the victim might be feeling. The hangman had a heavy responsibility; he was likely to be attacked himself if he bungled the job by tying so tight a knot the head was severed and the crowd missed the show. The body was left swinging for an hour, before being cut down and buried in an unmarked grave, or being handed over to a hospital for dissection. There were medical complaints that the number of hangings was reduced towards the end of the eighteenth century, partly because potential victims were deported to Australia, partly because criminals were offered the alternative of fighting Bonaparte.[7]

The reduction in the number of executions may explain why 'the Other Chamber' became so popular. It was a taste that Tussaud's exploited but did not create. At eighteenth-century fairs the gingerbread men on sale were shaped into famous felons, while puppets performed mock executions.[8] The French Revolution turned death into a daily, prominently displayed street theatre. The British were eager to find out more about the horrors of multiple deaths during the Revolution. They had read accounts of the Terror and seen cartoons of the guillotine.

Tussaud's started with guillotined revolutionary heads and a small model of the guillotine Marie had brought from France in 1802. The French flavour of this part of the exhibition was seasoned by a growing crop of home-grown murderers and villains. One of the most popular was a scene showing the murder of Maria Martin at the Red Barn in 1828. 'Red' was an arresting title, though it referred to the barn's roof tiles, not the unfortunate girl's blood. The daughter of a farm labourer, Maria had hoped that her lover, and the father of her child, William Corder, would marry her. He promised to do so and arranged to meet her at the Red Barn, near Bury St Edmunds. Maria was never seen alive again. Corder wrote to the parents assuring them that they were married. Maria's mother, however, dreamt so often that her daughter's remains were buried in the Red Barn that eventually an investigation was made. This apparent supernatural element in the story intrigued people, ten thousand of whom saw Corder hang. Madame Tussaud took a model of his features from a death mask made by the surgeon at the Bury St Edmunds hospital. Hers was not the only representation of the murder. In London seven years after the death there were still five panoramas or phantasmagoricas retelling the tale.

The Burke and Hare body-snatching murders were also good for business. There was a perpetual shortage of dead bodies for surgeons and their students to practise on and this void was for a time filled by the activities of grave robbers. William Burke and William Hare, both Irish and labourers, took to a different trade when they parcelled up one of their fellow lodgers, who had died accidentally and sold him to Edinburgh hospital, with the conniv- ance of the two women who ran the lodgings. They did so well that they subsequently killed sixteen rough sleepers in their lodging house, carried them in a sack to the hospital and sold the bodies. When other lodgers found one of the bodies, Hare and one of the women denounced Burke and the other woman. They were tried and Burke was executed in 1829. Madame Tussaud modelled Burke during the trial, her sons completed Hare, and also acquired a cast of Burke's head done three hours after the execution.[9] This display proved so compelling that it is still part of the exhibition.

Tussaud's next moved from King's Cross to a more elegant London venue, the Lowther Arcade in King William Street, near the Strand. In August 1830 Tussaud's set up for a three month season at Old Grove House, an inn in Camberwell, then a fashionable pleasure garden. Their final show of the year was in the assembly rooms of the Mermaid Tavern in Hackney. Just after Christmas they returned to Gray's Inn Road and three months later took a lease at the Bazaar, the former King Street barracks at the junction of Baker Street and Portman Square, an elegant and very desirable central location. For over a year the Tussaud's assumed they would move on and Joseph put on a show at the town hall in Brighton as an insurance policy. They repeatedly took only short leases on the Baker Street premises, in case the business took a down-turn. The crucial factor was always financial. The Tussauds explained their decision to stay put by a specific event. London profits doubled in a single week in 1836 when everyone rushed to see the model of an extremely popular young opera singer, Maria Malibran, who had died suddenly. Madame Tussaud anticipated public interest and ordered five hundred posters advertising the new figure. Yet Marie's artistic skills and sensitivity to public demand would have been little good without her control of money and awareness of where they stood from day to day. She retained close financial control of her business and operated the cash desk herself. She clearly had well-developed economic antennae. There were still no free tickets and she employed her family where possible and their wages were very modest.

The decision to stay in Baker Street, in a highly fashionable central district, close to the most prestigious cluster of retail streets in the world, was determined by day by day profits. In 1833, when they were still touring, average weekly takings were £45, by 1837 they stood at £102 a week.[10] The decision to stay was astute. Tussaud's were very sensitive to the impact of changes in methods of transport on their business, partly because they had been a travelling show themselves for so long. The revolution in transport, in respect not only to speed but frequency and also cost, made it easy to persuade people to travel to entertainments rather than expect the entertainments themselves to move constantly. Even before the railways, road improvements had made coach journeys shorter. In the 1820s London to Brighton was cut to six hours, but even an outside seat cost 12 shillings, so only the rich could ride. Mass movement came about with the railways. In 1835 117,000 made the trip to Brighton by rail during the year. By 1850 the same journey was made by 73,000 each week. On Easter Monday 1862 132,000 crowded into trains to Brighton. The journey time had shrunk to two hours. Surprisingly, although it was cheaper, the price was only one-third less than the coach price of the 1820s. Passengers were drawn mainly from the existing leisured classes. The reduction in journey time to towns like Brighton and Bath, where the rich had previously spent the entire season, was dramatic. The elite no longer thought of spending a season in Brighton when they could go for a day, a week or a fortnight. Indeed Queen Victoria was so appalled by the crowds that she decamped from the Royal Pavilion to the Isle of Wight. Other wealthy leisured families also began to look further afield to retain privacy and exclusivity. A day at the seaside became an exciting novelty for the less well off, although they tended to prefer different resorts. There were special excursions for working people from the industrial towns. In 1846 a mill in Swinton negotiated the first trip to Blackpool for its workers for 1s. return, plus 1d. for a band. Two soldiers playing a fife and drum roused the passengers at 3 a.m. to catch the train, a little earlier than they were used to getting up for work.

Horse buses brought Londoners to the front door of the new Tussaud venue and, as demand increased, prices fell. A ticket from Charing Cross to Camden Town came down from a prohibitive 1s. to 3d. and then 1d. Within a few years the rapid development of the rail network meant customers could travel from all over the country. By 1848 all eight main London rail terminals were built. There was no need to transport the exhibition to people; they came to it. Families who had visited the travelling show made the new venue part of a trip to the capital. The Baker Street site could be reached from all of the new main stations on the 'New Road': Marylebone Road and its continuation, Euston Road. The permanent exhibition was less than two miles from King's Cross, St Pancras, Euston and Paddington, while Marylebone station, built towards the end of the century, with its new commuter traffic, was no more than a mile away. The models could now lead a more sedate and restful life. The culture that assumed that customers travelled to places of entertainment, to the new municipal art galleries and museums, as well as theatres and waxworks, was quickly accepted. The most rapidly expanding section of the entertainment market was the salaried, rather than the leisured, middle classes. The construction of the rail network, and in London the building of an underground system, tempted them to move their homes out of the centre into the new suburbs. The Tussaud's exhibition was in easy reach by a variety of forms of transport.

The Baker Street Bazaar was on the west side of Baker Street between Dorset Street and King Street. The building had originally been the King Street Barracks, and the Life Guards had set off from it for Waterloo. Madame Tussaud was always proud to recall that her main showroom had been the Guards' mess room.[11] The Tussaud exhibition occupied the upper floors of the three-storey building. Downstairs horses and carriages were offered for sale and later the area was used for the annual Royal Smithfield Club Cattle Show and regular poultry shows. Upstairs was a different world. Unlike the average wax show housed in cramped, dark quarters, the Tussaud exhibition did its utmost to resemble a visit to a large, elegant and dazzlingly lit salon. Visitors entered by a small ground floor hall, ornamented with sculpture, in both antique and modern styles. A wide staircase led to the salon, decorated with artificial flowers, scrolled and twirled arabesques and enormous mirrors. Here they were greeted by Madame Tussaud herself,

25. Madame Tussaud.

sitting at a small table, waiting to take their money and welcome them, for all the world like the hostess at an elegant salon. Then they were encouraged to 'mingle with the mighty'. 'This is one of the most delightful salons in London; the first people of the day (past and present) appear as if attracted by the hospitality of Madame. It is true that they remain silent, but an acquaintanceship with phrenology supplies that defect to logicians.'[12]

The first room was the focal point of the Baker Street exhibition, the 'Great Room', which was 100 feet by 50 feet. The walls were covered in plate glass and decorated with draperies and gilt ornaments, in the style of France at the time of Louis XIV. There were statues and groups on all sides, with large tableaux in the centre. There was plenty of space to move around, and ottomans and sofas for rest and conversation, just as one would expect in an art gallery, or indeed a private drawing room. A balcony over the main entrance housed the orchestra that played during the evening session. At the other end you entered the 'Golden Chamber', the embryo of what was soon known as the 'Hall of Kings', including Henry VIII, Elizabeth, Mary Queen of Scots, Charles I and Cromwell, plus all the Hanoverians. Coronation displays were now a focal part of the show. Such tableaux made a small contribution to forming opinion about monarchy.

26. The Baker Street Bazaar, interior.

The detested Prince Regent, who finally became George IV, had come close to persuading the British to abandon monarchy. His brothers were not much more reassuring, even though William IV, who succeeded him, had served in the Navy. The image of monarchy was restored partly by surrounding these unpleasant characters with elaborate formal ceremonial. The divine right of kings was dead and gone, but some distance and spectacle was urgently needed if the institution was to survive.

Tussaud's played their part in publicising the ceremonial of monarchy and popularising the institution. Even George IV was 'made over' to perfection and beyond. His coronation in wax was breathtaking. Judging by the crowds, a lot of people admired it, although Dickens was critical both of the opulence of the garments and the approval signified by the Tussaud display. It was rumoured that George had spent £18,000 on his coronation robes. In 1840 the Tussaud's bought the originals for £300 to adorn their model. The king was surrounded by an odd assortment of attendants, including 'allegorical figures ... in the most splendid costume, of the value, we should imagine of £150 to £200';[13] one resembled a medieval knight in chain mail, another was in a full suit of armour, with the visor closed. Another seemed to be dressed as a Roman centurion, while mere mortals were decked in more predictable ermine robes.[14] The 1846 catalogue lauded

27. Tableau of George IV in his coronation robes.

the skill of the British craftsmen and paraphrased Shakespeare in praise of the king, 'the glass of fashion and the mould of form'.

As the landed elites in Britain had held a profound distaste of republics since the days of the Levellers and Cromwell, a view reinforced by the violence of the French Revolution, a credible successor to William IV needed to be found after the death of Princess Charlotte and her baby. A niece of George IV and William IV, Victoria, gave Marie double scope for combining sentiment with profit. Within a few months of Victoria's coronation in June 1837, the full scene, including a papier mâché reproduction of the interior of Westminster Abbey, became the centre-piece of the Tussaud show. The cartoonist, George Cruikshank, included a painting of the tableau among his ten aquatints, 'London Fashion Plates'. Victoria understood the value of wax publicity. Apparently after her own visit to Tussaud's in 1833, she encouraged Sir George Hayter to make a copy of his painting of her coronation for Tussaud's and allowed exact copies of her robes to be made for the Tussaud tableau.

Victoria's marriage in 1840 provided another spectacular opportunity to mould and echo popular sentiment; the Tussaud tableau showing Albert as he put the ring onto his new wife's finger. Tussaud's scored another marketing triumph. With the queen's permission, Madame Tussaud had an exact copy of her satin wedding gown made by the same Spitalfield weavers. Tussaud's were delighted to inform their customers that the price of their gown was £1000. The young Victoria appeared on the cover of the 1841 Tussaud catalogue, with her name emblazoned above her head, in case anyone did not recognise her. She had become Tussaud's' biggest attraction. The birth of nine offspring made it even easier to portray this queen as a familiar and endearing British institution. In 1848 Victoria (incognita) took her brood to see Tussaud's. After the death of the Prince Consort in 1861, however, she refused to appear in public, even to open Parliament, and republican criticism revived. The Tussauds' devotion to the wax Victoria and her family helped maintain an illusion of her visibility and accessibility. Waxen Princesses Alice and Louise appeared in glamorous Worth gowns, copies specially made for Tussaud's. Princess Louise's wedding was rendered in wax. Tussaud's did their best to make yet another Prince of Wales, Albert Edward, acceptable with constant reworkings of his model. Despite the real Albert, Victoria herself and her eldest son, royalty in wax proved to be a far more reliable money-spinner than it had been in France. The royals continued to return the compliment. In 1879 massed ranks of royalty visited their wax selves, including the Prince and Princess of Wales and the Princesses Louise and Victoria. Another visit of multiple royals took place in 1882.

Royals continued to rub shoulders with famous opera singers and well-known preachers.[15] Journalists noted approvingly that Madame Tussaud herself stood amongst her models like a hostess receiving her guests. She had become as much an attraction at the exhibition as the models themselves, 'one of the national ornaments of the feminine species', according to *Punch*.[16]

Tussaud's 'Adjoining Room' became so famous that some villains donated their own clothes for their models before their execution. Sometimes the Tussauds bought the entire contents of a room where a particularly memorable murder had occurred, and reconstructed it in what *Punch* christened, in 1846, the 'Chamber of Horrors'. In 1835 Fieschi and his 'infernal machine' proved a compelling novelty. The Corsican Joseph-Marie Fieschi, a thief who had served in the Neapolitan army, and two French republican associates constructed a machine to which twenty-four rifles were attached which could be fired by one man. Their plan was to assassinate Louis-Philippe, king of the French, while he was reviewing the national guard. The killing machine was assembled in the third floor of a house in the Boulevard du Temple. The king survived, but eighteen died and twenty-two were injured. The three main conspirators were executed; in addition Fieschi's thumb was chopped off beforehand. Tussaud's soon had a model of Fieschi's guillotined head, and one of the detestable machine. They acquired their own working scale model of the official Paris guillotine and the actual blade and lunette used during the 1790s. The story of how this happened is ambiguous. When the Terror ended in 1794 the guillotine and the official executioner, Sanson, were far less busy. Sanson was always haunted by the scale of his revolutionary operations, but the family were hereditary executioners and he was succeeded by his son. His grandson, Clément-Henri, was less successful. He was thrown into the Clichy prison for debt in 1847. He had no son to follow him and so, for him, his instruments of death were superfluous. Clément-Henri tried unsuccessfully to sell the original guillotine. In 1847 he sold the plans used to make the original guillotine to the Tussaud's for £220 and a substantial functioning replica was made.[17] In 1879 the shah of Persia tried, unsuccessfully, to persuade one of his officials to lie in the lunette to show him how the blade functioned.[18]

The British treated Madame Tussaud's French origins with the rather bemused affection that has been part of their profound love-hate relationship with their nearest neighbours. Safe in England, where no one was likely to check the claim, she never failed to assert that she had been artist to Madame Elizabeth, sister of the last three Bourbon kings.[19] When the revolutionary wars were over, with the emperor safely dispatched to St Helena, she also gradually began to amass a Napoleonic collection, which became a favourite with British customers. Napoleon had been at the head of a massive empire, which the British had taken the dominant role in destroying. Promenading around Napoleonic artefacts cut the emperor down to size, like domesticating a dangerous animal. It was a sure-fire winner in bringing in the crowds to the exhibition. Marie already had the models of Napoleon and Josephine she had brought over from France. She made a new statue of Napoleon in 1815 after Waterloo. A stunning publicity stunt was staged when Madame Tussaud was allowed to model his face aboard the *Bellerophon*, anchored in Torbay and awaiting his final journey to St Helena.

London exhibitions were struck by Napoleon mania in 1815. There were at least three displays dedicated to Britain's enemy, one of which included the emperor's white horse Marengo, complete with five wounds and a bullet lodged in its tail. At Bartholomew Fair for 6d. you could see the carriage Napoleon had used during his brief exile on Elba. William Bullock acquired what clever marketing turned into the *pièce de résistance*, the carriage in which Napoleon escaped after Waterloo – he had something of a penchant for deserting a battle he could not win. Prince Blücher presented the carriage to the Prince Regent, who himself saw its potential and, as ever short of cash, sold it to William Bullock. Bullock created a Napoleon Museum in

28. Crowds swarm over Napoleon's coach at Bullock's Museum.

the Egyptian Hall, with the carriage, complete with the original horses and coachman, the last of whom had been presumed dead. Bullock made £35,000 from the carriage in London and on a subsequent tour. It was claimed that 800,000 people went to see it.[20] A famous Cruikshank cartoon shows visitors swarming over it, with several chubby ladies climbing on its roof showing their underwear.

The coach was surrounded by works of art from the Louvre and other places, taken when the Allies invaded Paris in 1814. When Bullock later failed to sell the art to the British Museum, he auctioned the lot, making £9974 13s. The twelve foot high original statue of Napoleon, which the Allies removed from the Vendôme column, was sold to William Beckford for Fonthill Abbey for a mere £33 12s.[21] The Tussauds acquired some of the items. Marie could not fail to be aware of the marketing potential of the fallen emperor and artefacts associated with him.

It was not until the exhibition was settled in Baker Street that the Tussaud show acquired a pronounced Napoleonic emphasis. This may have been partly due to problems in transporting a large array of relics, but it seems to have been more a matter of timing. By the 1830s an increasing number of Napoleon's possessions were appearing in auctions and the Napoleonic myth was well developed. Napoleon himself died in 1821, leaving behind a memory of French military conquests and an empire equalled only by the Romans. His memoirs, dictated to Las Cases on St Helena, went through six editions between 1823 and 1842 and were one of the best sellers of the century. He was remembered in songs, especially those of Béranger, flags, medals, the popular woodcut *images d'Epinal* and countless other illustrations.

The legend might have begun to fade after the death of Napoleon's son, Napoleon II, in 1832, but in the 1830s the new citizen-king, Louis-Philippe, and one of his leading ministers, Adolphe Thiers, consciously cultivated and exploited the Napoleonic legend. The Arc de Triomphe was completed between 1833 and 1836, and in 1833 a new statue of Napoleon was placed on top of the Vendôme column, built to commemorate the 1830 revolution. Louis-Philippe transformed Versailles into a Napoleon museum, commissioning numerous massive portraits of the emperor's battles.[22] Victor Hugo, Alfred de Musset, Balzac and numerous playwrights celebrated his glories. In 1840 Napoleon's ashes were brought back to France and installed in Les Invalides by the king's eldest son, the duc d'Orléans, with immense ceremony.[23] In 1836 and again in 1839 the emperor's nephew, Louis-Napoleon, tried abortively to seize power on the tide of growing Bonapartism.

At one level the Tussauds exploited a Romantic Bonapartism invented by the French themselves. The British were fascinated by their former enemy, perhaps even more so now that he was safely dead. In the late 1830s worsening Anglo-French relations made it topical to feel aggressive towards the French. The Tussauds' own views may have been more reverential. Madame Tussaud patiently built up her Napoleonic collection at auctions when those to whom Napoleon had given his possessions, or who had acquired them by other means, died. In 1834 she bought some of Napoleon's eagles and a battle flag for £12 13s. 7d. at a sale of Waterloo trophies. The previous owners of her purchases included one of the emperor's elder brothers, Prince Lucien, whose effects were dispersed after his death in 1840, and Dr O'Meara, a naval surgeon who was Napoleon's doctor on St Helena.[24] O'Meara's collection was auctioned after his death in 1836. Madame Tussaud bought some silver and other items in a sale after the death of Major von Keller. He was the Prussian officer who had failed to capture the emperor after Waterloo, but seized his carriage and its fittings, after Napoleon escaped on horseback. Keller handed the carriage over to his superior officer, as it was too big to purloin, but he kept most of its numerous fittings. In 1841–42 the Tussaud ledgers recorded the accelerating pace at which they bought Napoleonic memorabilia, including the mantles of Napoleon and Josephine (£105) and the camp bed on which the emperor had died. In total the Tussauds claimed to have spent £6000 on these artefacts.

Two rooms dedicated to Napoleon opened in 1843 with a special catalogue in French, but no additional entry fee.[25] The extra 6*d*. for the Chamber of Horrors also allowed entry into the two new Napoleon rooms. This may have implied that the emperor was himself a horror for the British.

> Madame Tussaud and Sons' New Rooms of the Relics of the Emperor Napoleon are opened to the Public without Additional Charge, although at a cost of nearly £6000 fitted up after the designs of Isabey and Fountain, the Emperor's artists forming a SERIES OF NATIONAL REMINISCENCES of great interest … everything connected to the late Emperor belongs to British history; it therefore follows that these extraordinary Relics cannot but be highly interesting to every reflecting mind, as they are such ought not to be, with propriety, in private hands, but should take their place in the INVALIDES in Paris where rest the Body of the Great Soldier, General, Consul and Emperor of the French.[26]

The catalogue went on to give details of every object, who had owned it, a certificate attesting to its authenticity, and often the price the Tussauds had paid for it. The first of the new rooms was known as the Golden Room or the Shrine of Napoleon. It included a wax model of the emperor, based on David's paintings, in clothes he had worn on St Helena. Also on display was a glorious blue velvet cloak which Napoleon had worn at the battle of Marengo, which had been used to cover his body in his funeral procession. He had bequeathed this treasured possession to his son, the king of Rome, by then a teenager growing up in Vienna, under the care of his mother, Marie-Louise, now the ruler of the Italian province of Parma and the mistress of the Austrian army officer appointed to guard her. A wax Napoleon stood next to his wax son in his original cradle, fashioned by the leading metal workers of the day.

The second room contained the even more precious table of the marshals, a Sèvres porcelain masterpiece presented by Napoleon to the city of Paris, for which he had paid £12,000. In the centre was a portrait of the emperor in his state robes and around the edge were stylish images of thirteen of his marshals, all the work of Isabey.[27] At the Restoration Louis XVIII exchanged the table, unwelcome in the Louvre, for some antique bronzes. When Isabey heard that Frochon, an antiquary, had bought it, with the intention of breaking it up and selling the miniatures, he persuaded Marcel de Serres to buy it, this time for 60,000 francs. One appreciates just how much this was by a comparison with the voting qualification in France at the time. A man had to pay 300 francs a year in tax to qualify and that there were only about 100,000 individuals rich enough to do so. In 1839, when his affairs were less buoyant, de Serres shipped the table to London where Joseph Tussaud acquired it at auction. It was a star attraction in the relics collection, but only for a few years. The 1843 and 1844 catalogues listed it for sale at 4000 guineas. Subsequent catalogues merely provided a description and its history, and in 1861 and later a facsimile. Apparently Joseph Tussaud and two associates, Michel and W. O'Brien, had each initially put up 2193 francs 75 centimes, but had never completed the purchase. When she reclaimed the table, de Serres's widow lent it to Malmaison, the Napoleon museum, with the hope of finding a purchaser. The rest of the exhibits in the second relics room included portraits by David, Gérard and others of Napoleon, Josephine, and Marie-Louise, and of Lucien and Caroline Bonaparte, the emperor's brother and sister.

The exhibition was dominated by Napoleon's Waterloo carriage. After its glory days with William Bullock, interest in Napoleon relics faded for a time. The carriage was sold on several times, and there was an abortive plan to exhibit it in America. Eventually it was ignominiously passed on as part payment for a debt of about £150 to a coach builder based in the stables of the Gray's Inn Road Bazaar where Tussaud's had a show before they moved to Baker Street. The Tussauds spotted it mouldering away and bought it for £52. Renovated, it turned out to be as much a treasure for the Tussauds as it had been for William Bullock. In 1843 Tussaud's reprinted the brochure Bullock had published telling the story of the carriage.[28]

The carriage was a special design beloved by the fast-moving emperor, who had ordered three identical ones between 1812 and his final defeat in 1815. The one Tussaud's secured was a rush order, built in April 1815, for which Napoleon had paid £639. The poet Lord Byron had a replica constructed in London a year later for a mere £500. Napoleon's carriage had dark blue bullet-proof panels, emblazoned with the imperial coat of arms. It was strongly built and equipped for war, with several compartments stuffed with loaded pistols. The carriage was a convertible and its design was novel. The upper parts could be folded towards the front and back and the window supports were also collapsible. It was referred to as a *dormeuse* and adaptable for use as a kitchen, dining room, study, bathroom as well as sleeping quarters. All the eating utensils were gold or silver and embossed with 'N' and the imperial arms. A desk could be drawn out, complete with secret drawers for jewels and money and compartments for telescopes and maps. There was a *nécessaire*, a toiletries box, given to Napoleon by Marie-Louise before the Russian campaign. Included underneath the seats was a commodious folding camp bed on castors that could be erected in a minute. At the rear a curved projection served as a small en suite bathroom, with outside access for easy emptying.

SEASON OF 1846.

M^ADAME TUSSAUD & SONS

Have the high gratification to state that THE GROUP of the

ROYAL FAMILY AT HOME !

CONSISTING OF

Her Gracious Majesty, Prince Albert, and their Four Lovely Children, the Prince of Wales, the Princess Royal, the Princess Alice, and Prince Alfred, HAVE GIVEN COMPLETE SATISFACTION TO THOUSANDS. The novelties for the present season consist of a

Magnificent Display of Court Dresses,

OF SURPASSING RICHNESS,

Comprising TWENTY FIVE LADIES' AND GENTEMEN'S COSTUMES, intended to convey to the **MIDDLE CLASSES** an idea of **REGAL SPLENDOUR**, a most pleasing novelty, and calculated to convey to young persons much necessary instruction. Amongst them will be noticed the FULL DRESS of His Majesty

LOUIS PHILIPPE, AS LIEUT. GEN. OF FRANCE

As King of the French, worn by himself on all public occasions, with the Grand Star, Cordon, &c., of the Legion of Honour.

The truly beautiful

GREEK WARRIOR COSTUME,

Of surpassing worsmanship, conveying an idea of a GREEK OFFICER in full Costume, of matchless beauty, and a curiosity for the ladies, as a specimen of NEEDLEWORK. The Ladies' Dresses comprise such as are Worn at Court by the Highest Classes. The Collection now contains upwards of ONE HUNDRED AND TWENTY PUBLIC CHARACTERS. Also, THE MAGNIFICENT

CORONATION ROBES of GEORGE IV.

Worn and designed by himself, and which cost upwards of £18,000.

THE RELICS OF NAPOLEON,

OF SURPASSING INTEREST. The GOLDEN CHAMBER containing the Camp-bed on which he Died, the Coronation Robes, the Cloak of Marengo, and the highly celebrated MILITARY CARRIAGE, taken at Waterloo. The magnificent Rooms fitted up for the purpose, at a great expense. The recent Novelties are

THE NATIONAL GROUP OF EIGHTEEN FIGURES,

IN HONOUR OF THE DUKE OF WELLINGTON,

The Group of the House of Brunswick,

CONSISTING OF FOURTEEN CHARACTERS;

Showing the whole of the British Orders of Chivalry, never before attempted ; consisting of the Robes of the Garter, Bath, St. Patrick, Thistle, and Guelph, with their Orders, &c. ; the whole producing an effect hitherto unattempted.

"THIS IS ONE OF THE BEST EXHIBITIONS IN THE METROPOLIS."—*Times.*

Bazaar, Baker-street, Portman-square.

Admission, **1s.**   Children under Eight Years, **6d.**   Napoleon Rooms and Chamber of Horrors, **6d.**
OPEN FROM ELEVEN IN THE MORNING TILL DUSK, AND FROM SEVEN TO TEN.

G. COLE, Printer, Carteret Street, Westminster.

29. Advertisement for Madame Tussaud's, 1846.

30. Characters at Madame Tussaud's come to life.

At Tussaud's, unlike the still new public museums, visitors were allowed to touch and, in the case of the coach, climb aboard. Some families took the opportunity to relax in the coach and eat their sandwiches. Strips of the dark red interior of the coach, described as 'squashed flea' colour, were hacked off by souvenir hunters. As a consequence accessibility had to be abandoned. The carriage was so popular that the Tussauds assiduously collected a small fleet of vehicles associated with the emperor.

A Tussaud's poster of 1845 was written, unusually for their advertising at the time, in French, indicating that the Napoleon collecting was attracting substantial numbers of French visitors. The leading article of *Chambers's Edinburgh Journal* for 3 June 1843 unfavourably compared a new Napoleon museum in the Egyptian Hall, Piccadilly, with the 'rich addition' of Madame's Napoleon collection to her Baker Street establishment.[29] George Cruikshank recorded Madame's attachment to the emperor with a cartoon, 'I dreamt that I slept at Madame Tussaud's', which showed Napoleon and Madame Tussaud dancing together, a fantasy still echoed in the design of the wallpaper on the stairs that leads down to the Chamber of Horrors.

Why was the Napoleon shrine so popular? Entertainment or edification? In her catalogue Madame Tussaud insisted she was contributing to the understanding of history, offering direct evidence from the past. Most of the items in this collection carried certificates attesting their authenticity. Madame Tussaud's claims to historical accuracy were eagerly tested. British newspapers loved to pinpoint errors in the recollection of the events of the 1790s in her memoirs, although they never questioned, and frequently referred to, the actual autobiographical content.[30] Her catalogues were mine-fields of misinformation.[31] Successive catalogues claimed in romantic, but erroneous, detail how Marie-Louise had ordered the coach to provide her husband with a safe, movable home to withstand the privations of the invasion of Russia.[32]

The items in the collection ranged from the strictly informative and reasonably historical to those likely to satisfy merely a morbid curiosity. Napoleon's atlas, which became a collector's item after it was inadvertently left behind at a hotel in February 1814, contained the plans he drew up for his different battles. While the dominating presence of the Waterloo coach and the blue death robe might be said to be evocative of time past, there were also voyeuristic and tasteless object such as the emperor's camp deathbed (marked by his own blood left after autopsy), his toothbrush, a tooth and a lock of his hair. Napoleon asked for his hair to be distributed among relatives and friends after his death. In the early twenty first century the hair has proved arsenic positive, provoking a rather sterile claim that Napoleon may have been poisoned, forgetting that at the time hair pomades contained all manner of toxic material.

Madame Tussaud set great store on the collection as relics, entitling the rooms a shrine to the emperor. As a convinced monarchist, she helped to build up the image of Napoleon as an alternative royal 'transcending genius'.[33] She could not delve into his psyche but she could buy up items of his wardrobe and reinvent his body. Appearance always dominated her consciousness, as indeed it did the physiognomists and phrenologists of her day, although for her the main criteria was simply what a person wore. Describing Napoleon's return to Paris before he became First Consul in 1799, she confined her account to a superficial catalogue of the equipment captured during the Italian campaign and a list of his clothes. 'He was dressed in the costume of a mameluke, in large white trousers, red boots, waistcoat richly embroidered, as also the jacket, which was crimson velvet.'[34] The garments may have been trophies from his victory in Egypt a few months earlier.

Madame Tussaud's sons and heirs exploited the image of Napoleon, aided by the emperor's nephew's success in reinstating the empire in the ruins of the republic of 1848. Napoleon III and Victoria enjoyed reciprocal state visits, which were also good for the wax business. The Napoleonic shrine earned a sufficient reputation for Napoleon III to dispatch two emissaries to try to recover the relics, which were considered the best collection of Napoleonic memorabilia in the world. The Tussauds were

31. Advertisement for Madame Tussaud's following the death of the duke of Wellington, 1852.

willing to part with their treasures for £30,000 but the emissaries left empty-handed complaining that the objects were being 'prostituted' by being displayed for gain in a foreign country. The *Times* gloated at the failure. 'Our gallant allies might be proud to possess so important a collection of souvenirs of the Great Empire.'[35] If Napoleon III was offended, it did not last and the Tussauds continued their purchases. Two years later the Tussauds modelled the Empress Eugénie from life and in 1871, when the empire had been replaced by a republic, Louis Napoleon and Eugénie visited the exhibition. When the former emperor died in England in 1873 an authentic death mask, made by the Tussauds, adorned a hastily assembled lying in state tableau. When Napoleon III's heir the Prince Imperial was killed fighting in the Zulu War in South Africa in 1879 his wax image was mounted on a specially made wax horse. The popularity of the Napoleon shrine at Tussaud's was long lasting. In 1883, on the day when the exhibition moved to the Marylebone Road, the *Daily Telegraph* commented in detail on how 'with an enthusiasm that never abated, [Madame Tussaud] kept alive the memory of the Napoleonic Legend'. The paper, however, distinguished admiration for Wellington's main enemy from the 'shabby and self-seeking imposture known as latter day Bonapartism'.[36] Napoleon III may have died in England, but some British people never thought him a worthy heir.

In 1913 the Napoleon 'shrine' rooms were revamped in green and gold with new fittings to display the burgeoning collection of small Napoleonic memorabilia which John Theodore Tussaud, Madame Tussaud's great-grandson, had accumulated. Like his famous ancestor, John Theodore was entranced by the empire, and wrote biographies of the generals who had followed their master into exile. In 1925 the Napoleon rooms, along with most of the exhibition, were destroyed by fire. All that remained of the coach was a single badly-warped axle, which was eventually presented to the Napoleon Museum at Malmaison.[37] The 'relic of a relic' finally made it to a real museum.

With the consolidation of a permanent exhibition site, Madame Tussaud and her collection became a familiar part of the London scene. A much-read survey of London attractions, published in 1841, noted that the Tussaud's investment in models, their costumes and other artefacts totalled £60,000, and that the exhibition drew thousands, from princes to babies.

> Impressions conveyed to the mind in this vivid manner, become permanently fixed in the memory, and in after years are found very materially to influence the imagination ... Hence it is, that with old and young, 'waxworks' have become universal favourites.
>
> Madame Tussaud has built her fortune on these common sympathies; to the

little folk she has given 'wonders'; to the star-gazing countrymen glories of scarlet, and glories of gold; to the historian, portraits of the great political actors of modern Europe ... We are of opinion that the curiosity that was at the root of this love of pictured history might be directed to higher and better purposes, and that for educational uses it might be made to illustrate not merely the races of man, but the whole natural history of the earth.[38]

The Tussauds in fact never considered reaching out into natural history, although later in the century they did show a 'caveman' tableau. The increasing size of the catalogue gave a clear signal that the exhibition was prosperous. An 1840 edition, now headed 'Madame Tussaud and Sons', carried the first illustration of the interior of the exhibition.[39] In July 1844 Tussaud's sold 8000 copies of their catalogue. From 1845 advertisements appeared and they immediately took up as much space as the information about the exhibition. The advertisements confirmed that Tussaud's were triumphantly targeting a prosperous and educated clientele with money to spend on luxuries to make their lives comfortable, and that advertisers were confident that the catalogue would reach a large audience. The advertisers included restaurants, insurance companies, a firm selling illuminated texts for use in churches, as well as portmanteaus, cocoa, and a variety of patent medicines with details of the incredible range of illnesses they could cure.

In her touring years Marie had always been willing to pay for the best publicity available. In London it came free. The enthusiastic approval of a succession of members of the royal family had always been quoted on posters and might have been totally disregarded, except for the huge focus on royalty in the exhibition itself. In London there was a greater concentration of other famous and strategically important individuals who were prepared to applaud the merits of the exhibition for nothing. The duke of Wellington, an irrepressible museum addict, delighted in visiting and studying his own statue, which faced that of Napoleon. When the Baker Street show opened in June 1835 the *Times* commented approvingly:

MADAME TUSSAUD'S EXHIBITION

A completely new arrangement of the figures which comprise this splendid Exhibition has taken place, and the effect is much improved; the whole appearance on entering, especially in the evening, when the whole is brilliantly illuminated, is peculiarly imposing and splendid.

The *Court Journal* was equally impressed: 'this is a scene for a pleasant and instructive hour'. Most evocative was *Chambers's Journal:* 'we can walk, as it were, along the plank of time'.

Several amusing Cruikshank cartoons which achieved wide circulation

helped, but the best publicist was Dickens, who became a veritable enthusiast. In 1840 a version of Madame Tussaud's appeared as 'Mrs Jarley's
Waxworks' in a complete serial issue of the *Old Curiosity Shop*. Mrs Jarley,
like Marie, was determined to convince the world that waxworks had left
the fairground, although her own life did not quite correspond to the
bourgeois respectability that Marie cultivated. When Dickens's central character, the innocent and gullible Nell, and her devoted but gambling-addicted
grandfather run across Mrs Jarley, her caravans and her touring waxworks,
Mrs Jarley is shocked that neither has seen a wax exhibition.

> Instead of speaking, however she sat looking at the child for a long time in
> silence, and then getting up, brought out from a corner a large roll of canvas
> about a yard in width, which she laid upon the floor and spread open with her
> foot until it nearly reached from one end of the caravan to the other.
> 'There, child,' she said, 'read that.'
> Nell walked down it, and read aloud, in enormous black letters, the inscription,
> 'JARLEY'S WAXWORKS.'
> 'Read it again,' said the lady, complacently.
> 'Jarley's Waxworks,' repeated Nell.
> 'That's me,' said the lady. 'I am Mrs Jarley.'
> Giving the child an encouraging look, intended to reassure her and let her know,
> that, although she stood in the presence of the original Jarley, she must not let
> herself to be utterly overwhelmed and borne down, the lady of the caravan
> unfolded another scroll, whereon was the inscription, 'One hundred figures the
> full size of life', and then another scroll, on which was written 'The only stupen-
> dous collection of real waxworks in the world', and then several smaller scrolls
> with such inscriptions as 'Now exhibiting within' – 'The genuine and only Jarley'
> – 'Jarley's unrivalled collection' – 'Jarley is the delight of the Nobility and
> Gentry' – 'The Royal Family are the patrons of Jarley'. When she had exhibited
> these leviathans of public announcement to the astonished child, she brought
> forth specimens of the lesser fry in the shape of handbills, some of them couched
> in the form of parodies on popular melodies, as 'Believe me if all Jarley's
> waxworks so rare'- 'I saw thy show in youthful prime'- 'Over the water to Jarley';
> while, to consult all tastes others were composed with a view to the light and
> more facetious spirits as a parody on the favourite air of 'If I had a donkey,'
> beginning
>
> > If I know'd a donkey wot wouldn't go
> > To see MRS JARLEY'S waxwork show
> > Do you think I'd acknowledge him
> > Oh no no! Then run to Jarley's
>
> besides several compositions in prose, purporting to be dialogues between the
> Emperor of China and an oyster, or the Archbishop of Canterbury and a Dissenter
> on the subject of church-rates, but all having the same moral, namely, that the

reader must make haste to Jarley's, and that the children and servants were admitted half-price. When she had brought all these testimonials of her important position in society to bear upon her young companion, Mrs Jarley rolled them up, and having put them carefully away, sat down again, and looked at the child in triumph.

'Never go into the company of a filthy Punch any more,' said Mrs Jarley, 'after this.'

'I never saw any waxwork, ma'am,' said Nell. 'Is it funnier than Punch?'

'Funnier!' said Mrs Jarley in a shrill voice. 'It is not funny at all.'

'Oh!' said Nell, with all possible humility.

'It isn't funny at all,' repeated Mrs Jarley. 'Its calm and – what's that word again – critical? – no – classical, that's it – it's calm and classical. No low beatings and knockings about, no jokings and squeakings like your precious Punches, but always the same, with a constantly unchanging air of coolness and gentility; and so like life, that if waxworks only spoke and walked about, you'd hardly know the difference. I won't go so far as to say, that, as it is, I've seen waxworks quite like life, but I've certainly seen some life that was exactly like waxwork.'

Having discovered that Nell, although penniless, can read and write, skills which Mrs Jarley herself lacks, she hastens to offer her a job guiding visitors around the wax figures:

'The duty's very light and genteel, the company particularly select, the exhibition takes place in assembly-rooms, town-halls, large rooms at inns, or auction galleries. There's none of your open-air wagrancy at Jarley's, recollect; there is no tarpaulin and sawdust at Jarley's remember. Every expectation held out in the handbills is realised to the utmost, and the whole forms an effect of imposing brilliancy hitherto unrivalled in this kingdom. Remember that the price of admission is only sixpence, and that this is an opportunity which may never occur again!'

Nell is persuaded fairly easily to take the job as she and her grandfather are penniless. She watches the waxworks display being set out.

When the festoons were all put up as tastily as they might be, the stupendous collection was uncovered, and there were displayed, on a raised platform some two feet from the floor, running around the room and parted from the rude public by a crimson rope breast high, divers sprightly effigies of celebrated characters, singly and in groups, clad in glittering dresses of various climes and times, and standing more or less unsteadily upon their legs, with their eyes very wide open, and their nostrils very much inflated, and the muscles of their arms and legs very strongly developed, and all their countenances expressing great surprise. All the gentlemen were very pigeon-breasted and very blue about their beards; and all the ladies were miraculous figures; and all the ladies and gentlemen were looking intensely nowhere, and staring with extraordinary earnestness at nothing.

Handbills were pushed through doors, posters put up and Mrs Jarley toured the town in her brightest shawl.

> Mrs Jarley had waited upon the boarding schools in person, with a handbill composed expressly for them, in which it was distinctly proved that waxworks refined the mind, cultivated the taste and enlarged the sphere of human understanding.

Unfortunately the teacher at the local girl's boarding school scorns both the waxworks and Nell as lowlife, threatening them with the full force of the law if their very pointed attempts to persuade her to visit with her pupils do not stop. The general public also fails to appear. Mrs Jarley, sustained by her 'suspicious bottle', remains optimistic, but Nell and her grandfather, who has gambled away every penny Mrs Jarley has paid Nell, abandon the promising career in wax. Dickens, hemmed in by the need to write a new episode every week, forgot to explain why. [40]

There is no record whether Madame Tussaud knew about Mrs Jarley, who personifies an image of waxworks she herself shunned, but the free advertisement must have been useful. Dickens made frequent references to the Tussaud exhibition itself, for instance 'A History of Wax', in his *Household Words* and 'An Eyewitness in Great Company', in his *All the Year Round*.

In 1841 *Punch* became an enthusiast for the wax exhibition, 'the real Temple of Fame', but Madame Tussaud's did not always please the editor. During the potato blight and accompanying severe economic depression in 1846, *Punch* was incensed by the unusually (even for Tussaud's) snobbish tone of the exhibition's advertising.

> A Magnificent Display of Court Dresses of surpassing richness, comprising twenty-five ladies' and Gentlemen's costumes intended to convey to the MIDDLE CLASSES an idea of the ROYAL SPLENDOUR; a most splendid novelty and calculated to display to young persons much necessary instruction.

Punch responded with a reminder about the famine in Ireland and misery in England too. Its article was headed 'A Great Moral Lesson at Madame Tussaud's'.

> The collection should also include specimens of the Irish peasantry, the hand loom weavers, and other starving portions of the population all in their characteristic tatters; and also the inmates of the various workhouses in the ignominious garb presented to them by the Poor Law. But this department of the Exhibition should be contained in a separate Chamber of Horrors and half a guinea should be charged for the benefit of the living originals.

An accompanying cartoon showed how such exhibits might appear in Tussaud's, and how the customers might react. The biting criticism was

Mr. Pips his Diary.

Wednesday, September 5, 1849.—To please my Wife, did take her this Evening to MADAME TUSSAUD her Wax Works; a grand large Room, exceeding fine with Gilding, lighted up very splendid, and full of People, and a Band of Musique playing as they walked about: cost 2s., and a Catalogue 6d. The Wax Figures a pretty Show: but with their painted Cheeks and glassy Eyes—especially such as nod and move—do look like Life in Death. The Dresses very handsome, and I think, correct; and the Sight of so many People of Note in the Array of their Time, did much delight me. Among the Company Numbers of Country Folk, and to see how they did stare at the Effigies of the Queen, and the Prince, and the Duke of Wellington, and the King of the Belgians, and the Princess Charlotte that was, and George the Fourth in his Coronation Robes, magnificent as a Peacock! The Catalogue do say that his Chair is the very one wherein he sat in the Abbey; but how like a Play-House Property it do look, and little thought the King it would come down to figure in a' Raree Show! A Crowd of Dames and Matrons gazing at the Group of the Royal Family, calling the Children "Dears" and "Ducks," and would, I verily believe, have kissed their Wax Chaps, if they had been suffered. My Wife feasting her Eyes on the little Princes and Princesses, I did fix mine upon a pretty, modest, black Maid beside me, and she hers on me, till my Wife spying us, did pinch me with her Nails in the Arm. Pretty, to see the Sovereign Allies in the last War, and bluff old BLUCHER, and BONAPARTE and his Officers, in brave Postures, but stiff. Also the two KING CHARLESES, and OLIVER, together; CHARLES THE FIRST protesting against his Death-Warrant, and his Son backing him; and CARDINAL WOLSEY looking on. LORD BYRON in the Dress of a Greek Pirate, looking Daggers and Pistols, close to JOHN WESLEY preaching a Sermon, was likewise mighty droll; and methought, if all MADAME TUSSAUD's Figures were their Originals instead, what Ado there would be! Many of the Faces that I knew by Recollection, or Pictures, very like; and my LORD BROUGHAM I did know directly, and LISTON in *Paul Pry*. But strange, among the Kings to see him that was the Railway King; and methinks that it were as well now if he were melted up. Thence to the NAPOLEON ROOMS, where BONAPARTE's Coach, and one of his Teeth, and other Reliques and Gimcracks of his, well enough to see for such as care about him a Button. Then to the Chamber of Horrors, which my Wife did long to see most of all; cost, with the NAPOLEON ROOMS, 1s. more; a Room like a Dungeon, where the Head of ROBESPIERRE, and other Scoundrels of the great French Revolution, in Wax, as though just cut off, horrid ghastly, and Plaster Casts of Fellows that have been hanged: but the chief Attraction a Sort of Dock, wherein all the notorious Murderers of late Years; the foremost of all, RUSH, according to the Bill, taken from Life at Norwich, which, seeing he was hanged there, is an odd Phrase. There was likewise a Model of Stanfield Hall, and RUSH his Farm, as though the Place were as famous as Waterloo. Methinks it is of ill Consequence that there should be a Murderers' Corner, wherein a Villain may look to have his Figure put more certainly than a Poet can to a Statue in the Abbey. So away again to the large Room, to look at JENNY LIND instead of GREENACRE, and at 10 of the Clock Home, and so to Bed, my Wife declaring she should dream of the Chamber of Horrors.

Printed by William Bradbury, of No. 13, Upper Woburn-place, in the Parish of St. Pancras, and Frederick Mullet Evans, of No. 7, Church-row, Stoke Newington, both in the County of Middlesex, Printers, at their Office, in Lombard-street, in the Precinct of Whitefriars, in the City of London, and published by them at No. 85 Fleet-street, in the Parish of St. Bride's, in the City of London.—SATURDAY, SEPTEMBER 15, 1849.

32. *Punch*'s description of the Chamber of Horrors, 1849.

possibly deserved, but it did nothing to dent the snobbery or popularity of Tussaud's; indeed such critical attention was almost certainly at least as beneficial as praise. Incontrovertible proof of Madame's success came in 1844, when the American fairground entrepreneur Barnum tried to buy Tussaud's to transfer it to New York. Madame Tussaud and her sons felt sufficiently confident and prosperous to refuse.

Some of the figures above give an idea of the value placed on the Napoleonic collection. The 1838 catalogue in the archives offers clues of the value they themselves placed on their exhibits at a time before most of the Napoleonic memorabilia was acquired. Estimates of the insurance value of models and costumes were added in ink next to the list of models. Seventy-seven figures were listed at £35 each, a total of £2695. Frocks, ornaments and the remaining figures came to just over £2000, which put the total value of their stock at £8000. Henry IV's shirt was insured for £100, the mummy for £200, Marie-Antoinette's Rose Bertin frock was rated £22, but no price was suggested for the models of the guillotine and the Bastille.

In 1841 Marie's husband must have heard of her prosperity, for he made another attempt to extract money from her. He sent a widow friend to London to ferret around. The friend reported that his wife had made all the proceeds of her exhibition over to her sons and was not at all well-disposed to her husband.[41] Marie had made her sons joint owners to put her British assets completely out of reach of her husband and, from 1842, they took over the business. Two years later the sons wrote in French to their father reminding him that since 1802 he had had total control and all the benefit of the three properties in Paris including the wax exhibition. He had never sent money, or an account of how the business was progressing, to his wife, in total contrast to Marie's detailed letters.[42]

Joseph and Francis quarrelled over whether their father deserved help and did not speak to one another for three years. Francis, who had been raised by his father and always maintained that his elder brother was their mother's favourite, lent his father money to pay the rent. Although Francis assured his father that he did not want to hurt him in his old age, he asked that the loan be repaid, though there is no evidence that it was.[43] To ensure that their father could make no claim on their British property, in 1847 both sons applied for British naturalisation, although Marie never did. Major-General Sir Charles Napier, a national hero in Britain, was Francis's sponsor. In the upheavals of the 1848 Revolution, both sons rallied round to pay the old man's rent, and also visited him, although they promised their mother they would not talk to him. In the end Francis spoke to him, while Joseph watched from behind a screen.[44]

When Marie died in April 1850 numerous obituaries appeared in the national press which confirmed her stature in the entertainment industry. Obituaries commonly referred to her move to London in 1802 as an escape from the horrors of the French Revolution.[45] The *Times* spoke of 'this lady whose name has long been familiar to the public'. It mentioned Curtius, Marie's association with Madame Elizabeth, her models of the heads of revolutionary leaders, her 'well-known' exhibition in Baker Street and her large family.[46] The *Illustrated London News* carried a copy of her own wax image and began its unusually lengthy obituary, 'This famous exhibitor of the greatest collection of waxworks ever known'. It noted that her career was familiar to everyone, her 'reputation unrivalled' and her exhibition 'of cosmopolitan renown'. Her links with the French royal family and French writers, including Rousseau and Voltaire, were remarked on. It noted, following the lead of Marie's own memoirs, that, visiting Curtius's house, Voltaire had patted Marie on her cheek and told her she was 'a pretty dark-eyed girl'. Phrases such as these reveal how much contemporaries had been convinced by the image of Madame and the 'old' French Revolution invented in the memoirs.[47]

The recognition of national biographical dictionaries, if this is a guide to lasting fame, came later. In 1888 Madame was referred to in an entry on wax figures in the *Encyclopaedia Britannica*. She earned her own entry in the eleventh edition (1910), while the *Dictionary of National Biography* included her in 1890.

As was fitting for the founder of the most famous waxworks and Chamber of Horrors in the world, a minor horror story developed around Madame Tussaud's own burial. She was first buried in the Catholic chapel in Pavilion Road, Chelsea. When the chapel was demolished in 1890 her body was moved to the crypt of St Mary's, Cadogan Gardens, nearby. A weird newspaper rumour circulated that she had actually been moved to Kensal Green Cemetery, favoured by the fashionable elite and where the rest of the family was buried. There were rumours that she lay in jewels worth £50,000, presents from the crowned heads of Europe. (The perpetrators of this tall tale could not have known the strict economy of the family.) In consequence two villains decided to try their luck. They opened the Tussaud family tomb and broke into four coffins with no reward. They were interrupted when one of them accidentally pulled a bell rope and set bells ringing. The gang left empty-handed, swimming across the canal in their haste to escape. It was said that within a year three of the gang had died mysteriously.[48]

Madame Tussaud set the Tussaud claim, which survived until the final family member in the firm died in 1967, that the exhibition was strictly a family concern, even if this was no longer the case in reality. Both of Marie's sons became thoroughly anglicised and married English girls. Joseph married

Elizabeth Babbington, who came from Birmingham. Their only son, Francis Babbington, was born in 1829 and named after his uncle and grandfather. Two daughters, Marie and Louisa, completed the family. Madame Tussaud's younger son, Francis, married Rebecca Smallpage. They had eight children, the eldest of whom was named Joseph Randall. The Tussaud children were carefully educated in their mother's traditional, though not prominent, Roman Catholic faith. (It was said that when someone gave her a crucifix in her old age she used it as a hat stand in her bedroom.) One of her favourite sayings to the younger Tussauds was, it seems, 'Beware, my children, of the three black crows, the doctor, the lawyer and the priest'.[49] Her great grandson, John Theodore went, first to St Charles's College, Bayswater and then to St Augustine's, a Benedictine boarding school in Ramsgate, enjoying the upper-class snobbery of both – much as Madame Tussaud would have done.

The Tussauds' business triumph was closely related to the biological success of the line. An early nineteenth-century family business could only thrive if the founder lived a long, active and healthy life. Marie survived until her ninetieth year and was at work in the exhibition until a few months before her death. Her two sons inherited her talents and business acumen to a sufficient degree to keep things going. They married women who would work with them and bred a large new generation of workers. Victorian family firms depended upon vigorous breeding. Necessary skills, loyalty and a willingness to sacrifice personal interests for the good of the business were more likely to exist within a close-knit family. In the entertainment world the idea of employing managers from outside the family was undeveloped. Firms like that of Tussaud's stressed the artistic quality of their exhibition and such talents were bred, not bought in.

Madame and her successors encouraged artistic talent among their offspring. Francis Babbington (1829–1857), Joseph's eldest son, was an artist who died young of tuberculosis in Rome. Joseph Randall, Francis's eldest son, attended the Royal Academy School to train as a sculptor, and then entered the family business. His younger son, Frank, worked in the exhibition but was also a composer, of among other things a Great Exhibition Polka. There were always plenty of family members; Joseph Randall had thirteen children and his son John Theodore produced ten. Tussauds were employed in the firm at all levels, from managers and model makers (the men) to paintresses, embroidresses and seamstresses (the women and wives) and were paid as little as possible. After Marie's death no woman ever occupied a senior post permanently. At first this was a matter of chance. Madame Tussaud's daughter died in infancy. Subsequently there were plenty of female Tussauds, but none achieved a position of authority.

Joseph and Francis divided the work. Joseph made the models of kings and queens for the main exhibition. Francis had a studio in St Johns Wood where he lived and did all the heavy modelling. [50] By 1847 both of their eldest sons were also apparently involved in modelling. Information on how they apportioned their work is taken from an old attendant's brief account of his life at Tussaud's. Luke Bevan worked there from 1832 to 1872 and died in 1895. His handwritten memoir reads like a fairy story, and an old man trying and failing to sort out the large number of Tussaud progeny of different generations. [51] That numerous typescript copies of this memoir have been retained in the archives is perhaps an indication of how much the Tussauds valued workers who spent their whole life with them.

This large family was kept so busy running the exhibition that they had little time to leave any record of the extraordinary woman who had started it all. While there are silhouettes, wax model and portraits made by various family members, Madame did not write her own memoirs and what she recollected to their author, Francis Hervé, tells us more about what she wanted people to think of her than what she actually thought. She was happier with figures and some of her very practical business accounts survive. Above all we have her numerous models. The most telling image recorded of her by several observers was of an old lady taking the money at the cash desk at the entrance to the exhibition. Her grandson, Victor, who only knew her when he was a young child, wrote down his memories of her but only after 1901, when his recollection of the 'facts' was somewhat hazy. Although Madame learned enough English to cope, she always spoke with a strong German accent. Victor remembered her sitting at a small table, on which sat six silver watches which she wound up daily. He recalled that she gave him and his brothers and sisters each a half sovereign at Christmas and at New Year, together with oranges and cakes. [52]

In what ways did the Baker Street exhibition outclass its numerous rivals? Many of the waxworks, the royals, assorted witches and criminals and aspects of history, were similar to those in other shows. What made Tussaud's distinctive was Madame's ruthless determination to go one better. Her show was always up to date, and she never stopped emphasising the fact. She was determined to instruct her visitors in history as well as current affairs. New models were added constantly and ones that people walked past without a glance were melted down. Visitors could never say that they had 'done' Tussaud's. She also avoided the embarrassment of other establishments whose figures were given new names but imperfectly modified. Her premises were large, impressive and elegantly fitted. They provided excellent opportunities for the middle class to promenade in a fashionable and protected environment, just a short walk from Oxford Street. The exhibition prided itself on its respectability and suitability as family entertainment. Pleasure gardens, like Vauxhall and Cremorne in Chelsea, offered the opportunity to walk, dance and eat a meal, but pleasure gardens at night also attracted elegantly dressed prostitutes. Victorian middle-class society became more and more censorious of visible immorality. There was never any question of finding whores at Tussaud's, aside from a few famous wax examples. There was also never a risk that Tussaud's would fall foul of the Obscene Publications Act of 1857. They were careful to exclude anatomical models, on show elsewhere in London and at fairs, which were criticised as salacious, devoid of any real scientific or medical justification.

Unlike many of her upmarket rivals, Madame was aware that museum-gazing made people both hungry and thirsty. She was careful to position a buffet as a social focus between the main exhibition and the Horrors. She also scored on the question of the demon drink. The buffet provided only tea and soft drinks, to quaff with buns and other snacks, something that must have delighted the temperance movement. This organisation waged war on other popular entertainments, particularly music halls, which sold alcohol and food as well as song and became very popular with working people. Tussaud's fitted in well with the often puritanical public morality of the Victorian middle classes.

Distinct from all other wax shows, Tussaud's met the new museums head on. Tussaud's competed brilliantly with institutions like the British Museum. Within a short time of the opening of the Baker Street Exhibition, Tussaud's was universally acknowledged to be a 'must' for any tourist, on a par with the Tower of London and Westminster Abbey. Marie assembled the most comprehensive collection of Napoleon relics in the world, at a time when Bonapartism was in the news. Tussaud's was also the first interactive museum. People could get close to the exhibits and touch them, an opportunity still denied by most museums today. Tussaud's concentrated on presenting an exhibition free of the prolific criticisms made of other museums. Madame Tussaud cheerfully admitted anyone proffering the required 1s., confident that this substantial sum would exclude 'undesirable' elements, because she was more of a snob than most. Paying customers could wander around freely. The catalogue sold at the entrance told them everything Madame wanted them to know about the figures and their history. Customers never risked feeling inferior, ignorant or patronised. They were presented with information that was familiar and easy to un-derstand. Unlike the British Museum, Madame concentrated on presenting her collection to its best visual advantage. Whereas public museums seemed committed to keeping the public out, Tussaud's never forgot that com-mercial survival depended on people lining up at the front door, indeed almost enjoying the fact that they might have to queue. After all, a queue confirmed that the exhibition was worth a visit. Above all, Madame Tussaud remembered that her visitors were human. They needed interaction and amusement, and some delighted in being made slightly afraid, but in a safe environment. Natural history collections had bags of potential, but their curators seemed determined to keep their treasures obscure, for a highly educated and wealthy elite.

Madame Tussaud had the unique distinction of building the most successful commercial tourist attraction by her own efforts, although there is no record of just how wealthy she became. She was a showman and an artist, but in the final analysis her success lay in her dedication to money management. She kept precise daily accounts of income and expenditure and made certain that each day produced a healthy profit. The basic accounting practices she developed, obviously recorded daily from the grubby state of the little notebooks in which she entered the figures in her own hand, may well have been the real secret of the survival and success of her business. Yet she did not stint on the exhibition, aware that expensive gowns, paintings, hangings and other fittings were appreciated by her customers, who thus felt they had value for money. She and her heirs were always careful to give full publicity to the fact that gowns, carpets and so on were either original or exact copies of the originals made by the original designers. Customers and the press were invariably told precisely how much such items cost.

Her employees, as far as possible drawn from her own family, were a different matter. Madame set a Tussaud's tradition of paying workers as little as possible. She also tried to encourage her workers to budget carefully, paying them on a Friday rather than a Saturday, judging that this would give their wives a better chance of getting their hands on a fair share. Until very shortly before her death, Madame sat at a table at the entrance to the exhibition, taking the money, and here too she set a Tussaud's tradition. Every visitor had to pay, even kings, queens and tsars. There were no exceptions. When someone pestered her repeatedly to see their collection of curios, she replied, 'See you sare, I nevare visit gentlemen and when dey visit me dey pay dare shilling'. When the dean of Westminster Abbey asked her to renovate their collection of dilapidated wax figures, she answered, 'I have a shop of my own to look after and I do not look after other people's shops'. These somewhat rude replies were recounted with obvious pride by her grandson, Victor Tussaud.

This was, of course, the tale told by Tussaud's publicity and newspapers, keen to jump on the bandwagon of evident success. Tussaud's have always been adept at securing the best possible publicity. A temporarily resident

American, Benjamin Moran, secretary to their legation in the 1850s had a more sceptical view.

> The untravelled countryman and his rustic daughters there see the sovereign in regal robes, and her descendants represented in yellow wax, and look with admiring wonder on the stupid show. Wretched figures of more wretched kings and queens are judiciously disposed for exhibition, and the spangles on their faded robes glitter in the gaslight, and astonish and delight the loyal crowd. A whole host of the line of Brunswick stand around like wooden men and women, with eyes agape, staring upon the throng who stare again at them. Miserable caricatures of Napoleon, Washington, Cromwell, Shakespeare, and Byron occupy niches, and the soul sickens at the contemplation of the figures, they so outrage humanity. Each one looks as if ophthalmia were a distemper of the atmosphere, and all suffer from the sad disease. Shakespeare is represented as a modern dandy, 'who cultivates his hair'; and Byron as a Greek, with a belt around the waist containing a whole arsenal of arms ... But this is not all. The 'room of horrors' invites attention next, as if there were not enough of *horrors* in the first apartments to horrify any decent, well-disposed individual ...
>
> So much for Madame Tussaud's exhibition of wax figures, the resort of the curious, and a sham to please or alarm children. It is, without misrepresentation, the most abominable abomination in the great city, and the very audience-hall of humbugs. Barnum ought to have it.[53]

Perhaps Moran did not realise that Barnum had actually tried to buy it. Maybe Moran was annoyed that he had not been modelled. What is certain is that the Tussaud's archives, assiduous acquirers of public comment on their collection, have not bothered to photocopy his opinion of their show whereas they assiduously collected information on their rivals.

6

Wax Rivals

Madame Tussaud's did not become a national institution because it was unique or even particularly unusual. What was different about Tussaud's was scale. Tussaud's amassed a huge collection of upwards of five hundred models, which no one else could rival. Secondly, Tussaud had the imagination to create a 'museum' image, buying paintings, actual royal robes, Napoleonic relics and many other artefacts. No other waxworks could match the size, relevance and richness of the Tussaud exhibition. Marie Tussaud made the daring leap from the traditional association of waxworks with fairs and invented a wax museum catering for a clientele that was middle class and highly respectable – the audience dreamt of by Dickens's Mrs Jarley.

When Marie Tussaud moved to Britain she cut out much that other waxworks retained. She left behind in Paris the fairground 'freak' trappings of the Curtius *salon*, the piebald children, the improbably and grotesquely fat man, the 'anatomical ladies' whose insides could be touched by gentlemen for an extra fee. Marie did not make erotic waxes for private orders; instead Joseph Tussaud produced respectable family silhouettes which could be displayed in the sitting room, rather than models that had to be concealed in the boudoir. Marie stressed education, but in her British exhibition there were no anatomical waxes and no weird and unlikely representations of humans. She made her British exhibition a quintessentially family entertainment, blending 'rational' recreation, undemanding education and highly moral fun. Marie was one of the first entrepreneurs of amusement to anticipate and exploit the Victorian obsession with the family and overt public 'respectability'. She turned her four-year-old child, who could have been an impediment, into an advantage; a wax child Joseph greeted customers. There was no ambiguity or innuendo in Tussaud's. Marie provided a totally non-titillating feast for the eyes, and equally 'respectable' music in her innovative promenade concerts.

There were other waxworks for all budgets and tastes in the nineteenth century. The fashion for buying full-size private wax models faded, while, from the 1840s the development of photography provided a novel, less cumbersome and cheaper way of representing people that could be displayed on the top of the piano. Waxworks survived the competition of the camera far better than anyone expected, however, particularly in Britain. Prices for waxwork shows ranged from 1s. to 1d. As with most things, the customer got what he paid for. Itinerant shows continued, as did wax booths at fairs. Wax was also used to make some of the 'dummies' used to display clothes in the new department stores that began to spring up in mid century. Wax could be subversive. Wax pears were made in France in 1834, echoing the caricatures in which Louis-Philippe, king of the French, was ridiculed.[1] Wax was also used for single-event shows. For instance an Oriental and Turkish Museum opened in the St George's Gallery, Hyde Park Corner, in 1854 as British troops were leaving for the Crimea. Its organisers hoped to profit from the novelty of the army being engaged in a little-known part of Europe. Different aspects of Turkish life were shown – a harem, a wedding and baths. All the figures were made of wax and the *Times* was quite lyrical about the real hair visible on arms and legs (of the males of course) and drops of sweat on the foreheads of the porters. Unfortunately for the proprietors, Oscanyan and Aznavour, single-event wax shows tended to reach meltdown fast and the Crimean War was a cause of scandal rather than self-congratulation.

Wax anatomical models played a significant role in the development of modern medicine in the nineteenth century, as well as being shown for commercial gain. Many hospitals in Britain and on the Continent held collections of anatomical waxes that were used for teaching. Joseph Towne (1808–1879) made over 600 coloured wax anatomical models, specialising in dramatic skin disorders and the human brain, which enhanced the Gordon Museum at Guy's Hospital. In France, when the National Museum of Natural History, the Musée Orfila and School of Medicine were set up to replace the old colleges and academies in 1793, they took advantage of the execution of the duc d'Orléans to requisition his extensive collection of anatomical waxes. The collection was enlarged and the models restored by their original sculptor, Pinson.[2] Opportunely, a substantial additional number of wax models were acquired for the Paris School of Medicine as booty during the revolutionary wars by Desgenettes, a doctor attached to the French army in Italy, who also promoted the use of anatomical waxes in teaching. Napoleon himself was so aware of the need for anatomical waxes in medical schools and the new museums of natural history that he set up a school of 'artificial anatomy' in Rouen, where sculptors were trained in the skills of anatomical wax modelling. The school was opened at the Rouen hospital in 1807 by Jean-Baptiste Laumonier (1749–1818), its chief surgeon. Despite its usefulness, ever more stretched military budgets kept Laumonier short of funds and only four students were trained. Laumonier was succeeded as the head of the school by his son-in-law, Achille-Cléophas Flaubert, father of the novelist. It was closed after Napoleon's defeat in 1814, perhaps a sign that the restored monarchy had little interest in scientific education, or maybe because fewer military surgeons were needed. Some of the models survive in the Musée Flaubert, which is also the museum of the history of medicine in Rouen.[3] During his Italian campaigns Napoleon acquired wax anatomical models made by the Italian specialist, Felice Fontana, and some found their way to the Montpellier school of medicine.[4]

The nineteenth-century anatomical wax sculptors abandoned the poetic and erotic style of their eighteenth-century counterparts in favour of more functional and prosaic products, whose sole aim was to inform and instruct students how the body worked. Jacques Talrich (1789–1851), on his retirement as military surgeon, became a wax modeller for the Paris School of Medicine. He also sold and showed anatomical models in London, Birmingham, Dublin and Edinburgh. His son Jules (1826–1904) was well known as a modeller in London and Vienna and in 1876 established an anatomical museum in Paris, 5 rue Rougemont, close to where the Musée Grévin later opened. The Paris School of Medicine also bought wax models from the Maison Tramond, conveniently located next to their anatomy theatre in the Rue de l'Ecole de Medécine. In the same street lived Louis Auzoux (1797–1830), who made anatomical models in papier mâché. These were very expensive: a whole man, complete with his internal organs, cost 3000 francs.[5]

Broadly speaking nineteenth-century wax shows can be divided into the anatomical and the general. We will consider the appeal of both to their contemporary audiences. Public anatomical waxworks, operating for profit, had always been ambiguous in their pursuit of scientific enquiry and blatant titillation. They occupied an increasingly ambivalent position between science and eroticism. There seems to have been a renewed interest in the 'men only' variety in the middle of the century, particular in Soho's red-light district; there was even a 'women only' show for a time. Mechanical waxworks also persisted.[6]

Why were so many wax uteruses, penises and associated organs produced and so few eyes and ears? For a time after Rackstrow's death anatomical waxworks had little appeal in England, although they thrived in France, particularly, for a time in the Palais Royal, by then increasingly a favourite haunt for prostitutes, whose activities were the delight of caricaturists. During the Revolution, when the Palais Royal was briefly renamed the Palais Egalité, a Piedmontese, Orsini, displayed a Venus rising from her bath.[7] In 1808 there was a 'Cabinet of Professor Bertrand' in the arcades, which seems to have focused on voyeurist items for men. It took the fancy of the right-wing playwright Kotzebue, who, according to Madame Tussaud, was one of Curtius's dinner guests,[8] but is chiefly remembered because his murder in 1819 provoked Metternich to issue reactionary decrees throughout the German Confederation. Kotzebue commented, with obvious pleasure, 'Here all the dreadful consequences of libertinism are represented in the most lively manner in wax, with a truth which excites utmost horror'. The high point of a detailed wax investigation of venereal disease was a model of a young man near to death, 'in whose languid eyes and distorted features, pain, death, shame, repentance and despair are eloquently displayed'. A whole range of colourful and unpleasant conditions was shown, from an abortion, a Caesarean operation to the plague, cancers and 'various female diseases ... the whole internal structure of the human body, the head dissected horizontally and perpendicularly ... in short it is impossible to see a greater number of instructive objectives for 30 sous only'.[9] As a further incentive to customers, Kotzebue concluded, 'All that I have to regret is, that persons whose nerves are too delicate, will scarcely be able to endure the sight'.[10]

Phrenology helped to give nineteenth-century anatomical wax exhibitions a new 'scientific' aura. In the first half of the century phrenology seemed an exciting new, somewhat exotic, branch of science. In an age when many believed in progress, both of countries and of human beings, scientists were eager to understand the workings of the mind. In 1791 a Viennese doctor, Franz Joseph Gall (1758–1828), claimed that it was possible to analyse an individual's intelligence and character from the shape of the exterior of the skull. He called this cranioscopy, but the term phrenology soon became more popular. By careful measurements of the skull Gall claimed that twenty vital mental faculties could be precisely located in both humans and animals, and that some of these were shared between the two. This was never proven and eventually was ridiculed as quackery. Gall's basic hypothesis, however, that it was possible to establish the precise function of different areas of the brain, was both new and was the starting point of modern brain mapping and genetic science. When the Roman Catholic Church grasped that his ideas on the brain refuted their claims that a supernatural power rather than an organ in the body dominated mental functions, and that Gall was claiming that there were similarities between human and animal minds, the Austrian emperor banned him from lecturing in Vienna. By then Gall was an eminent physician, a noted anatomist and an excellent public speaker. He and his student, Dr Johann Christophe Spurtzheim, migrated to give lecture tours in the

German states. Gall won many supporters and influential patients, including Goethe and Metternich.

In 1807 they moved to Paris, where Gall's fame added to the impressive list of his subjects, including the novelist Stendhal (Marie-Henri Beyle, 1783–1842) and the radical writer and inspiration to the early socialists Henri de Saint-Simon (1760–1825). Gall's lectures were fashionable and very popular. He was criticised because he sold tickets for his lectures, but he was more concerned to convince his audience than fleece them and was a generous host. Unlike Mesmer, who had held Parisian audiences in thrall a generation earlier, there was some scientific basis for his theories. Despite his weighty publications and exhaustive empirical research to test his theories, including the dissection of brains of executed criminals, the Parisian medical establishment was never convinced.[11] Gall made the mistake of noting the inadequacy of the measurements of Napoleon's skull. Nonetheless Gall had an enthusiastic following among students in the Paris *Ecole de Medécine*, particularly those who were members of the radical secret society, the *charbonnerie*.

For a generation after Gall's death phrenology remained influential; many phrenological societies sprang up in Britain and throughout Europe and North America. People consulted phrenologists about everything, from whom they should marry to whom they might employ, as well as mental and psychological illness. There were undoubtedly charlatans among them who traded on people's gullibility, charging a fat fee for measuring their skull with a cheaply acquired wire frame. Spurzheim moved to England and created a considerable following. By the middle of the century phrenology was no longer at the cutting edge of fashion and its radical trappings were decidedly out of favour in the autocratic empire of Napoleon III. Gall's questioning of the literal interpretation of the Bible would soon be taken up and definitively challenged by Charles Darwin and Gall would only be remembered as a man who measured bumps in skulls. Phrenology was never accepted by established experts and the developing science of physiology rejected all but basic idea that different areas of the brain were responsible for different responses.

Stripped of its claims to be accepted as serious science by the mid century, phrenology was left to popularisers on the fringe of science, particularly the proprietors of anatomical wax shows. Gall himself had made wax and plaster models of skulls, some of which survive in the Musée de l'Homme. A wax model of a skull was a useful tool to 'prove' that the external shape of the head was indicative of character and psychological disposition. In 1865 there was an ethnological and anatomical museum in the Salle Beethoven, situated in the Passage de l'Opéra in Paris. Despite the claims of its name, it appears to have focused on royalty, politicians, literary figures and a clutch of murderers. There was also the Harthoff collection, made by Professor Schwartz, a phrenologist from Stockholm, which was advertised as a modern scientific museum, but serious visitors were presumably warned off when they realised that the show only admitted men. The main attraction seems to have been a model of indeterminate sex, a Mexican dancer, Julie Pastrana, complete with full beard and an 'excellently proportioned' body covered in hair. Another room was filled with examples of surgical operations in the style of the school of medicine collections designed by Dupuytren and Orfila.[12]

The rationale and marketing opportunity behind the sexually explicit wax exhibitions of a self-styled doctor, the Alsatian P. Spitzner (1833–1896), was increasing concern about the spread of sexually-transmitted diseases. By the late 1870s there was a panic when it was calculated that syphilis was escalating with five hundred new cases a year to a total of 85,000 in Paris alone.[13] Spitzner bought, rather than made, the models he showed. In 1856 he opened a *Grand Musée Anatomique et Ethnologique* in Paris in what was to become the Place de la République, near where the Curtius exhibition had been held. Following a fire in 1885, he toured the fair circuits in France, Britain, Germany, Holland and especially Belgium. Anatomical waxes did well at fairs. The Spitzner family indeed toured fairs in France until the Second World War and developed an American offshoot. Spitzner's motto 'Science! Art! Progress!' became famous. His show was a mixture of serious science and of fairground oddities: wax models of Aztecs and Hottentots, monsters, foetuses and mummies. There were wax body parts and bodies that opened. Although himself unqualified, Spitzner employed qualified doctors and nurses to give lectures, illustrated by his models. The section on reproduction was advertised as educational for adolescents. Advertisements expressed the hope that their horrifying models, showing the effects of sexually transmitted diseases, would have an impact in limiting the spread of syphilis, which, they claimed (surely with more than a little exaggeration) affected eight million people in France by 1900. The central feature of Spitzner's show was a typically ambiguous anatomical Venus in a white frock, who could be stripped and split into forty sections. When Spitzner died, his widow toured the show until her death in 1939. Another family took it over for twelve years until such exhibitions were thoroughly out of fashion. In 1980 the collection was, however, rediscovered and shown in Paris.[14]

No anatomical collection was complete without a Venus. They were even included sometimes, as in the case of the model in the Josephinium in Vienna, in otherwise very serious professional collections. The Josephinium

Venus was obviously a later inferior addition, and not even made of wax. It is impossible to look at them without being reminded of the most horrific murders.

In Italy anatomical modelling was a serious and highly refined scientific skill. Some of the best models were made in Italy, particularly in Florence. There was an *Istituto di Anatomia Patologica* in Florence where twenty rooms contained wax models of every organ and physiological conditions, fit, on the turn and desperately ill. Wax showmen in Britain ruthlessly used the label 'Florentine', much as 'organic' is used by processed food sellers in the early twenty-first century. Venuses were made in Florence. In 1825 the first 'Florentine' Venus was shown in London. Critics would have none of it.

> Under the pretence of imparting anatomical knowledge, this filthy French figure, the property of one Monsieur Esnaut, is exhibited. It is a large, disgusting Doll, the alvus of which being taken off like a pot-lid, shows the internal parts, heart, liver, lungs, kidneys and as remotely from anatomical precision or utility as any of the sixpenny wooden dolls which you may buy at Bartholomew fair ... The thing is a silly imposture, and as indecent as it is wretched.[15]

Eighteenth-century Venuses may have been treated as objects of scientific edification, but nineteenth-century critics were quick to identify them as a threat to morality and decency.

On the other hand, wax anatomical models as such were regarded with approval, because they protected the dead, and the living, from exploitation. In 1828 an indignant British press had condemned the body-snatching of Burke and Hare. More sensitive attitudes towards corpses made anatomical waxworks vital for teaching and research. By 1830 two anatomical shows were running in High Holborn, those of Simmons and of Madame Hojo or Hoyo, which apparently hailed from Italy. Madame Hojo had earlier put on a show at the Rotunda, near Blackfriars Bridge, where the Leverian Museum had ended its days, and in a number of other towns. Her major anatomical masterpiece was Samson. The model opened up to show his head and breast, also the muscles, veins and arteries of the left arm. The handbills claimed that the model was made of 300 pounds of wax, had taken two years to make and was valued at 500 guineas. This was a very high and unlikely price, but at that weight (also unlikely) there was little fear that anyone would make off with Samson. The advertisement pointed out how such figures could replace dead bodies in teaching, although there is no evidence that the Hojo Samson could be taken apart. Hojo also included an old favourite of the fairground that proved even more distasteful to the press than the Venuses, a 'Grecian daughter and her father', in which the father, condemned for some unexplained reason to die of starvation, is saved by being breastfed by the daughter, as a consequence of which the father forgives the daughter.[16] A very similar show 'just arrived from Italy', also included Samson, with the additional information that Napoleon had presented the artist, Caballi, with a Belles-Arts medal when he saw the model in 1815. In addition to inviting the general public, the exhibitors hoped that their show 'will be acceptable to the Professors of Surgery and Sculpture, to whom it is particularly recommended'.

Samson seems soon to have gone out of favour, but Venus thrived. Soon there were copies in the Cosmorama rooms, Dubourg's Saloon of Arts and opposite Exeter Hall on the Strand, where the handbills suggested that ladies might appreciate private showings. In 1844 a Parisian 'Venus' openly boasted a taste for a mixture of death and sex, a combination that fascinated Victorians:

> We see what seems to be the corpse of a handsome female who has just expired. It is moulded in wax; the face is removed like a mask, and the exterior of the limbs and bosom being lifted, representations of what would appear in a real subject are pointed out. Anatomical explanations are provided with great clearness by the gentleman who attends ... Young medical students would be likely to derive considerable benefit from the inspection.

Adonis joined Venus in 1839 in an exhibition run by Sarti, a Florentine, at 27 Margaret Street that seems to have had a genuine scientific purpose. Even the *Times* admired the result. Both models could be taken apart, Adonis from the rear. Around them were smaller models showing a foetus, the structure of the female breast, the sense organs, an ectopic pregnancy and how cholera affected people. There was a special session for ladies run by a woman between 5 and 7 p.m. In 1847 Sarti came back to London with a Museum of Pathological Anatomy held in the Cosmorama Rooms. There was a 'Pathological Room' with three full-size figures and examples showing sixty diseases. There was also a 'Physiological Room' with a full-size model of a 'Moorish' female that could be taken into seventy-five parts. The handbill claimed that the exhibition would enable non-professionals to explain their symptoms better to their doctor and have more faith in his competence. The exhibition was open to women on Tuesdays and Thursdays so that, as mothers and nurses, they would be better able to care for the sick.

The most active self-publicist among these anatomical wax entrepreneurs, and by the sound of it one of the most ambiguous, was Dr Joseph Kahn. He claimed support from numerous faculties of medicine in Europe and from the queen of the Netherlands. His show was part wax, part preserved real body parts. His Venus was divisible into eighty-five pieces. Conception to birth was illustrated by 103 tiny preserved foetuses. The dangers of syphilis were demonstrated, as were those of tight-laced stays, shown on a model of a pregnant woman who had died while dancing. Travellers' tales had talked of people in Abyssinia having real tails – so Kahn had wax models made with tails. Kahn also gave lectures at the exhibition and published pamphlets, including a set of nine lectures, *The Philosophy of Marriage.* His main living seems to have been made giving confidential advice about sexually transmitted disease and his show was conveniently located on a busy prostitute beat. When a music hall, the London Pavilion, blocked light from his premises, Kahn took off for New York, where he opened a 'Museum for Men Only'.

In the same district in 1853 Reimer's Anatomical and Ethnological Museum appeared in part of Saville House. It consisted of three hundred anatomical wax figures, which later grew to five hundred. The ethnological side consisted of a Gallery of All the Nations, a subject which attracted a lively interest in this age of exploration. The show was strictly for men over eighteen and cost 6*d.*, half price for workers. Other men only exhibitions were the Institute of Anatomy and Science in nearby Oxford Street and Dr William Beale's Museum of Science, Anatomy and the Wonders of Nature in Berners Street. In 1859, also in Berners Street, a Madame Caplin set up an Anatomical and Physiological Gallery, for ladies only.

In the twentieth century anatomical wax models were made irrelevant in medical and surgical education by the development of X-rays, scanning and laser investigation. Since 1893 formaldehyde has been used to preserve bodies, and anyone who has studied biology at school has been repulsed by rows of tiny white wet foetuses in glass cases. From 1914 it has been possible to infuse bodily tissue in a dry state using paraffin. From the 1950s water-soluble polythylene glycol did the same job. Samples of human and other formerly living tissues have been preserved in hard, transparent plastic blocks since the 1930s. The human body can be preserved by infusing the tissues with silicone rubber. Such models are not displayed for paying customers.

In consequence medical school wax anatomical collections lay neglected.[17] Anatomical waxworks remained popular, however, particularly at fairs, well into the twentieth century. Gradually, whether the prime attraction for customers was enlightenment or titillation, they were superseded by film, and, for those who need tactile stimulation, by plastic and rubber. Few collections are still intact. In December 2001 350 anatomical wax models were auctioned at Christies, London. A private collection amassed by a

33. Handbill for Reimer's Anatomical and Ethnological Museum, 1854.

Swiss painter, Léonce Schiffman, and mainly produced in late nineteenth-century Germany, the models were apparently moved to Switzerland during the First World War. In the usual overblown dramatic style of waxworks, the Schiffman catalogue claimed that the van that transported them to Switzerland was used as a cover by the German secret service. William Bonardo and his wife Lily Bindi showed the models in fairs in Switzerland for many years. The collection consisted of the usual erect fleshless male bodies, accurately demonstrating muscles and sinews, and a standard horizontal Venus, complete with flesh, silver bracelet, long dark wavy hair, lacy shoes, corset and petticoat (discreetly covering the vaginal hair) and an open uterus revealing a part-formed embryo. Advertised as a pregnant lady who had laced herself too tightly into her corsets in order to go to a grand ball (almost as common a feature in waxworks as the inevitable Venus), Christies expected her to sell for up to £12,000, and she did indeed attract a high price from an American customer. A second pregnant woman, naked, with visible uterus and masses of hair on both her head and her vagina was expected to reach £8000. In an array of black wooden boxes with glass fronts there were numerous examples of limbs to illustrate bandaging, part bodies to show surgical techniques, including circumcision, the development of the embryo from very early stages and various very unpleasant illnesses, especially sexual.[18] An indication that interest in such models has dissipated was that, although such a sale is rare, 40 per cent of the models remained unsold.

There are, however, radical challenges to wax, particularly in the exhibition of real preserved bodies. In the 1990s plastination allowed whole and part bodies to be preserved, not for scientific or medical research and teaching but for public show at competitive prices. Individuals apparently donated their bodies to be stripped of their flesh and, like wax anatomical models, displayed to show the relationship of the various organs, muscles and blood vessels and the impact of a variety of diseases. Unlike anatomical wax models which simply stand erect, plastination allows the whole bodies to be displayed in action, fencing, swimming, playing chess, even riding a plastinated horse. Slices through vital organs are set in resin.[19]

To turn now to more 'general interest' or family waxworks. Fairs were still the place where most people went to see wax models. In 1825 Bartholomew Fair showed a mixture of royals, including George IV, Mary Queen of Scots and Queen Elizabeth, plus Othello; also stock characters such as Mother Shipton and Jane Shore, plus a topical murderer for good measure. In 1839 Signor Francisco showed moving waxworks of figures about to die, including John the Baptist, Mark Antony and Cleopatra.

There were still sculptors making wax models for individual orders.

Among others, Peter Rouw (1770–1852) made numerous religious and political waxes, including Lucien Bonaparte (1814), Princess Charlotte and the duke of Wellington.[20] There were many permanent wax shows in London when Madame Tussaud was building her reputation. On the Strand in 1812 was the London Grand Cabinet of Figures, which sported seventy models, including assorted politicians, the actress Mrs Siddons and Napoleon. In 1830 the Oxford Street Bazaar, which considered itself high class, added wax figures including a life-size copy of Rubens's *Descent from the Cross*. There were also penny shows such as the Royal Waxworks at 67 Fleet Street, with five rooms and two hundred figures, while Simmons on High Holborn insisted it had the only genuine models of the body-snatching murderers Burke and Hare.

In the later 1850s you could see all the crowned heads of Europe on the Strand at Springthorpe's Waxwork Figures and Grand Cosmoramic Views. Springthorpe's also had some mechanical humming birds, fresh from the Crystal Palace, and its own Chamber of Horrors, mainly occupied by a pair of mummies. At some point Madame Tussaud no longer included mummies in her show. Perhaps they migrated to Springthorpe's. Another show, that of Napoleon Montanari, displayed Victoria, Albert and their brood entertaining Napoleon III and the Empress Eugénie in the state drawing room at Windsor Castle, together with models showing civilised and savage Mexican society and bull fighting. You could enjoy 'The Awful Tortures of the Inquisition, with the Authentic Instruments of that Dreadful Institution', plus yet another Chamber of Horrors. Some waxwork shows specialised in mechanical devices. In 1833–34 the Cosmorama Rooms had a French wax model of Napoleon lying on a couch in all his uniform, breathing, while he was the leading item in another show at Saville House at the same time. John Dubourg's Saloon of Arts in Great Windmill Street had five hundred totally automated figures, including Androcles and the lion.

In nineteenth-century Britain the number of family waxworks grew. As Tussaud's became established as a household name, rivals often imitated them. Like Tussaud's, Ewings stressed the 'superior brilliancy of the lights' and their band. One novelty in their show in Beverley was that 'A BALLOON will ascend from the interior at Seven O'Clock'. Ewings focused on the contemporary English royalty, and on political and cultural figures. Napoleon only appeared in disguise, making his escape from Moscow.[21]

A back-handed tribute to Marie Tussaud was that wax entrepreneurs liked to boast on their posters that their show was comparable to Tussaud's, printing the name Tussaud's in such large, bold print that a casual reader might think it was a Tussaud's exhibition. Or sometimes, like F. H. Bradley, they imitated the design of the Tussaud's posters and models so closely that a prospective customer could easily confuse the two. In Manchester in 1817 Bradley claimed to have put on his collection with *éclat* in London, Bath, Bristol, Oxford and Cambridge. 'Modeller to the late Princess Charlotte', he included 'A most superb Representation of her Royal Highness Princess Charlotte and her Royal Infant, as they Lay in State at Windsor.' Princess Charlotte (1796–1817) was buried in St George's Chapel, Windsor. Showing the wax models was good marketing. Interestingly, Madame Tussaud did not include a model of the tiny baby. The death of this young mother and tiny daughter was more than a personal tragedy. Princess Charlotte was the only child of the Prince Regent (who became George IV in 1820) and therefore would have become Britain's next queen after her father's death. In May 1816 the wedding of Charlotte to her cousin, Prince Leopold of Saxe-Coburg, caused a stir among the fashion-concious. Newspapers included lengthy descriptions of her silver and gold lamé dress, and the equally stunning outfits worn by the guests. Princess Charlotte, however, lacked the dignity of a future queen. The *Lady's Magazine* described her appearance at the wedding ceremony in Westminster Abbey.

> Her appearance and her manners were shockingly vulgar, particularly when she stood up. She took very little notice of the service, and seemed, from her uneasiness to wish that it were ended.[22]

Charlotte quickly fulfilled her constitutional duty by becoming pregnant, but tragically she and her tiny daughter died in childbirth.

Bradley's show of seventy-two models contained many of the same characters as Tussaud's; Napoleon, Marie-Louise, their son the king of Rome, 'The Unfortunate late Queen of France', the Princess Elizabeth and Voltaire, and the usual quantity of English royals. There was also 'a striking figure of JANE SHORE who Died of Hunger in the Streets of London', a model which appeared in a number of exhibitions. Bradley also claimed to have two spotted Caribbean negroes. They may have been the same pair who had lurked in the basement of Curtius's Palais Royal establishment in the 1770s. Bradley boasted that his was the only show that was candlelit in the daytime. Customers could also order a model of themselves, for from between 15 and 30 guineas.[23] It is unclear whether the price depended on the size of the sitter or of the model.

Bradley himself faced competition in Manchester in 1817 from Churchman's 'Reduced Price' show, apparently on tour from the Strand, London. The great attraction was Princess Charlotte and her baby in their coffins, 'covered with Crimson Velvet, and lined with White Satin, with rich Gold Ornaments ... executed by the same Artist who made the originals'. In 1825 Bradley performed at Nottingham Fair. A new and important attraction was the 'Death of the Immortal Nelson', another ubiquitous item. 'Over his head is a Cherub preparing to invest him with the LAUREL of Conquest, and BRITTANIA in tears for the loss of her darling SON'. In the intervening years, Bradley had added substantially to his collection. Although he included no villains, in other respects he followed the Tussaud example by emphasising the contemporary English royals, and in presenting a virtual pageant of British history, 'from the signing of the GREAT CHARTER, which renders an Englishman's fireside so dear to him'. King John is portrayed, 'bearing those marks of anxiety his situation would naturally excite'. Foreign history is not forgotten, from Julius Caesar to Napoleon, 'a striking instance of the futility of human ambition'.

In 1850 a former Tussaud's employé, Lambert d'Arc, set up on his own. It took him six weeks to make a collection of models, which he showed first in Manchester. He was at the Rotunda in Dublin in 1876. During his six years there he built up a marionette show which employed thirty operators. They moved to Cardiff in 1884. His wife and son ran a waxworks there until 1931, when they sold out to another company which ran the business until 1936. Lambert himself embarked on a series of world tours with his marionettes. This Welsh establishment, Grand French Waxworks and Marionettes, including Freaks of Nature, was known as 'Madame Tussaud's of Wales'. For a time Louis Tussaud showed his wax models on the same premises.[24]

Mr Major's 'Splendid Collection of Wax Figures Acknowledged Equal to Madame Tussaud' went on show in Portsmouth in 1841 as the 'French Mechanical Theatre of Arts, Grand Cosmoramic Views'. Admission was half the price of Tussaud's, 'Ladies and Gentlemen 6d. each; Working People, Servants and Children 3d.'.[25] In 1849 a different outfit set up in nearby Portsea, 'never before in this town'. W. Allsop was eager to assure his customers (1s. each for Ladies and Gentlemen) that he had no connection with any other concern. Allsop promised his clients all the usual royals in predictable yards of silk velvet. He also offered 'Pius IX Pope of Rome in his Morning Robe and Cardinal Wiseman, Attired in Robes of Scarlet Silk'. There were a healthy crop of murderers (a correct likeness) and a 'Grand Series of Cosmoramic Views, of the most Costly Description ever witnessed in this Town', was assured including, in addition to views of Rome, Paris and Napoleon's death bed, 'the Extraordinary Leap of a Horse and Rider over a Dinner Table, at a Hotel, at Aylesbury, for the wager of £5000, plus the Interior of a Convent with Monks at their Devotions'. A year later Allsops were performing in Bristol with 'an Efficient Band'. A number of wax shows, including those of Mr Morell, like Tussaud's, flaunted a spurious royal crest at the head of their posters.[26] In 1834 a

Milanese waxworker, Signor Francesco, held a show in the Minories in London which included the last moments of Mark Anthony and the coronation of William IV and Queen Adelaide, complete with 'three most beautiful figures, representing BRITANNIA, HIBERNIA AND CALEDONIA', perhaps the same trio Tussaud's had in their collection, but which had actually ornamented George IV's coronation not the less grandiose coronation of his brother ten year's later.[27]

In addition to Italian exhibitions, there were waxworkers who had trained in Italy, notably Alfred Reynolds and his son Charles. They ran one of the leading provincial shows, 'Reynolds' Exhibition and Musical Promenade' at the Freemasons Hall in Liverpool, opposite Lime Street Station, from 1854 to 1923. Dubbed (by themselves), the 'Tussaud of the Provinces', their models of Disraeli and the actor Henry Irving were photographed and sold as pictures of the living person. (Disraeli himself hated being photographed.) In imitation of Tussaud's, Reynolds included a breathing Sleeping Beauty, Madame Amaranthe and, a very large collection of military and royal scenes, which by the early twentieth century also included explorers and sportsmen. Reynolds specialised in a side of the trade Tussaud's shunned, freaks of nature, from very heavy, very light, to two-headed. Like Tussaud's, he had an impressive Criminal Chamber, mostly cast after execution, and a selection of anatomical models. Reynolds was probably the closest British rival to Tussaud's. In 1923 he sold off some of his collection and Tussaud's were careful to acquire the detailed sale catalogue.[28] In 1937, its surviving Museum of Anatomy was sold to Louis Tussaud's Blackpool show.

The nearest equivalent and international rival to Tussaud's appeared in France. For a large part of the nineteenth century, however, apart from anatomical and fairground wax shows, French waxworks appear to have been far less vibrant than the British. Curtius was acknowledged at the time and since as the founder of modern wax showmanship in Paris and his *salon* continued to dominate there, long after his death. A substantial number of nostalgic enthusiasts for the Boulevard du Temple noted that the *salon* was still using Curtius's name long after François Tussaud had sold it to clear his debts. Indeed some commentators seemed unaware that Curtius *was* dead. It survived as a dusty, rather neglected exhibition. One apparently frequent visitor recalled how the only noticeable change in the *salon* in sixty years was the uniform of the wax model at the entrance. Since the Revolution he had been dressed as

chasseur in the Imperial Guard, National Guard drummer; last Sunday he was in the uniform of the municipal guard ... When you enter the *salon*, you notice that it is just as it always was, black and smokey. New figures are pushed behind the old ones ... you get the impression that they have merely changed the costumes not the figures themselves ... what has never altered is the dinner table, around which all kings have dined in turn. First we saw Louis XVI and his illustrious family; the Directors and their illustrious families, the three Consuls [etc etc] ... today we get the chance to see Louis-Philippe ... I need hardly mention the fruit bowl that represents their dessert; I can swear that the apples, pears, peaches and grapes spread out on this illustrious table are exactly the same that I gazed on thirty years ago ... I don't believe that they've been dusted in the meantime; it seems somewhat unfair to put before these crowned heads a bowl of fruit that the meanest merchant in the rue Saint-Denis would not dare to offer to his assistant.[29]

As today, people tended to take their young children to see an exhibition they remembered from their own youth, perhaps as a way of creating a shared memory of childhood, or recalling past times. Surviving illustrations show a rundown exterior and a very uninteresting display of wax busts inside.

In 1847 the process began of truncating the Boulevard du Temple and demolishing the buildings to make way for the Place de la République. The Curtius *salon* and all of the theatres disappeared; today there is only a tiny rump of the old heart of Parisian popular theatreland and a few pathetic trees, relics from the formerly tree-lined boulevard, with a very busy *cirque* hosting a variety of very well attended shows clinging on in a side street. No one knows what happened to the Curtius models. Yet even in the 1870s the Curtius show and the boulevard were still recalled nostalgically by elderly *flâneurs*, wistfully trying to recapture their childhood and youth. 'Curtius perfected the art of sculpture in wax ... In the Palais Royal he focused on politics and science; on the boulevard he specialised in infamous villains and celebrated individuals from the lower ranks of society.'[30]

After the Curtius *salon* disappeared the main Parisian waxworks were anatomical collections.[31] There were also some provincial shows, mainly at fairs. A frequently told story, which may indicate that there were very few surviving waxworks, was of an exhibition in a pink tent in Limoges in the 1840s. For two *sous* people could gawp at a wax model of a young girl, wearing the red head scarf she had worn on the day she was murdered. The girl's parents had agreed to the model being shown.[32] Mazagines like *L'Illustration*, the French version of *Illustrated London News*, and the *Grand Dictionnaire Universel* (1867) claimed that the fashion for wax models fizzled out when the Curtius *salon* closed and that there were no waxworks in the capital, only a few in the provinces. Given the timing, the absence of family wax shows cannot be explained by a popular interest in photography, which was still in its infancy. It was also in sharp contrast to London, where waxworks emphatically did not lose their audience.

How can the difference be explained? The answer must lie to a large

16. Winston Churchill. (*Madame Tussaud's Archives*)

17. Charlie Chaplin. In his day, perhaps the most widely recognised man in the world. (*Madame Tussaud's Archives*)

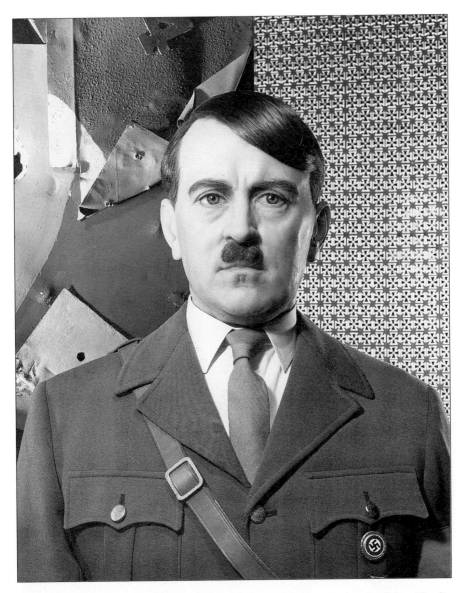

18. Adolf Hitler. It is unclear whether his moustache was inspired by Charlie Chaplin's. Chaplin repaid the compliment of imitation in his film *The Great Dictator*. (*Madame Tussaud's Archives*)

19. The King – Elvis Presley. (*Madame Tussaud's Archives*)

20. The Greatest – Muhammed Ali. (*Madame Tussaud's Archives*)

21. Robespierre's head, modelled by Madame Tussaud in 1795. (*Madame Tussaud's Archives*)

22. Dr Henry Hawley Crippen, the poisoner, hanged in 1910. (*Madame Tussaud's Archives*)

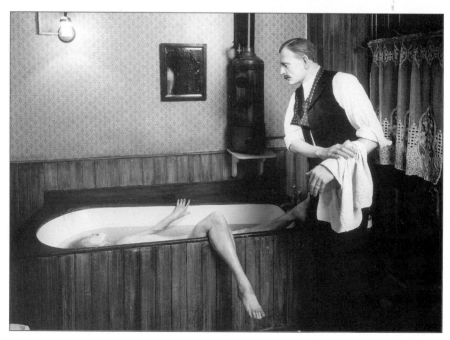

23. George Joseph Smith, drowning his bride Margaret Lofty. He was hanged in 1915. (*Madame Tussaud's Archives*)

24. The Electric Chair, showing Bruno Hauptmann, electrocuted at Trenton State Prison, New Jersey, in 1936. (*Madame Tussaud's Archives*)

25. Princess Diana. (*Madame Tussaud's Archives*)

extent in personalities. Marie Tussaud was a determined, energetic, forceful woman who built up a very successful business to leave to her heirs. In France Curtius had been the outstanding wax entrepreneur of his day and his legacy was recalled long after his death, but no one of equal stature replaced him. The main explanation for the big difference between France and Britain may well lie in the presence or absence of a dynamic show person. After Madame Tussaud's death, even her exhibition gradually slid into difficulties. It may also have been that the British were more willing to travel to seek amusement, a consequence of London serving a larger catchment area than Paris. Parisians may have thought themselves too sophisticated to visit a waxworks; apparently most visitors to the Musée Grévin in the 1980s were provincials, not Parisians. It may have also been that recent French history had been too divisive to make an historical exhibition acceptable to many Frenchmen. Perhaps some people thought of Tussaud's as a French exhibition. From the fact that there were French-language versions of Tussaud's posters and catalogues in the 1840s, it appears that French tourists visited Tussaud's, drawn particularly by its substantial French historical content. Tussaud's profited mightily from the twin cults of Napoleon and of monarchy, and both were visually compelling. A wax show in Paris might have exploited the former, but Paris did not need wax exhibitions to sustain the Napoleonic legend. The very architecture of the city, the history exhibition at Versailles and, after 1840, the shrine of the Invalides were more than enough. The glorification of all the glamorous trappings of monarchy, which was so central to Tussaud's, would have been embarrassing in Paris, indeed totally alien to the French, especially after the fall of the Orléans monarchy in 1848.

After Curtius the first successful attempt to create a substantial non-anatomical waxworks in Paris came in the early 1880s. The new wax gallery was founded by Arthur Meyer and Alfred Grévin, both quintessential *boulevardiers*, men with leisure to live a life of conversation in the elegant cafés of the capital and eager to recreate that culture in their waxworks. [33] Grévin was its main artistic inspiration. Grévin (1827–1892), very briefly a bureaucrat on the Paris-Lyon-Marseille railway, dreamt of being an artist. To start the process rolling he dressed the part, wandering around the boulevards in a red beret and blue jacket. In his spare time he made silhouettes of *grisettes*, the traditional seductive young worker mistresses of penniless poets. He became a caricaturist successively for *Le Charivari* and *Le Journal Amusant*. In 1869 he published an *Almanach des Parisiennes*.[34]

Their first attempt, to be known as the Eden *musée*, at 17 Boulevard du Strasbourg, planned to focus on famous contemporaries as well as infamous villains. A full range of rulers, including Victoria, would stand alongside the likes of Bismarck, Victor Hugo, de Lesseps, von Moltke, Garibaldi, Liszt and Wagner. There was to be a special Mexican exhibition and a Chamber of Horrors, modelled on Tussaud's, which would include Fieschi, who had tried to blow up Louis-Philippe. The publicity literature sounded compelling, but apparently this project did not come to fruition. [35]

There were at least two other Eden *musées* at the time, one in Belgium, the owners of which were initially investors in the Paris scheme, and another in New York, run by a Frenchman, Professor Constant Thys, and his wife,[36] which also seemed also to specialised in contemporary affairs. Thys may have worked with Grévin, or he may simply have borrowed the name, or vice-versa. Precise details of wax exhibitions are mostly now lost. The New York show boasted a large and frequently changing collection of both contemporary and historical figures. When famous characters lost their appeal, they were recycled as 'extras' in newer tableaux; in 1890 'Napoleon' sprouted a long black beard to become part of a crowd scene.[37] At Christmas 1910, just as he had completed a jolly Santa Claus, Thys himself died suddenly of a heart attack and his museum closed.[38]

The plan for a Paris exhibition was revamped in 1880 as the Musée Grévin. Unlike Tussaud's, this did not start as a wholly family financed and run firm, although the banker Gabriel Thomas (1854–1932), whose family ran it and was the main share-holder, was Meyer's cousin by marriage. Thomas was also involved in the Eiffel Tower. Arthur Meyer (1844–1924), the initial business inspiration for the project, was a successful newspaper proprietor, notably of *Le Paris-Journal*. In 1880 he published a brochure to attract investment in a new waxworks radically different from its two closest rivals, Tussaud's and the Eden *musée* in Brussels, the latter of which was rapidly excluded from the project. The new Musée Grévin promised a 'living' or 'plastic' newspaper to focus on current political and cultural affairs, leavened by suitably juicy murders. The gallery aimed to focus on presenting current affairs accurately, 'to create a sort of theatre where the outstanding dramas as well as the great comedies of modern life will be replayed'. It aimed to attract the comfortably off, who liked to be shown and feel part of a city which thought of itself as the cultural capital of Europe, with a unique tradition of boulevard entertainment. Meyer hoped to acquire a large building at 27 Boulevard des Italiens. It had a magnificent entrance, forty rooms, a winter garden and a buffet. When shares went on sale in December 1880 with the hope of raising one million francs of capital, investors were promised a return of 50 per cent.[39] The company was named after its artistic director, Grévin. The wax newspaper, however, was nearly stillborn because Meyer withdrew soon after the gallery opened.

The Grévin opened, 6 June 1882, not in the Boulevard des Italiens, but in an equally stylish central location near to the offices of Meyer's newspaper, the Boulevard Montmartre, where it remains today. *Le Temps* welcomed the 'very modern and very Parisian' new enterprise as a 'Tussaud's in Paris'.[40] Publicity in Meyer's own newspaper and the articles he paid for in other leading papers guaranteed success. Like Tussaud's, but unlike many smaller waxworks, the models were made in an in-house studio, equipped with a sculptor, costume-makers and make-up experts. Grévin, and his successor after his death in 1892 Leopold Berstamm, always dressed models in the person's own clothes and modelled their hands from life. For this reason the Victor Hugo model was advertised as a 'precious relic'. The entrance fee for the gallery, 2 francs on weekdays and 1 franc on Sundays, was considered within everyone's range. Unlike Curtius and Tussaud's, a substantial number of free tickets were distributed. The catalogue, which sold at 1 franc at first, looked rather like a cross between an almanac and a theatre programme. Grévin had made his name drawing fetching young women. In tune with this, for years the cover displayed a pretty, rather worldly fairy, while inside were *fantaisies Parisiennes,* glamorous ladies fronted by risqué by-lines.

At first Grévin steered well clear of French history, perhaps because the last century had been so divisive and whatever political preference it chose would have alienated potential customers. Tussaud's held displays of the Franco-Prussian War, with genuine relics and a tableau of rival claimants for a monarchy to replace the new French Republic, but the Grévin did not. One of the most dramatic events of the previous decade, the revolutionary Commune in Paris, was never shown in the Grévin gallery, despite its visual potential and the huge success of Emile Zola's novel, *La Débâcle,* published in 1892. Louise Michel, one of the leading female Communards, was included in the gallery, not for her supposed fire-raising during the Commune but for her later work for charity. This blindness to controversial events was in line with moderate French republicans who, in the name of national unity, tried to pretend the Commune had never happened.

It was not long, however, before the *musée* or gallery, the names preferred by Grévin (neither Grévin nor Tussaud tolerated the fairground term 'waxwork') became more than a mere newspaper. Following the example of Tussaud's and other waxworks, and driven by the opportunity of the celebrations of the centenary of the 1789 Revolution, it began to range through selected aspect of French history. To test opinion, in 1886 they imitated Tussaud by making a tableau of the murder of Marat – by chance it seems Grévin acquired the actual bath in which Marat was assassinated. After his death Marat became a cult figure for republicans and his bath had been part of a funeral display in the church of the Cordeliers and then in the Place du Carrousel. When Marat went out of favour, it had been assumed that the bath had been melted down. In June 1885 the *Figaro* told how the abbé Le Cosse, vicar of Sarzeau in Brittany, had been left the tub by a very Catholic and royalist lady, whose father had bought it from a scrap metal merchant in 1805.[41] The Marat tableau was instantly popular and a substantial set of tableaux on Napoleon joined it, together with other aspects of the history of France. Unlike Tussaud's, there were tableaux of the life of Jesus. There was a full complement of horror, including 'the history of a crime' in four tableaux, which was so popular that Tussaud's imitated it.[42]

Like Tussaud's, for many years the entire Grévin gallery, including non-wax diversifications, remained within one building. A year after opening they set up the *théâtrophone*, which allowed their customers to listen to performances at one of the leading music halls in the capital. In 1884 they were one of the first entertainment venues to install electric lighting, at a cost of 80,000 francs. Both Grévin and Tussaud's installed cinemas, but neither made a commercial success of the venture. Far more profitable for Grévin was something Tussaud's never tried, a children's theatre, which filled a niche for the middle classes that traditional theatres neglected. From 1902 until the First World War, the Grévin *théâtre-joli* put on family shows on Saturday afternoons, between 4 and 6 p.m., with additional performances entirely for children. They showed a varied repertoire of 'morally good' material, vetted by a committee of the subscribing fathers and mothers, all presented, as they insisted, in a spacious, hygienic, well-ventilated and heated theatre. The management assured customers that a mother, or her governess, could safely go alone with the children: 'A mother's dream has been realised' – and all for 6 francs for a fortnight, including free entry into the wax exhibition. Little children were given toys, sweets and a free tombola at their own special sing songs and magic shows. Afterwards they were served snacks at little tables. Older siblings enjoyed operettas, short talks on current affairs and elegant teas in the foyer. Young women could visit alone, or with their teacher or a chaperon. The theatre was a great success. In 1902 it transformed itself into a *théâtre anglais*, with the whole programme delivered in English. Madame Tussaud would have regretted that she had not thought of such a moralising, ultra-respectable venture. Best of all, it ran as a commercial success for several years. In 1911 the theatre actually provided 40 per cent of Grévin's income. Another innovation, in 1908, was a *journal lumineux*, later named the *palais des mirages*. This used 2500 coloured electric lights and numerous large rotating mirrors, which gave the customer the impression of looking at 64,000 lights, brilliantly illuminating, successively, a Hindu temple, a forest, an Arab palace, and so on. Based on the now rather old-fashioned diorama concept, this venture did not attract many visitors.

In 1911 the Grévin welcomed just under 400,000 paying customers, including over 191,000 who bought joint tickets for the waxworks and the *théâtre-joli*. This was a fall of 24,000 on 1910 but, since 1909 had seen an increase of 60,000, the management was not downcast. Grévin like Tussaud's always saw themselves at the mercy of the weather and 1911 was a year of seemingly endless rainstorms. Their total takings were 435,748 francs, their costs 306,545 francs. Costs included publicity at 17,854 francs, costumes at 5940 francs, while a modest 671 francs was spent on decorations. The wax exhibition was the biggest money spinner, at 201,496 francs; the theatre took 167,428 francs, while the cinema brought in takings of 17,384 francs, the *palais des mirages* 26,611 francs and catalogues and souvenirs 25,634 francs. A major programme of modernisation was completed without the need to seek outside financing.[43]

It is tempting to conclude this snapshot of rival waxworks with the view that Grévin emerged as the most successful competitor because of the extent to which the gallery imitated Tussaud's. Grévin kept well away from anatomical and 'freak' models. Its recipe at first was the contemporary world, including crime, although history was added quickly. The manager and major shareholder, Gabriel Thomas, was as aware as Tussaud's of the need to sustain a respectable, middle-class image. He hosted masters' concerts, even more stylish than Tussaud's promenade concerts. The children's theatre was a brilliant idea, reflecting the theatrical aspect of wax as well as supplying a snobbish child care solution. Thomas did not slavishly copy Tussaud's however; indeed, Thomas considered Tussaud's rather dull and characterless and sought from the outset to make his gallery more exciting and fashionable. He wanted his gallery to echo the spirit of Paris and the elegance of its ladies. Glancing through the catalogues of the rival establishments at the turn of the nineteenth century, the predominant image of Tussaud's was masculine, while the Grévin catalogue has the air of being a blend of a mildly naughty gentlemen's magazine and a department store catalogue. Grévin did not try to be a museum, rather its claims were to represent contemporary Parisian popular culture. It always called itself a gallery.

Both exhibitions diversified by adding a cinema, and in the case of Grévin a theatre and other amusements. Both put on extensive war tableaux. There was a threat during the war that falling attendances would force the *musée* to give way entirely to the cinema. The offer of free tickets to soldiers and their families, however, and the extra business this brought, saved the day. In 1918 the Grévin was still predominantly a waxworks. It appeared that a nineteenth-century bourgeois amusement had, rather surprisingly, withstood the challenge of photography and film. An important common feature of the two exhibitions was their assertion of family and middle-class values, expressed somewhat staidly at Tussaud's, more flamboyantly at Grévin.

7

From the Great Exhibition to the
First World War

In 1851 an enormous exhibition was held in Hyde Park in a temporary glass structure, the Crystal Palace. Around two hundred people paid 5s. just to watch the prefabricated panels being draped around the trees. Frustrated sparrows struggled to hold on to their nests in the elms, now under glass. They were eventually dislodged (if not by sparrowhawks at the duke of Wellington's suggestion). The wonders of the British and other economies were displayed. The French were thought to have cheated by putting their exhibits up for sale. A group of wax figures of American Indians and Mexicans won a prize medal.[1] There was also a line of kings and queens of England in wax, which do not seem to have won any medals. The initial price of admission to the Great Exhibition made Tussaud's seem very reasonable. A season ticket to the Exhibition cost its 25,000 purchasers three guineas. In the first three weeks a single visit was 5s., but it then fell to 1s. from Monday to Thursday, 2s. 6d. on Friday and, 5s. on Saturday, when working people might have been able to attend. Over six million people visited the exhibition, nearly 4,500,000 of whom were 1s. ticket holders. Middle-class observers commented on the vulgarity of the poor who went and there was a great deal of debate over whether they would arrive drunk and wreck the palace. None of these worries was merited and a very healthy £356,000 profit was made.

All London's tourist venues gained from the Crystal Palace. There were more exhibitions than ever before. In 1851 the Tower of London, the most expensive tourist attraction at 12s. 6d. per person, had six times as many visitors as the previous year. Attendance at the two publicly owned free exhibitions rose from just over 720,000 to 2,230,000 at the British Museum and from nearly 520,000 to almost 1,200,000 at the National Gallery, although people still remarked on the filth and chaos of the displays in the museum. There were, as always, frequent complaints that Westminster Abbey and St Paul's were even more commercial than Tussaud's, the total cost of visiting each exceeding 5s. in tips to assorted vergers. Worshippers would even be charged for their pews if they overstayed the hours of the

34. Wyld's Great Globe, 1851, exterior.

divine services. An American visitor calculated that Tussaud's had nearly a million visitors in 1851.[2] Their publicity reassured customers that 'the most timid need not fear visiting the promenade with their families, being sure to find ample space and ventilation'. There were also at least a dozen dioramas and panoramas on show in London alone. Their most popular theme was the Holy Land, not to mention assorted balloon ascents in search of a more direct route to heaven.

One of the most innovative ventures was Wyld's Great Globe. The idea was not entirely new. Maps were a very fashionable item. In 1823 a giant globe or georama had appeared in the Boulevard des Capucins, Paris. James Wyld, a Member of Parliament and geographer to the queen, was a well-known globe maker and map-seller in London. He offered a huge walk-in globe for installation in the Crystal Palace, but the organisers refused because they did not want exhibitors trying to sell their wares. Wyld erected his globe in a brick rotunda in Leicester Square, by then run-down and seedy. The central dome was painted blue and ornamented with silver stars in their correct constellations. Inside there were steps to four viewing platforms where people could survey the various land masses and oceans on a spherical coloured relief map constructed out of six thousand plaster casts. Live volcanoes were painted red and had bits of cotton wool stuck in their vents. Wyld's maps and globes were prominently displayed and sold. The Globe was the single most visited place next to the Crystal Palace

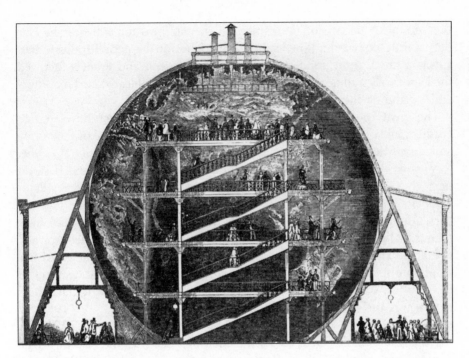

35. Wyld's Great Globe, 1851, interior.

itself. No one seemed bothered that they were looking at the outside features of the earth from the inside of the globe, or that the map was actually erected outside in.[3]

The Crystal Palace finally closed on 11 October 1851.[4] The South Kensington Museums were launched with £186,000 of the profits that went to the government. There was pressure to keep the palace in Hyde Park, until Prince Albert complained that the horses from the neighbouring barracks had had problems reaching their usual exercise routes. A vastly expanded Crystal Palace was re-erected on Sydenham Hill, but it was never a comparable stimulus to London tourism and indeed did not pay its way.

Anticipating that the Crystal Palace would bring an increased number of visitors to the capital, as the 1844 Exposition had done in Paris, Joseph and Francis Tussaud took the opportunity of at last having money that they could call their own to expand their exhibition. Their mother had left no will, instructing her sons to divide everything equally. Following her example they budgeted by regularly putting aside cash for rent, gas, insurance and wages. The rest they divided into two, half to be split between them, half for investment in the business. Victor Tussaud, Francis's son, claimed that they doubled the size of the exhibition in readiness for 1851, but he was only a little boy at the time and the catalogues of the period indicate that it was a much more modest reorganisation.[5] Joseph and Francis followed their mother's traditional recipe, adding more royal tableaux, current affairs and expanding the Horrors.

The great room, with its crimson drapes, huge mirrors and elaborate cornices, now had Victoria's coronation centre-stage. In praise of the family and domesticity, there was a nearby tableau of the royal family at home. Royals were arranged by popularity not chronology; Charles I and II stood next to Oliver Cromwell, opposite Richard III, with a seated William Cobbett, perpetually nodding and taking snuff. A model of Madame Tussaud herself looked on approvingly. Cobbett was one of very few Tussaud's wax figures that moved. Unlike many other waxworks, they had few mechanically operated exhibits, perhaps Madame's detestation of Philipstal deterred her from automation. The pope had just made a very controversial decision to install a full Catholic hierarchy in Britain, so a new addition to Tussaud's in 1851 was their superior, Cardinal Wiseman.

The great room now gave onto three interconnecting rooms which together measured 243 feet by 48, the chief of which was the Hall of Kings. For comparison the Hall of Battles, which had been blazed through the whole of the south wing of Versailles by Louis-Philippe, to make a memorial to the military pomp of France, was 394 feet by 43. The Hall of Kings was lit by five hundred gas lamps, which provided brilliant lighting but also not always welcome heat. When it was warm outside, the rooms were filled with the smell of warm wax and old clothes. Madame Tussaud insisted on washable garments being laundered regularly, but many of the outfits could not be easily washed.

The Hall of Kings celebrated what Tussaud's always called the House of Brunswick. The central group depicted an even more sophisticated tableau of George IV's coronation, with the monarch now arrayed in his original robes, thanks to the economy of his brother who sold his sibling's robes and throne and wore a much simpler outfit for his own coronation. The walls were also hung with crimson drapery, which helped to deaden sound from outside. There were a number of famous portraits by contemporary artists, some of which had been the templates for neighbouring tableaux. There was Victoria, painted by Sir George Hayter, his own copy of the original painting; Albert, painted by Patten; George III and George IV, the latter painted by Sir Thomas Lawrence; William III and Louis XIV and two paintings of French duchesses by Sir Peter Lely. The ceiling was set with panels painted by Sir James Thornhill, restored, the catalogue tells us, by Mr Holden of Holborn. All the wax royals were grouped in harmony, flanked by four wax figures whose costumes had been commissioned by George IV for his coronation. Dressed in ornate 'medieval' style costumes were representations of 'the four National Orders, the Garter, Bath, Thistle and St Patrick'. In the centre was George IV in the coronation regalia he had designed.

> The figure of His Majesty, wearing the Orders of the Garter, Bath, and Guelph, was modelled from life; the attitude copied from a picture by Sir Thomas Lawrence; the Robe, complete in every respect, was worn by his Majesty, and used in the Procession to Westminster Abbey and measures seven yards long, was borne by nine eldest sons of peers. The Robe, placed on your extreme right, was used at the opening of Parliament; that on your left, similarly placed, was, the purple, or Imperial Robe, used on His Majesty's return from the Abbey. The three robes contain five hundred and sixty-seven feet of velvet and embroidery, and, with the Ermine lining, cost £18,000. The splendid Crown, Sceptre, Orb, Orders etc., were faithfully copied from the originals. The Throne is the original one, from Carlton Palace, in which His Majesty received the Allied Monarchs. The Chair of State is the original used at Westminster Abbey, at the Coronation, sitting on which the King received the homage of the Peers.[6]

This was the Tussauds' biggest coup, next to the Shrine to Napoleon, which led off from the Hall of Kings. Between the two Napoleon rooms and the Chamber of Horrors was a buffet, which served tea, fizzy 'effervescents', buns and pies. The Horrors itself, previously a tiny room reached by a narrow staircase, with space for no more than fifteen figures, was the main area of expansion. Although the cost of the expansion was considerable, visitor fees covered it within a year.

A substantial printed catalogue continued to be a valued component to a visit to Tussaud's. Until after the First World War the price stayed at 6*d.*, although the amount of detail and therefore the size of the catalogue increased. Presumably in anticipation that the Great Exhibition would attract more French visitors eager to see the Napoleonic relics, a French version that highlighted the Napoleonic collection in its title was produced in 1851.[7] On the front page, instead of the usual Shakespearian quote, was a royal coat of arms.

At Christmas 1852, when the Shakespeare quote ousted the coat of arms again in the catalogue, another shrine was opened opposite the entrance. This was to the much revered and recently deceased duke of Wellington, 'A National Subject which has given general satisfaction and elicted the highest enconium, the Magnificent Shrine or Memorial in honour of the late illustrious duke of Wellington'.[8] In 1856 there were a number of changes, including the addition of the gun Curtius was awarded as a *vainqueur de la Bastille*. Presumably Francis brought it back from Paris after his father's death. Whatever the explanation, the gun never appeared in catalogues after 1862. There was an enhanced emphasis on political and especially royal subjects and in 1856 a dedicated Hall of Kings was inaugurated. The Hanoverians still dominated. Apart from isolated stars like Queen Elizabeth and Mary Queen of Scots, the earliest royal was George I. Then in 1861 a group was added that was to be one of the most durable and popular: Henry VIII surrounded by all his wives in a renamed 'Marriage Room'. Wellington and Napoleon were put in the Hall of Kings in 1851, presumably as honorary royals. An assortment of European monarchs joined them, including Victor Emmanuel I of Savoy, king of Piedmont, soon to be king of the whole of Italy, Elizabeth, empress of Austria, the Empress Eugénie, wife of Napoleon III, and, a year after his death, the Tsar Nicholas I. Therein lay a tale. Apparently General Popoff, the Russian Minister of Police visited Tussaud's and, on his return reported to Alexander II that the model of his father was a poor likeness. Years later, around 1870, Alexander II sent Tussaud's a huge packing case containing a correct military uniform, a statuette and a massive oil portrait of Nicolas I with instructions to Tussaud's to try again. Victor Tussaud, the family publicist, claimed that before his accession the late Emperor Alexander himself visited the exhibition to check the result with his wife and her sister 'our queen then Princess of Wales'.[9] The portrait is still on display in the lobby of Madame Tussaud's, as is Victor's explanation of how they acquired the painting.

British royals also maintained a close watch on their waxen selves, but were more inclined to 'borrow' items rather than donate valuable paintings. In 1889 Tussaud's received a letter from Buckingham Palace complaining that the model of the duke of Clarence was in a disgraceful state.[10] The boot, or rather the royal robes, were on the other foot in 1904 when another letter from the palace asked John Theodore for the loan of a complete set of Garter robes and the Tussaud coloured engraving of the correct Garter insignia. Poynter was to paint the new king, Edward VII, who seemed to be bereft of suitable garments. The insignia were returned, but five years later Poynter still had the robes and asked to borrow the engraving again.[11]

The exhibition was always quick to reflect contemporary interests and issues. In the eighteenth century and early in the nineteenth, when only a tiny minority were able to travel large distances, but travellers' tales, real and imaginary, were very popular, customers were fascinated by representations of primitive peoples and their dress. Because Tussaud's always portrayed specific and notable individuals, their exhibition might include Indian princes but never anonymous people. They missed opportunities to satisfy the public's curiosity about 'primitive' people, but the race to colonise Africa later in the century made wax heroes of Livingstone, Stanley and the latter's native boy, Kalala, in 1872. Indian and African themes were popular. Tussaud's put on special displays of the Zulu Wars and the Egyptian campaigns. They highlighted a tableau of the viceroy of India, Lord Lytton, and the Indian tributary sovereigns. Predictably the empire occupied a growing space. In 1857 Felice Orsini, who had continued the well-established, but not very successful, tradition of trying to murder French rulers, was added to the Chamber of Horrors. To draw attention to the cause of Italian nationalism, Orsini, an Italian revolutionary, tried to assassinate Napoleon III and Eugénie as they entered the Opéra. Despite his failure and execution, ironically, Orsini was successful, as Napoleon III subsequently did turn his attention to Italy.

The Chamber of Horrors was revamped and expanded again in 1860 in response to public demand. Joseph Randall tried to upgrade it into a 'Chamber of Comparative Physiognomy'. Like phrenology, which George Combe (1788–1858) had made into even more of a cult in Britain than it was in France, physiognomy had a considerable following; indeed many people accepted both theories. In France, Britain and throughout those parts of the world dominated by the self-designated superior white 'races', since the last quarter of the eighteenth century physiognomic theories had claimed to be a development of physiology. Physiognomists studied not merely the skull, but the expression of the face and the shape of its individual features. Enthusiasts for physiognomy were convinced that one could divine a person's character from facial muscles, expression and features. A criminal could be identified by the shape of his nose, mouth, chin and ears, as well as by the cast of his expression. Such assumptions became commonplace, extending beyond criminals even to political opponents. Henri Wallon, a member of the French National Assembly in 1848, illustrated the influence of physiognomy in his description of socialist opponents, who were dubbed reds by conservatives like him.

> A red is not a person, merely a red ... He is not a moral, intelligent and free individual like you and I ... but a depraved being without human rights. He carries the signs of his degeneracy all over his body. His physiognomy is feeble, moronic, expressionless; his eyes wandering, evasive, never daring to look anyone in the face, lacklustre like those of a pig; his features, with their lowering forehead, are coarse, unbalanced and compressed; his mouth is as dumb and insignificant as that of a donkey; his thick, prominent lips suggest gross instincts; his nose is crude and huge, as if it were hammered onto his face; these are the features you find on most of these 'sharers' [socialists]. Their whole body and appearance shouts out the stupidity of their doctrines.[12]

After 1871 Wallon had the distinction of proposing the acceptance of a republican constitution. Little wonder that the result was distinctly conservative. At the end of the nineteenth century, eugenicists such as Herbert Spencer extended some of the broad assumptions of phrenology and physiognomy in their doctrines which claimed that intelligence was defined by birth and therefore race.[13]

The Chamber of Horrors thus offered enormous potential, not just for idle curiosity and a few shudders but as wax proof of theories, some of which may seem outlandish and outrageous today, but which attracted a great deal of support in the nineteenth century. Part of the fascination of being able to look at length at the faces of criminals might be, in comparing them, to assess whether there was such a thing as a criminal face, ears or shape of head. Gall had undertaken extensive research among prisoners as well as on the skulls of executed criminals. Despite the continued fascination with phrenology and physiology in Britain and his own enthusiasm, Joseph Randall failed in his attempt to rename the Chamber of Horrors. Although journalists occasionally linked the exhibition with phrenology, Tussaud's accepted that customers did not want popular scientific contemplation forced upon them – and they liked the existing name.

On the other hand, criticism from clergymen and journalists that Tussaud's were glorifying and immortalising crime forced them to stress that their best money-spinner also had a moral purpose. In 1880 *Punch* decided the Horrors was 'nasty, demoralising and ought to be closed', which almost certainly made the queues even longer. Tussaud's were careful to insist that gazing at murderers and criminals 'creates a contrary tendency to imitation'. What is fascinating is that, for all the moral outrage that murderers were being celebrated, protesters did not complain that acquiring items linked to murders was vulgar, tasteless and showed no concern for the survivors.

Tussaud's were unusual among waxworks in the comprehensiveness of their coverage of British royal history. The Musée Grévin was at first exclusively contemporary, as was the New York *musée*, although touring waxworks in Britain always had their quota of royalty. Tussaud's displayed, and in their catalogues described, a very special kind of history. They had almost no interest in trying to narrate or explain events. Their history was one-dimensional biography, stripped down to physiognomy and style of dress. For their customers, this was enough. Biography, after all, is still the most popular form of history, and appearances still count for a lot, especially in the media. From the start in Britain, Madame Tussaud both cultivated members of the British royal family and installed their models in her exhibition. From 1859 to 1864, however, a massive expansion of historical royals was added to complete the Hall of Kings. In quick succession Elizabeth was joined by Mary, William I, Mathilda (1859), William II, Henry I,

Henry II, Stephen, King John, Richard I, Edward III, the Black Prince, Henry V, Edward IV (1860) and Henry IV, Henry VI and Richard II (1864). The Tussauds were proud of this achievement and believed that the completed Hall of Kings was the climax to their efforts to educate young Britons in their own history.

> The proprietors beg to state that they have now completed the line of English kings and queens from William the Conqueror to the present reign; to serve as a *vade mecum* for the rising generation, and to give them greater interest in their historical studies.[14]

At the same time a not inconsiderable number of contemporary foreign royals including the Prince Imperial (1868), plus clerics and political figures, including Gladstone (1866), also appeared.[15]

Like all waxworks, Tussaud's delighted, and delight, in trying to confuse illusion and reality. In the second half of the nineteenth century visitors could still touch the models and sit and stand very close to them, making the confusion of real and wax more likely, and highly entertaining. At Easter 1872 the *Illustrated London News* carried a half page, 'Holiday Time at a Wax Exhibition', in which the seated figure of William Cobbett is almost smothered in admiring women and puzzled small girls. A second large illustration showed crowds around Napoleon I lying in state, several studying their catalogues.[16] The *Illustrated Sporting and Dramatic News* carried a full page of sketches showing how easy it was to confuse illusion and reality as people took the models of Madame Tussaud herself and of a policeman for real. This was an old chestnut, but the illustration also included a neat sketch of two elegant top-hatted gents gazing through their lorgnettes at two lovely young things resting on a couch, and searching in vain in their catalogue for the relevant entry.[17]

Illusion and reality mingled to make Tussaud's a great attraction for ladies keen to study and imitate the latest court fashions. Tussaud's became part of the fashion plate industry. In 1831 plates made for the Royal Pavilion in Brighton included Tussaud's models in the latest gowns. These fashion plates were such a success that people bought them, trimmed off the advertisement and displayed them as pictures. When the fashion industry needed an image of Victoria's wedding gown, it used the Tussaud's tableau. Tussaud's became the owner of a unique collection of costly and fashionable gowns bought from the actual royal dressmakers. They bought copies of court dresses made for Princesses Alice and Louise and other members of the royal family from Worth, Tissier and Bourlay. The collection was applauded by fashion magazines as 'not only interesting, but in a certain sense instructive as manifesting the progress in artistic taste'. In 1878 Tussaud's held a display of fashions and manners, 'as much a refined reference as an elegant novelty'. A second purely fashion show was held two years later.[18]

Tussaud's had to buy their copies of royal gowns, but many subjects, from politicians to murderers, were delighted to donate a suit of clothes to help convert their wax self into an illusion of reality. Occasionally the reverse happened. Tussaud's lent a suit of court dress to the sculptor Joseph Durham so he could attend the unveiling of his bronze statue of the Prince Consort as the centre-piece in the Albert Memorial. Tussaud's continued to buy original paintings by famous artists. Tableaux might be copied from paintings, but sometimes the compliment was returned. Sir George Hayter, whose painting of Victoria's coronation hung in the entrance of Tussaud's and who had painted Wellington gazing at Napoleon's shrine, took lessons in wax modelling from Joseph Randall.

Tussaud's were in touch with more terrifying reality. In 1868 they felt obliged to hire a guard to protect the building (and the customers) from Fenian attack. The Fenians, or Irish Republican Brotherhood, were founded in America in 1858. In 1865 its main Irish leaders were arrested, but one, James Stephens, escaped to America and terrorist incidents occurred in Canada, England and Ireland. In December 1867 twelve were killed and many others injured when a bomb exploded at the London prison where the Fenians were being held. Gladstone came into government at the end of 1868 'to pacify Ireland'. Tussaud's were aware that the Irish Question was good for business and added a waxed Michael Davitt, a former Fenian and founder of the more law-abiding Land League. In May 1882 Fenians murdered the new Irish chief secretary Lord Frederick Cavendish and the British under secretary for Ireland in Dublin's Phoenix Park. Some months later Davitt's wax model was found adorned with a fine diamond ring. Tussaud's quickly acquired the jaunting car alleged to have been used by the murderers. Curiously such macabre purchases have not been made in recent years, despite the fact that television ensures that viewers are aware of such details.

The rapid growth in the number of people with the money, leisure and opportunity to travel had an impact on popular culture and in time on the Tussaud exhibition. From the 1850s the location and nature of London leisure activities changed dramatically. Leicester Square, no longer the heart of entertainment, became increasingly disreputable. Big enterprises appeared on the periphery: following the migratory example of the Crystal Palace, Alexandra Palace was built on Muswell Hill, while Olympia appeared on the western edges of the capital. The comparatively expensive and decidedly immoral pleasure gardens at Vauxhall in the south and Cremorne in the south west of town could not compete with these free rival open spaces and eventually closed. The royal parks were also opened to the public and new public parks were created, including Primrose Hill (1842) and Victoria Park (1849).

The completion of the rail network had a major impact on leisure activities everywhere. At the time of Madame Tussaud's death the exhibition was gaining from the development of omnibuses. Very soon it was reaping the benefit of rail transport. Within fifty years most of Britain was accessible by rail. In 1835 there were 471 miles of track. This had grown to 13,411 miles in 1850 and 30,843 by 1885. While the early excursions tended to be to the seaside, Thomas Cook organised day trips to the Great Exhibition, and then developed group visits to more distant places.[19] In 1851 Prince Albert himself contributed to the trend when he demanded that all schoolchildren in southern England should have a day trip to the Great Exhibition. Railways also took Londoners away from the city and made it easier for exhibitions to travel to provincial towns.

Special excursions ran to organised entertainment, most spectacularly to prize fights. In 1845 a prize fight at Newport Pagnell, which went to ninety-three rounds, witnessed almost as much violence outside the ring and at the station as between the two pugilists. Although the combatants were working men, boxing was, of course, a sport patronised, like horseracing, by both rich and poor. Excursions to public hangings were even more popular than boxing matches. They drew large crowds long before the railway. In 1807 45,000 crammed the area around Newgate to see a double hanging. The excitement was so intense that twenty-seven of the onlookers were crushed to death. In 1840 trains from Wadebridge carried 1100 passengers, equivalent to half Wadebridge's population, to Bodmin to watch a local man hang. Rail transport meant that up to 100,000 would congregate for a hanging in London and other large towns. Hangings attracted more people than any other public entertainment.[20] Although they were good for railway profits, the huge crowds were impossible to police and control. Mounting injuries, plus moral indignation that so many people thrilled to such a scene, brought public hangings to an end in 1868. Little wonder in this context that the Chamber of Horrors was Tussaud's biggest attraction.

Apart from special excursions, until the 1870s (when third class carriages appeared) railways mainly catered for the recreations of those who had the most money as well as the most leisure. Horse-racing meetings expanded rapidly in response to available rail travel. Before the age of the motor car trains proved a superb means of travel to country house weekends and for trips to rural hunts.[21] The upper and middle classes eagerly deserted their carriages for rail transport. It was no coincidence that both the Baker Street wax exhibition and its successor in Marylebone Road were very well located for trains, and later for the underground. By the 1880s steamships were also bringing increasing numbers of foreign tourists, including 50,000 annually from the United States.

The gradual extension of more leisure to working people had a clear impact on entertainment. In 1847 the ten-hour hour act limited the working day. Some workers began to have a half day on Saturday, usually knocking off at 3 p.m. Sunday was also formalised as a day off for everyone except essential workers like maintenance men. Sunday Observance ensured, however, that Sunday would not become a day of organised leisure, and establishments such as Tussaud's remained closed. In 1861 the Crystal Palace, which despite its average annual attendance of two million never paid its way, tried a Sunday opening, distributing free tickets on stations, trains, and (perhaps unwisely) at local hostelries. The 40,000 who crowded in as a result apparently behaved so badly that the experiment was not repeated.[22] Although the notion that working people at leisure were invariably drunk and riotous persisted, Christmas, New Year and Easter were recognised as regular holidays in many trades before the Bank Holiday Act of 1870. This legislation, plus the beginnings of paid annual holidays, provided more custom for the entertainment industry. Whilst many Londoners rushed to the coast at the August Bank Holiday, London tourist attractions could soon reckon on about 360,000 day trippers from out of town for this holiday alone. Tussaud's began to put on special tableaux for the Bank Holidays, Santa Claus in season, and where possible a juicy addition to the Horrors. The impact of paid holidays, even before the Bank Holiday legislation, was clearly shown in takings. On 27 October 1866, an average day, the cash desk took £40. Boxing Day raked in £245. On 5 January 1867, when they reopened after the New Year closure from 1 to 4 January, they took £221, but quickly slipped back to the £40 average.[23] Large Bank Holiday crowds gradually increased and reports of large attendances in newspapers must have made the queues even longer.

From the 1850s, when the Tussaud exhibition expanded, providing popular recreations became a major industry in Britain. This was partly because working people now had both the money and the time to pay for leisure activities. Wages rose 40 per cent between 1860 and 1875 and another 33 per cent by 1900. This brought Tussaud's within the budget of prosperous workers. It was still an expensive day out. In the 1850s, when it began to put on organ concerts for the 'labouring population', Birmingham Council priced the events at 3d.[24] Music halls, specifically catering for working-class families, mushroomed after 1850. By 1868 there were twenty-eight in London. They provided song, music, food and (to the intense displeasure of moral reformers) alcohol. In the 1850s the Manchester music halls attracted 25,000 visitors a week with 4000 for each performance at Rochdale Circus of Variety. Rochdale had a population of only 40,000.[25] Until towards the end of the nineteenth century the music hall audience was almost entirely working class. Blackpool, inspired by the Eiffel Tower, opened its own tower in 1894. Circuses and fairs were also popular with working people.

Leisure activities changed in response to other factors besides transport and worker income. Technical developments had their impact. Photography, which was making its mark by the 1840s, made some entertainments, whose attraction was representational, irrelevant. It was the end of the 'ramas', whether cosmoramas, panoramas or dioramas. Tussaud's might also have been a victim because reality could at last be reproduced and the customer could test the accuracy of the models. A respected guide to London, published in 1868, praised the three hundred Tussaud's 'fine specimens' of waxwork in detail.[26] However a careful reading reveals that there had been few changes to the show since the time of the Great Exhibition. Indeed a popular, multi–volume tour of London, published in the early 1880s, reproduced an almost identical account of the exhibition.[27]

Tussaud's recognised the changes in the world of entertainment and tried tentatively to respond. Family firms had considerable strengths, but the ability to change was not one of them. The dominance of family members was obviously important for transferring skill and expertise and for economy, because relatives worked for lower wages. The firm remained entirely in the hands of the family until the 1880s. It was a close and closed network, not only because it was run by the family but because a tradition developed of children following parents into the workforce. On the artistic side, this meant that skills were fostered and enhanced. Madame made her last figure in 1842 when she was eighty-one, a self-portrait which is still on display. Children learned the wax craft early, and artistic talent was fostered. On the business front, caution predominated, with Madame's careful attention to the daily balance sheet. Madame's sons were content with very modest changes to the galleries for the Great Exhibition. Extensive and expensive developments were only attempted years after both had died and the stagnation of these years was acknowledged to have been a misjudgement. Joseph died first in 1865. Only Louisa, of his three children, was by then still alive. Francis Babbington had died in 1857, Mary in 1847. Joseph left Louisa, his only heir £40,000, with instructions to distribute £200 to the employees. When Madame Tussaud's younger son, Francis, died in 1873, he also left £40,000 to his three sons. That each son bequeathed identical amounts presumably indicates that the total had been carefully calculated and bore little relation to the value of the exhibition. By chance, only Francis produced heirs to run the exhibition. Francis's eldest son, Joseph Randall, took charge with two of his two brothers, Victor and Francis Curtius. There was no question of petticoat government. Their sisters worked in the exhibition, but they did not figure in the inheritance. Unfortunately Joseph Randall Tussaud was an unpromising character to lead Tussaud's in a world of rapid change. He lacked his grandmother's assertive personality. He complained perpetually about colds and depression. In 1879 he confessed to his diary that he was over fond of strong drink and put off making decisions.[28]

In the early 1880s Joseph Randall was persuaded by a builder friend with an available site and the eye for a business opportunity that the exhibition had been left behind by the rapid changes taking place in the entertainment industry. 'Thirty years had passed since we enlarged it [the exhibition] by so much as a superficial foot and the danger of such a stagnant state ... the transitions in regard to places of amusement are simply alarming.' People were no longer satisfied with an exhibition; they expected spacious open-air surroundings in which to stroll.[29] Part of the studio and workshops also had to be moved to the Tussaud family home in nearby Portman Square to make way for the exhibition.[30] Illustrations and descriptions of the Baker Street Bazaar suggest that by this time it must have been cramped, especially with all the Napoleon carriages. Lack of space when ladies wore such voluminous gowns was also a handicap. At the time of the Great Exhibition Tussaud's had felt obliged to produce leaflets assuring people that there was plenty of space to move around and sit and relax. Then there was the question of accessibility. Baker Street was wide, but the growth in omnibus and carriage traffic may have caused problems.

There were other considerations, not least of which was the lease on the Baker Street site. Tussaud's had always stuck to a short-term agreement, giving them the option, if the market went flat, to resume touring. In 1863, when the lease had been due for renewal, Joseph and Francis had tried to assess whether to retain a short lease or accept a ninety-nine year agreement. Their discussions took on a weird and pessimistic tone when they even calculated that, with a long lease, each would receive £16,000 if the collection was destroyed by fire. If they continued with the old lease for another four years, and then there was a fire, they would each save £8000.[31] They opted for a short lease. In the early 1880s Joseph Randall faced an even more difficult problem in renewing the lease because the value of the site had soared with the prosperity of nearby Oxford Street. The owners, the Portman Estate, demanded an increase, but refused to name a figure or negotiate until the last moment. Pushed into a corner, Joseph Randall finally made the most momentous decision since 1835, to move the whole exhibition to

36. Silhouette of the Tussaud family.

a completely different site and to a new, purpose-built establishment in the Marylebone Road, the frontier of the entertainment industry in north-west London at the time.

Joseph Randall's decision may have been influenced by the novel prospect of a competitor across the Channel. The opening of the Musée Grévin in Paris in June 1882 coincided with a spate of Tussaud's activity in addition to the construction of the new building. An unusual concentration of things French were acquired, including the keys to the fortress of Metz, abandoned to the German victors in the Franco-Prussian War and bought by Tussaud's for £250. In 1883 the republican politician Léon Gambetta, who had died unexpectedly a year earlier, and President Jules Grévy were added. The star of the Grévin show, the world famous poet Victor Hugo, was also installed in Baker Street.

There were other French additions which would have pleased Madame Tussaud. In the first decade of the new French republic some members of the conservative traditional elites hoped briefly, and ultimately vainly, for a restoration of the monarchy, which had been despatched by revolution in 1848. There were two families with a claim: the Bourbons, who had been dispossessed in 1830 and were represented by the middle-aged and childless comte de Chambord; and their cousins, the Orléans family, who had ruled from 1830 to 1848 and were represented by the comte de Paris. In 1883, on the death of Chambord, Tussaud's embarked on a collection of French Pretenders. First, since his death had sparked off this batch of models, came the comte de Chambord in August 1883, to be followed by the comte de Paris, the Orléanist claimant a month later, and by his son the duc de Nemours in October.

Finally, Joseph Randall stopped hesitating and made the decision to move. In 1883 Tussaud's took a lease on a very desirable site next to the new Baker Street station on the Marylebone Road. Their new landlord was the Howard de Walden Estate, which owned (and still owns) much of Marylebone. Their neighbour to the north in Regent's Park was the Crown Estate Commission. Tussaud's later bought the freehold. The existing building demolished to make way for the Tussaud establishment was the Gothic Granary. A large church-like building, it housed a granary and shops selling ice-cream and cakes. In the 1830s it had been an early socialist cooperative venture.[32]

The construction of the new building brought Tussaud's into acrimonious conflict with their local authority, the Marylebone vestry. They encroached into Marylebone Road beyond the agreed building line. Eventually the vestry agreed, as an 'act of mercy', to allow the construction to remain. The new building was of modern design, lit by electricity and passed the fire office's tests with flying colours. Tussaud's was a luxurious and distinctly upmarket affair, exactly the tone Madame herself would have liked. It was said that the building cost £80,000. In true Tussaud style, glamorous fittings were installed in the new building with maximum publicity. Their new galleries were adorned with ceiling panels which had been in the Bazaar since the time of the Great Exhibition. These had originally been painted by Sir James Thornhill (1675–1734), who had designed the ceiling for Greenwich Hospital in Queen Anne's time.[33] An elegant dome graced the building. Tussaud's acquired an imposing marble staircase, which had cost its original owner, 'Baron Grant', £20,000 for £1000. Grant, a self-made entrepreneur, was bankrupted by his development of Leicester Square. Tussaud's were far from pleased when the vestry decided that the Grant staircase was dangerous when used by large crowds and insisted on a central handrail, which spoilt the sweeping façade of the original.

There were seven major exhibition halls. The spirit of the exhibition was, as in Baker Street, the adulation of ornamental imperialism and monarchy. The ground floor entrance was flanked on one side by a model of the Prince of Wales, the future Edward VII, hunting a tiger. Beyond was a children's area with a bran tub and a toy stall. Later this section expanded to include tableaux of nursery rhymes such as Jack the Giant Killer. In the garden, where visitors could relax, there grew up a small zoo with live talking parrots, parakeets and monkeys and automatic piping bullfinches in gilded cages. Mounting the imposing staircase, visitors were in familiar territory. The two Napoleon rooms and the Hall of Kings dominated the first floor. In the Hall of Kings a non-stop relay of two orchestras, one of them made up entirely of ladies, the other a Rumanian band, entertained the enthusiasts of monarchy. In the afternoon visitors might hear snatches of a Chopin piano solo. Visitors then went downstairs, as they do today, to the Chamber of Horrors, which was directly beneath the larger of the Napoleon rooms. Beyond it was the restaurant with stained-glass windows and tessellated flooring, plus a big tea-room, and a bar serving beer and wine, where customers could recover after having gazed their fill at the murderers. Later a cinema was installed on the ground floor near to the tea-room.

Moving the figures to Marylebone Road took a week and some employees actually spent those nights sleeping among the four hundred sheeted models. The new galleries opened, appropriately given the nationality of their founder, on 14 July 1884, which six years later was to become France's national day. Members of both Houses of Parliament were invited to the champagne and strawberries and cream launch.

The opening inspired the *Daily Telegraph* into a positive eulogy. Their three-column spread began with a lament for the loss of popular cultural amenities in London. The Vauxhall Gardens, with its orchestra and jugs of foaming stout, and the Cremorne Pleasure Gardens had gone to property developers. The Surrey 'Zoo', the Adelaide Gallery, the Polytechnic and the Colosseum in Regent's Park had disappeared. The 'unrivalled collection of ceroplastics in Baker Street' (Tussaud's) were favourably compared with the 'desperately "seedy" gathering of wax figures which continue to lead a dingy and dusty existence in their glass cases in a remote eyrie in Westminster Abbey'. The building was 'a palatial edifice'. Access was superb, 'the Quality's coaches need not molest or be subject to molestation from anybody'. This 'most complete and the most splendid collection of waxworks in the world' could easily be shown off to country cousins and guests from abroad. Indeed the *Telegraph* cited a typical foreign visitor from Russia who successfully 'did' London, knowing only nine English words, one of which was 'Tussaud's'.[34]

The move was, initially, a triumph. Receipts quintupled and 'the place became more of a resort, especially in the evenings'.[35] The location was excellent and the fact that customers could step out of the exhibition almost into Regent's Park was a great advantage. In the summer of 1884 Joseph

Randall thanked their builder warmly for persuading him to make the move:

> You have given Madame Tussaud and Sons not only fresh energy and vigour, but a fresh lease of existence. In former years any great exhibition became a source of immediate profit to the smaller ones our own included, but now the exhibits are not only comparatively trivial but it is the surroundings which have become so attractive that all London and the country visitors are attracted by the light and music of the gardens.[36]

Above all, the new building was located at the centre of new transport opportunities. It was next door to the Baker Street underground station, which provided direct access to all the mainline railway stations on the north side of London. Omnibuses on the Marylebone Road were also plentiful. The road itself was twice as wide as Baker Street, so carriages could park easily. The new site thus allowed Tussaud's to exploit the transport revolution to the full.

Joseph Randall had, however, failed to follow his grandmother's strict accountancy maxims. The gap between profit and loss narrowed and went into reverse. Tussaud's financial difficulties were exacerbated by family quarrels. Louisa, Joseph's only surviving child, and heir to half the business, worked on the ledgers and in the wardrobe and ran the business in 1858 after the death of Francis Babbington when her cousin Joseph Randall was in Rome. She married, but soon tired of being Mrs Kenny, the wife of a physician. She kicked over the traces, in the eyes of her scandalised family, to such a degree that from then on her name was not mentioned. She left her husband and went to live a luxurious life in the south of France with a French nobleman, the marquis de Leuville. The marquis's funds did not match their lifestyle. To the great shock of the other Tussaud's, who had been drilled by Madame Tussaud into a proper sense of economy and wax loyalty, and continued to live close to the exhibition and work in it, Louisa insisted on being bought out in 1881. With her withdrawal, none of Joseph's side of the family was involved in the exhibition. Indeed for many years the page in the catalogue that listed the Tussauds who had run the exhibition left out Joseph and his children.[37]

In 1888, despite a record 400,000 paying customers the previous year, Louisa's demands, plus the huge cost of building and equipping the new galleries, forced Tussaud's to set up a limited company with a capital of £92,000. However Victor and Francis Curtius were unhappy and decided to take their shares out and bankruptcy proceedings began. The original company was dissolved and in February 1889 Tussaud's was sold for £173,000 to a group of businessmen including Edwin Josiah Poyser, John Michisson and Hubert Jackson. They set up first a public limited company, which in 1908 became a private company. The main shareholder was Josiah Thomas Poyser who became lifelong managing director, with total power as long as he continued to hold at least 20 per cent of the shares. The others were salaried directors at 200 guineas a year.[38] The Poysers, a Norfolk family, were in partnership elsewhere with the Allsop family of Burton-on-Trent brewing fame. The Allsops were at least as experienced in running wax exhibitions as they were in making beer. W. Allsop ran several provincial wax shows between 1849 and the 1880s, including Bianchi's, from 1864 to 1866, in the notorious centre of the pornographic book and picture trade, Holywell Street.[39] The Poysers were apparently on friendly terms with the Tussauds at the time of the purchase.[40] There is no indication whether the friendship survived the takeover. Some Tussaud employees were made redundant, although family members retained senior posts on the artistic side. The new company appointed John Theodore, Joseph Randall's son, as artistic adviser.[41] In 1891 he organised a family coup to take over from his father, which apparently Joseph Randall did not resist or regret.[42] John Theodore was delighted to be in charge and proved as domineering as his great grandmother.

A national institution seemed to be under threats from unsettled employees and a divided family. John Theodore received a parcel of enough gunpowder, complete with lucifer matches, to destroy the exhibition. The press rumoured that the sender was a disgruntled employee. The suspect, Ed White, was prosecuted, but all the evidence was purely circumstantial and he was acquitted.[43] The exhibition itself was still run by five Tussauds, now paid employees, but they were far from united. Under the new articles of association John Theodore became chief artist and manager, a position he held until his death in 1943. His uncle, Victor, continued to work on the company's publicity until his death in 1923, age eighty-two. Some members of the family objected to the change from family firm to private company, complaining that it involved too much outside interference. John Theodore's uncle Francis Curtius, who had specialised in colouring the wax heads, resigned. He lived to be ninety-two, devoting himself to the study of chemistry and electricity. Three of John Theodore's own brothers and sisters decided to withdraw from the business, although we do not know whether it was because they could not work with him or because they resented the change in ownership, or both.

Louis, one of the brothers who left, was an excellent modeller. With the help of another brother and a sister he opened an exhibition in Regent Street. Tussaud's tried to shut it down, but it was destroyed by fire almost as soon as it opened in 1891. Louis did not give up and the parent company

CONTENTS OF CATALOGUE.

———※※———

The following Numbers give the Name and corresponding Number affixed to the figures; further information will be gained by reference to the Biography.

CATALOGUE.

ENTRANCE ROOM.

1. MADAME TUSSAUD was a native of Berne, in Switzerland; at the age of six years she was sent to Paris and placed under the care of her uncle, M. Curtius (artist to Louis XVI.), by whom she was instructed in the fine arts, of which he was an eminent professor. Madame Tussaud had the honour of instructing Madame Elizabeth, sister of Louis XVI., to draw and model, and was employed by that amiable princess until October, 1789. Accordingly, Madame Tussaud spent a great portion of her time at the Tuilleries and at Versailles, where she had the best opportunities of becoming acquainted with the nobility and talent of the French Court, besides being occupied executing many commands. The most admirable specimen of her talent in the present collection is the portrait model of the famous wit Voltaire. In 1802 she left France, and from that period exhibited her collection of figures in the principal cities and towns of Great Britain and Ireland. Died April 15, 1850.

2. CHARLES DICKENS, novelist and humourist, was born at Landport near Portsmouth, Hants, Feb. 7, 1812, and partly educated at Cheltenham. He first became a reporter of the London press, in connection with the *Mirror of Parliament*, *The True Sun*, and the *Morning Chronicle*. To this latter paper he contributed his first literary effort, "Sketches by Boz." Next was published the "Pickwick Papers," "Oliver Twist," "Nicholas Nickleby," "Master Humphrey's Clock," (containing "The Old Curiosity Shop,") "David Copperfield," &c., &c. He afterwards visited America, and on his return published the "American Notes for General Circulation," "Martin Chuzzlewit," "Cricket on the Hearth," "Bleak House," and still more recently, "A Tale of Two Cities," and "Great Expectations." In 1845 he edited the *Daily News*, and in 1850 started *Household Words*, now continued as *All the Year Round*, the editorial chair of which is now occupied by his eldest son, Charles Dickens. "The Mystery of Edwin Drood," bore evidence that his vigorous pen and splendid imaginative powers were still unimpaired, and would, doubtless, have proved the crowning effort of his genius. He died at Gad's Hill, near Rochester, Kent, June 9, 1870, and was buried in Westminster Abbey, in Poet's Corner, within a few steps of "Old Chaucer," leaving a name that is "familiar in our mouths as household words."

ROOM OPPOSITE THE ENTRANCE.

3. THE LYING IN STATE OF HIS LATE HOLINESS PIUS IX. His Holiness Pius IX, the descendant of a noble family, was born at Sinigalia, in the Romagna, May 13, 1792. After receiving an education suitable to his high rank, he entered the Noble Guard, but soon after left it to enter the Church, of which he became one of its brightest ornaments. This representation of the scene at St. Peter's is as nearly as possible a fac-simile. The Swiss Guards on each side are habited in uniforms designed by the great architect Michael Angelo, and which they have continued to wear to the present day.

4. HIS EMINENCE CARDINAL GIACOMO ANTONELLI, late Secretary of State to His Holiness Pope Pius IX. Born of the respectable middle class at Sonnino, April 2, 1806. Having entered the Church, he was employed in several ways by the last Pope Gregory XVI. He was made a Cardinal Deacon by the late Pontiff, Pio Nono, in June, 1847. He held the following distinguished offices:— Secretary of State to the Pope, President of the Council of Ministers, Prefect of the Sacred Apostolic Palaces, of the Sacred Congregation of the Loretto, and of the Consulta. As we should say in England, he was at once Prime Minister and Foreign Secretary. Died November 6, 1876.

37. Madame Tussaud's catalogue.

kept track of his career, constantly trying to stop him and other members of the family using the Tussaud name. He was obliged to put in his catalogue 'no connection with Madame Tussaud Limited'.[44] Louis toured Sutton Coldfield and Crystal Palace in 1893, then Dublin, Belfast and Birmingham in 1894. He married a cousin, Minnie, but became bankrupt. In 1895 he was discharged and started out again. He shared the bill in Nottingham with a hypnotist and from time to time a 'Trance Lady' put on hypnotist sessions during the show. In 1900 he set up an exhibition that survives, with his name but in other ownership, on the Central Pier, Blackpool. On several occasions the Marylebone Road company considered buying the Blackpool outfit, but always decided that the price was too high and the quality too low. In 1915 Louis opened a wax show at Coney Island, near New York. Uninsured, he lost everything in a fire.

John Theodore Tussaud (1858–1943), who took over the senior exhibition, was keen to maintain the history and illusion of a Tussaud family business, even though financial control had gone. Like the rest of the clan, he had been born to work in wax. He started to learn how to make wax models when he was five and completed his first one when he was nine. From the age of fourteen he worked full time in the studio. He became chief modeller and remained at work until his death in 1943. His first major figure was that of Napoleon III for his lying in state in 1873. In his 'Chronicle', which he began to keep when he was ten, he kept a record of everything he produced, although it has been suggested that there was some exaggeration in his statistics. He claimed he made one thousand wax models, an average of roughly one per fortnight, including renovations to many existing models and private commissions, for which no details survive. He dominated all his employees, including his five sisters and other family members working in the exhibition. It was said his sisters always trembled when he entered the workshop. As well as rearing ten children, his wife found time to do high-quality embroidery and needlework for the costumes, but there is no record of how she coped with John Theodore's sharp tongue. A thrusting businessman, he exploited the new, large site in the Marylebone Road energetically. He was as eager as his great grandmother to make the most of publicity and was always willing to give newspaper interviews. He published *The Romance of Tussaud's* in 1920. The sections about his great grandmother are based on Marie's memoirs, but are even more incorrect and fanciful than the original. Otherwise the parts outside his own memory are largely based on weekly episodes of not always reliable recollections sold to him by his uncle Victor. John Theodore was obviously proud of the book and in 1920 sent Queen Mary a copy. He shared his great grandmother's passion for their Napoleon relics and continued to expand the collection.

John Theodore was also a moderniser. His favourite hobby was mechanical engineering. Under his forceful and irascible personality the exhibition added electric lighting (1890). A Rumanian band was taken on, but was later replaced by an organ, which was not popular. In 1908 the orchestras were supplemented with an 'auxetophone', an electric amplifier through which the customers could hear famous singers such as Caruso and Melba. In 1909 the north wing of the building was turned into a bioscope theatre which seated three hundred to watch moving pictures, then a new development. A seat at the back cost 3d. John Theodore was a keen photographer. Photography and film could have easily ruined the attraction of waxworks as an immediate record of how people looked. Instead John Theodore tried to bring the new mediums together in one exhibition and was careful to make no extra charge for the cinema. In the 1890s a photographic catalogue appeared and occasionally there were photographs in the ordinary catalogue and in special children's editions.[45]

In John Theodore's day Tussaud's began to face up uncertainly to the need to capture a more popular and numerous market, but they tried to do this without sacrificing their exclusive image. Their archives record the pleasure the Tussaud's still took in visits from heads of state and other notables. They were typical of the middle classes in being apparently alarmed that amusements and vices 'can be enjoyed by the base mechanical sort ... if this kind of thing goes on, there must in the end follow an effacement of all classes'.[46] Tussaud's tried to preserve elements of elitism while attracting the masses. This was particularly marked in their catering, their choice of music and their attempts to secure puffs in the best newspapers. The Marylebone Road restaurant was far more fashionable than the Baker Street buffet.

Tussaud's needed a large popular as well as elite audience and they depended on the press to help them bring in the crowds. There was a tendency for the papers to write about Tussaud's only when new models were added, or when they had spectacular visitors, such as the Maori king and his attendants.[47] To elicit publicity John Theodore spent far more money cultivating editors than his predecessors had done. A sign of the attempt to popularise was in 1891 when John Theodore copied (without acknowledgement) one of Grévin's most popular ideas the 'Story of a Crime'. Both resembled Hogarth's The Rake's Progress. For the first time in the history of Tussaud's it recreated an entirely imaginary story, designed for a popular audience. In the first scene a young man is reluctantly drawn into a game of cards. In the next he loses all. Scene three shows the wily victor with the sheriff's men seizing the loser's property. The loser retaliates by stabbing his persecutor in bed. A tableau of his trial is followed by the scene of the anguished murderer on the way to the gallows. To publicise the new tableaux John Theodore put on a special press invitation viewing and dinner. The tableaux were explained for the editors in a programme which was also their special dinner menu written in French. The dinner was far from 'popular' and included cavaire, lobster salad and pheasant. Extra entertainment was provided by Miss Graves's Ladies Orchestra which performed a cornet solo from Gounod's *Faust*, selections from Sir Arthur Sullivan's *Gondoliers* and other pieces.[48] Undoubtedly John Theodore hoped the newspaper articles would help him retain his middle-class audience as well as gaining a popular clientele.

John Theodore kept the exhibition a blend of history museum and visual newspaper, but, in the attempt to attract a wider audience, there was an increasingly emphasis on the latter. Models had to be topical, and were quickly removed when visitors showed no interest in them. If they were lucky, their heads might be stored. A *Punch* cartoon of 1889 indicates that the speed and rate of meltdown were increasing. In this case the victim was Georges Boulanger. In the 1880s Boulanger, a popular French general, attracted support from right and left in France for his strident demands for 'revenge' against Germany's seizure of Alsace-Lorraine in 1871. In 1886 he became Minister of War, lost office a year later, and at the beginning of 1889 was elected to the National Assembly in Paris and a number of other constituencies. People held their breath. Was Boulanger another Napoleon? Boulanger, however, had no stomach, and indeed inadequate popular support, for a *coup d'état*. In April 1889 he fled the country and disappeared from politics. In September, when a general election in France led to a republican victory, *Punch* published a drawing of Madame Tussaud clutching a newspaper with a prominent heading about the elections, gazing at Boulanger's wax self, predictably on horseback, while her carpenter asked, 'Where's he to be put now, ma'am?'[49]

The emphasis on topicality was a direct response to the great expansion of mass-produced newspapers and the use of photography, as well as the hunt for new visitors. Customers were more aware of people in the news and current affairs. Tussaud's must also have known that the Musée Grévin had focused successfully in this direction. When John Theodore Tussaud was asked what made Tussaud's decide to make a certain model, he replied: 'Our minds are made up according to the way newspapers deal with people. We always follow them, we never lead. We find the big celebrities as a rule very pleasant to deal with, although we cannot always get sittings, yet they never make objections.' As for villains, 'as soon as I see a *cause célèbre* is likely to come on, I go to the police court ... make careful sketches and take notes of the prisoner's demeanour and I can generally get the tailor's measurements. I am bound to add that criminals like Mrs Pearcey, Rush, Lefroy, Wainwright and the Mannings draw the biggest crowds'.[50]

In 1892 the Tussaud's catalogue, which had been virtually unchanged for many years, was completed revamped, but this does not seem to have been an effort to popularise the exhibition. It is true that the royal coat of arms was replaced on the front cover by a photograph of some of the new tableaux and one of the new building itself. The text was rewritten by a well-known journalist, George Augustus Sala (1828–1895). Using him to write the catalogue was an appeal to elitism and snobbery. His favourite was obviously Marie-Antoinette, who merited nine grieving pages, compared to a mere three for her husband. Sala was obviously regarded as a catch. He had been educated in Paris, and was an artist as well as a leading literary and art critic.[51] His catalogue remained virtually unchanged until the 1925 fire. Long before then customers must have wondered why they were paying good money for a catalogue written in 1892.

A real revolution in the exhibition in the last decades of the century was the proliferation of tableaux depicting leisure activities. The first appeared in 1891 and eventually a designated Hall of Tableaux was created. Group and team sporting activities were very popular. One tableau depicted a rugby international between the Scots and the English in 1894. There was a scene of yachting on the Norfolk Broads, one of a shoot and another of hunting, including a pack of hounds. The Oxford and Cambridge Boat Race was a mixture of painting and figures, including three wax models. The tableaux were all acknowledged in the catalogue as the work of John Theodore. Previously, catalogues had rarely attributed models to particular sculptors, unless they had been made by Madame Tussaud herself. Another novelty was that a contemporary artist Bruce Smith was employed to paint suitable backgrounds. Although at first glance it might be assumed that sporting tableaux were an attempt to develop mass appeal, they were not aimed at the working classes, but were a direct response to the change in how the leisured elites spent their time. In the second half of the century organised sports, particularly team games like rugby and cricket, had a high profile in the curriculum of the public schools and the grammar schools that aped them. While exercise and rational recreation were considered vital to contain the unruly passions of workers, organised sports, including at first soccer, were restricted to the elite. Boys in elementary schools only did drill, to prepare them for the discipline of work and military training. Workers were actually excluded from sporting organisations such as the Amateur Rowing Association and the Bicycle Union, on the grounds that the amount of physical labour in their jobs would put them at an unfair advantage in competitions. The real reason was probably

38. Cover of Madame Tussaud's catalogue, 1892.

that the middle classes did not want to share changing rooms with the 'great unwashed'.[52] The tableaux were designed for professional middle-class families, typified by the schoolboy who was heard to complain that all the players were offside in the rugby tableau. As well as sporting tableaux individual sporting achievements began to be noticed. Public baths were being constructed and swimming was growing in popularity. A model of the first man to swim the Channel in 1875, the merchant navy captain Matthew Webb, was shown in 1897, although in 1903 he spoiled his record by drowning in an attempt to swim the Niagara Rapids. In 1911 he was joined by another Channel swimmer, Burgess, who also sold Tussaud's the goggles, hat and drinking cup he had used.

Tableaux also emphasised education and history. Nelson was shown at the point of death on the *Victory* as was Mary, Queen of Scots at Fotheringhay. Robert Koch, the German scientist who contributed to the understanding of infections, particularly tuberculosis, was shown in his laboratory, with two live rabbits in a cage nearby. Perhaps because their exhibition was not far from the Zoo, Tussaud's decided that customers appreciated live animals as well as wax figures. They also had parrots and cockatoos, plus a shrunken head from Ecuador, on display.[53]

John Theodore continued to make tableaux. 1893 saw the completion of a North Pole Expedition tableau. Historical scenes included King John signing Magna Carta and Harold losing the battle of Hastings. Wars in the Sudan and South Africa afforded dramatic opportunities. Some tableaux were replaced; all the sporting ones seem to have disappeared in 1903. Between 1909 and 1912 three new tableaux were completed: Shackleton's Antarctic expedition, a miniature tableau of the Messina earthquake, and, in 1912, a Dickens scene.

It was the 'Horrors' that drew the largest crowds and did most to please the broadest cross-section of the population. Press criticism increased in the second half of the nineteenth century: 'It panders to a morbid, unhealthy, unfeeling curiosity', comparable to that which in times past drew people to cheer at the foot of the gallows.'[54] Despite the moralising of the middle-class press, the veneer of civilised modernity and the growth of mass education, what sold most tickets for Tussaud's was the long-established voyeuristic predilection of the masses for violent death and retribution. In 1878 Tussaud's bought the gallows from Hertford Prison when the prison was demolished and erected it in the Chamber, where it remains. The big attraction over the Christmas holidays in 1890 was Mrs Pearcey. 31,000 queued on Boxing Day,[55] and in all over three days 75,000 went through the turnstiles.[56] In October 1890 Eleanor Pearcey had battered her lover's wife and baby to death in her sitting room at 2 Priory Street, Kentish Town.

She then piled both corpses into the pram and dumped them on waste ground two miles away near Crossfield Road, Hampstead. During the trial John Tussaud reconstructed her sitting room and spent £200 on the fatal pram, furniture and other bits and pieces from the room, even the sweet the baby was sucking just before it was killed and the bloodstained cardigan which Mrs Pearcey would never need again. She met an inevitable and rapid fate and was in the Horrors in time for Christmas.

One of the most notorious murderers of the century, Jack the Ripper, was not added to the Horrors at this time. Although he disposed brutally of at least five East London prostitutes in three months in 1888, the Ripper was never caught. Tussaud's prided themselves on only modelling from life or death, not from the imagination. The Ripper therefore never reached Tussaud's' basement.

Tussaud's continued to buy the trappings of death. With electricity came the electric chair, and an example was quickly put centre stage in the Horrors. In 1903 the Old Bailey and the adjacent Newgate Prison were demolished. Tussaud's bought the Old Bailey fittings and its jury-box for a song. Tussaud's also acquired two Newgate cells, which cost far more to reconstruct in the Horrors than their purchase price, but remained popular until the 1970s.[57]

The reputation of the Horrors gave Tussaud's its best publicity. John Theodore liked to recount the unfounded tale that Tussaud's would give a substantial prize, people could not agree on how much, to the person who spent a night in the Chamber of Horrors.[58] The story was reinforced by a 1909 play, The Whip, in which one scene was set in the Chamber. On the opening night handbills offered £100 to anyone who would spend the night in the Horrors. The Tussaud's Archives are peppered with stories of people attempting to stay overnight and tales of terrified individuals who tried to hide in the Horrors and were found screaming to be let out because they thought one of the figures had moved. Some of the models are indeed inclined to shake as the Metropolitan Line trains pass directly beneath them, and this is more noticeable when the galleries are closed and empty. An inebriated policeman fell asleep in the reconstructed Old Bailey dock, to be found the next morning, but his visit was accidental. The War Office actually set a clandestine overnight stay in the Horrors as an initiative test for army cadets, until the scale of stowaways became so numerous that Tussaud's had to ask for the test to be withdrawn.

The process of reincarnating someone in wax did not change radically during the century. John Theodore was always willing to provide newspaper copy on how to make a model. If possible he worked from life. Ideally he had four sittings with the person, the first two to obtain the general

Madame Tussaud & Sons' Catalogue.

COLLECTION OF

INSTRUMENTS OF TORTURE.

THIS collection, which for authenticity is perfectly unique, has been brought together from various sources by a celebrated collector.

Monsieur Herbertte the Director of the French prisons, has made advances on several occasions for the purpose of acquiring several of the most important of these specimens, with the idea of establishing an historic museum of instruments which had been used for torturing men who figured in the history of past centuries. As the owner of these interesting relics, from whom they have just been purchased, was anxious not to deprive the collection of its characteristic features, he refused his offers, and decided to sell them to us, saying the Tussauds were the first to preserve to history and science relics like these, the most curious in existence.

No. 1 in the Collection. This iron chair, which is the most rare and unique specimen, was used for torturing Jean Calas in Toulouse in 1762, and, horrible to relate, three years afterwards his innocence was declared.

To proceed to the torture, the victim was seated and sustained by the front bar, then by another vertical bar, while two rings fastened the ankles below; in the upper portion there is a collar for the neck, and then another transverse bar passing through the first, and fitted at each extremity with a ring holding the wrists, while underneath the seat is a stove.

No. 2. The "Gressillon" hand crusher comes from Rouen, where it was used for several celebrated victims.

No. 3. Manacles, found at the Prefecture of Police in Paris during the time of the Commune.

39. Instruments of Torture.

Madame Tussaud & Sons' Catalogue.

No. 4. Mask of ignominy. This mask was brought from Chateaulire (Finisterre). It was used as recently as the end of last century for unfaithful husbands, on whom it was placed, and who were then marched through the streets. One man named Le Fevre was thus marched through the streets, and whipped in the public square in 1786.

No. 5. "Moltière." This rare specimen no longer exists in any of the collections of instruments of torture in the museums of the French Government.

No. 6. Bolt taken from the Bastille.

No. 7. Thumb screw. There are no specimens of this among the prison collections. This one was found in a dungeon during the Commune.

No. 8. Tongue pincers. This is the only specimen in existence; it was used for securing the tongues of the tortured victims. They were held for days together in this position; it was used for the celebrated Damiens, who was racked, tortured, and spread eagled in the Place de Grève, Paris, on the 28th March, 1757.

No. 9. Wristlet. This specimen is a very rare one, and was brought from the Chatelet. It was used like various other instruments on a number of celebrated victims whose names it would take too long to enumerate.

No. 10. The hog's mask. Unique specimen. Was procured from the same source as No. 4, and was used for marching the victim about the streets. Its shape sufficiently indicates that it was intended to degrade the victim.

No. 11. Branding irons. These two irons were used for branding the shoulder. They were taken from the Chatelet.

No. 12. Necklace used in the galleys at Toulon.

No. 13. The possessed mask. Unique specimen. This comes from Toulouse; it was used in a convent, and when they wished to punish the inmates they were placed in the passage leading to the church, from which they were excluded for a time. This mask, placed over the face of the victim, was supposed to resemble the evil one.

No. 14. Ring and chain from Toulon, used as recently as 1871 for Alphonse Humbert, condemned by the Commune and now a Municipal Councillor of Paris.

Madame Tussaud & Sons' Catalogue.

No. 15. One of these doors belong to the dungeon in which Le Chevalier de la Barre was incarcerated before his execution. A judge of Abbeville, wishing to be revenged on him, accused him of having mutilated a wooden crucifix placed on the bridge of the town, and of having sung impious songs and passed in front of the procession without taking off his hat.

The tribunal condemned him to have his tongue cut out, his right hand cut off, and to be burned alive; a decree of the Paris Parliament ordered that he should be decapitated before being thrown into the flames.

Before the execution of the sentence the unfortunate man was submitted to the torture. He suffered in Abbeville on the 1st of July, 1766, at the age of 19. The Convention afterwards re-instated his memory.

No. 16. Instrument for leading condemned victims to execution. This instrument, which is unique in France, and which was used for leading several celebrities to execution, among others Cartouche and Madrain, was still in use in Versailles in 1871.

No. 17. "Cubitoire." Curious and unique specimen. This instrument was used about the year 1600 for holding the arms firmly by squeezing the shoulders. It was brought from the Spanish office.

No. 18. Engraved cincture for women. This cincture (which is a unique specimen) was used during the inquisition in Spain on several celebrated women.

No. 19. "Tenaille Mammère" (torturing tongs) from the Chatelet. It is said they were used for torturing the temples of Damiens in 1757.

No. 20. Two pulleys found at the taking of the Bastille.

No. 21. Spiked cincture (unique specimen) used for placing round the loins of the victims under torture. Procured from a museum in Barcelona.

No. 22. Necklet and bracelet found at the Bastille by the conquerors, and sold afterwards by one of the old combatants; it is believed these were used on Latude.

No. 23. Handcuffs with chain, found in the office of the famous Raoul Rigault at the capture of the Prefecture by the Versailles army.

Madame Tussaud & Sons' Catalogue.

No. 24. Two handcuffs without chain, procured from same source as No. 23.

No. 25. "Tape-langue." An instrument procured from a convent in Spain.

No. 26. Torture girdle found in the cellars of the convent of Saint Denis, having been used by various courtesans in former centuries who had become converted to religion.

No. 27. Necklace. Authentic specimen, used for exposing condemned criminals in the public square at Pontoise (Seine et Oise).

No. 28. Grating found at the demolition of the prison of St. Denis.

No. 29. Thumb-screw from the Chatelet, used for Montalli, Damiens, etc.

No. 30. Leg chains found in the Bastille dungeons.

No. 31. Chains from the same source.

No. 32. " Jambière d'angoisse" (very rare specimen) used at the Paris Chatelet for extorting confessions from the victims.

No. 33. Bar, rings, chains, necklace, forming part of Chair No. 1

No. 34. Alarm mask. Mask fitted with bell for warning the jailer when the prisoner awoke or moved.

No. 35. Chains found at the Bastille and used for chaining prisoners.

No. 36. Dungeon Door. This door was taken at the time of the demolition of the Abbey Prison, situated near the Church of the same name (still extant). This prison played a prominent part in the history of the Revolution. It was here that most of the great dames and several gentlemen of the Court of Louis XIV. were incarcerated.

No. 37. Fetters with lock and key brought from the galleys, used for punishment, as also for condemned prisoners during the Commune —Lisbon, Allemane Lecipial, etc.

No. 38. A piece of iron with notches. This piece came from the dungeons at the Bastille.

No. 39. A cannon ball. This ball was attached to the feet of Brissac, the French journalist, who was condemned for writing against the Versailles Government.

appearance, the third to model the precise features, and the last to capture the expression, although he sometimes completed the head after a single sitting, if the subject was important and pressed for time. After sittings, he had to rely on photographs, which in those days would have been either newspaper shots or studio portraits. He placed more store on the numerous pencil sketches he made during interviews, none of which unfortunately survive. John Theodore sketched his candidates for the Chamber of Horrors during their trials. Cameras were and are still banned at the Old Bailey, so he took photographs with a small device concealed in his bowler hat.

Tussaud's always prided themselves on making all their own models. Many smaller waxworks bought figures and there were later complaints that John Theodore spent a disproportionate amount of time on private commissions. There were also sculptors who worked to order, in wax or whatever material was required, either for individuals or for hospitals for teaching purposes. Some made display dummies for department stores. One of the victims in a novel by Austin Freeman, the father of detective thrillers in the early twentieth century, was a wax sculptor. Freeman delighted in explaining, obviously from first-hand knowledge, the intricacies of how a model was made.[59] Freeman himself was a qualified surgeon, so clearly surgeons themselves were still making anatomical models to help them in their work.

Towards the end of the century a completed model took about two weeks to make, but if necessary the process could be completed in three days. Madame Tussaud herself had worked very fast. Wandering around a waxworks, one might imagine that once a model was finished time stopped still and nothing more needed doing. In fact each of the five hundred models on show at the time had to be recoloured every six weeks or so. Although the models could not move around, their clothes, as well as their hair and bodies, had to be constantly cleaned, even renewed. Some costumes lasted up to seven years, others barely a year, depending on the material used and how frequently they were touched by the customers. Occasionally a model was damaged; Charles Dickens's head was broken by a crowd and young lads were inclined to become excited when they failed to chat up the model of a young female attendant near the exit.[60]

The acid test for survival in Tussaud's was whether visitors stopped as they passed a model. Tussaud's paid close attention to this and no stops meant rapid melt down. Public memory was all. John Theodore divided Tussaud's heroes into two classes, ephemerals and immortals. Serbian royals were fly-by-night waxes, while people actually stood and cheered the wax model of Robert Baden-Powell, founder of the Scout movement. Predictably, John Theodore thought Queen Victoria their most successful model.

The attempt to broaden the appeal of Tussaud's was reflected in the choice of subject. One model which caused quite a stir was that of the trade unionist and dockers' strike leader John Burns (1858–1943). His presence was a sign that Tussaud's were trying to attract a mass audience. In 1886, during a sharp economic downturn, a successful and popular dockers' strike gained a minimum wage of 6d. an hour, incidentally an indication of just how high the entrance fee still was to the Tussaud exhibition. Burns, waving a red flag, led a demonstration of the small Marxist Social Democratic Foundation, founded by the wealthy Cambridge socialist Henry Mayers Hyndman (1842–1921), marching with the unemployed in Trafalgar Square in protest at a Protectionist demonstration. It was a small-scale affair. A few windows of gentlemen's clubs in Pall Mall were broken and some expensive shops looted, but the leaders agreed to stop the march in Hyde Park at the request of the police. Along with Hyndman, Burns was tried for sedition but acquitted. In 1887 a larger march, protesting at a police ban on Trafalgar Square meetings, led to violence, prison for Burns, and his subsequent rejection of violent tactics. In 1892 he was returned to Parliament as an Independent, although he had lost his socialism by the time he entered the cabinet.

In 1889 when he sat for John Theodore, Burns proved to be his liveliest model, striding around the room constantly during his sitting, lecturing him on the sufferings of the dockers. When John Theodore asked him for one of the blue reefer suits he was wearing, and had worn during the riots, John Burns replied that he had only one suit of clothes. Tussaud agreed to have another suit made, to which the docker agreed with some nervousness, commenting that his men might think him outrageously rich wearing a new suit.[61] When he later became a cabinet minister, early in Asquith's government, his model moved to join other statesmen, still wearing the original suit. Such comments about the man's clothing sound snobbishly reminiscent of Madame Tussaud herself, until one realises that Burns was actually very vain about his appearance. When the model was first installed at the end of 1889, a large cartoon showed many of the figures, carrying a placard announcing they were on strike, and chasing the dapper but alarmed Burns out of the building.[62]

Militant feminists found a wax home, although they were unlikely to have appealed to a popular market. The Women's Social and Political Union was founded by Mrs Emmeline Pankhurst in 1903 and made women's rights a passionate issue. Women could already vote in municipal elections (1868) and for the newly-established county councils (1888). They could also sit on parish and district councils when the latter were started in 1894, and from 1907 they could be members and officials of county and borough councils.

40. Cover of Madame Tussaud's catalogue, 1897.

Only the parliamentary franchise eluded them, and this was the mission of the suffragettes. Mrs Pankhurst, her daughters and followers soon progressed from heckling politicians to destroying property, arson and bombing, and waging hunger strikes when they were imprisoned. They scorned three proposals to enfranchise single female property owners between 1910 and 1912. The suffragettes achieved a martyrdom when Emily Davidson threw herself to her death under the king's horse at the Derby.[63]

Tussaud's displayed four of the suffragette leaders, Mrs Emmeline Pankhurst herself, Miss Christabel Pankhurst, Mrs Pethwick Lawrence and Miss Annie Kenney. They were placed facing the current Asquith government, despite Annie Kenney's protest that the ministers might melt under their combined glare. Another of Mrs Pankhurst's daughters, Sylvia, was not included in the display. Sylvia was a socialist, rejected by her mother because she did not merely want the enfranchisement of rich women, while Christabel supported extreme violence.

Acknowledging that young customers had different interests to adults was part of the attempt to widen the social appeal of Tussaud's. In the late nineteenth-century Tussaud's made a positive effort to be children-friendly. The age of the elegant promenade was over. The exhibition developed a section of children's amusements and issued the occasional special children's catalogues with coloured illustrations. At the outset Madame Tussaud had been content to educate the young. Her successors responded to the need to entertain children, perhaps because compulsory schooling up to the age of fourteen seemed education enough. Late nineteenth-century children had more time to behave like children. They owned more toys than children had a century earlier and expected to see bigger and better ones when they were taken to an exhibition. By 1908 the ground floor children's gallery contained four tableaux, Jack the Giant Killer, Babes in the Wood, the Old Woman who Lived in a Shoe and Cinderella. In addition there was a large collection of non-wax amusements. These included two 'laughable' mirrors, a helter-skelter lighthouse, a model dolls' house, an electric railway, several displays of dolls, a ferris wheel, an Egyptian snake charmer, the Headless Man, a number of automated toys including a drummer, an electric switch-back, a miniature water chute and a tightrope dancer. An illustrated guide to the capital for children, reprinted several times early in the twentieth century and a popular choice for a gift from grandparents, included only one place of commercial entertainment, Tussaud's, which merited a substantial chapter.[64]

By 1914 Tussaud's seem to have taken some steps towards acknowledging that the entertainment market had changed and that its future lay in a popular, not a middle-class audience. An indication of the changing social position of Tussaud's clientele in the second half of the nineteenth century can be gauged from who sang about them and where. In 1868 W. S. Gilbert set part of his *Robert and the Devil* in the Chamber of Horrors. 'We're only waxworks … Artistic quack's works.' In the *Mikado* Gilbert and Sullivan suggested that a suitable punishment for off-key amateur tenors would be

> To exhibit their powers,
> During off hours,
> In Madame Tussaud's Waxworks.

Gilbert and Sullivan's well-heeled middle-class audience was obviously acquainted with Tussaud's. In 1878 the second of Edward Elgar's 'Six Promenades for a Wind Quintet' was 'Moderato at Madame Tussaud's'.[65]

Towards the end of the century a rash of music hall songs sang the praises of Tussaud's, attesting to the growing popularity of the show with the working-class families who formed the audience in music halls. In 1885 'A Model for Madame Tussaud's', a popular song at the Players' Theatre ran

> Every night when the clock strikes
> We all come to life, with a rum-tum-tum,
> Murderers, clergymen, thieves and lords
> All so jolly at Madame Tussaud's.

Hilaire Belloc also wrote ironically of the popularity of Tussaud's for the 'popular' classes:

> Every Saturday night at 8
> We want to drown our sorrows
> So off we goes to the Waxworks
> To look at the Chamber of Horrors.
>
> There's a lovely statue of mother there
> We like to see it rather
> Its nice to see her as she was
> The night she strangled father.

It would be interesting to know if Tussaud's gained its popular audience at the expense of its bourgeois customers. G. Thorne, author of *The Drunkard*, published in 1912, commented snobbishly 'this place is a national institution – people like you and me only come to it out of curiosity or chance'.

Tussaud's grasped the First World War as an opportunity to show how broad their appeal was to the British public. The day Germany declared war on France, Monday 3 August 1914, was a Bank Holiday, when traditionally the exhibition attracted a large crowd. Tussaud's deftly rearranged

its royals and politicians into a single display and sent out their walking
advertisers with sandwich-boards that read

THE EUROPEAN CRISIS
Life-like portrait models of
THEIR MAJESTIES KING GEORGE AND QUEEN MARY
H.I.M. THE EMPEROR OF AUSTRIA
H.M. KING PETER OF SERBIA
And other reigning sovereigns of Europe.
NAVAL AND MILITARY TABLEAUX
Delightful music
Refreshments at popular prices

Exceptionally the exhibition opened its doors at 8 a.m. and had bigger
crowds than anywhere else that day. Many people had hoped for a day at
the sea, but the stations were packed with mobilised troops.[66]

The exhibition continued to exploit its popular appeal throughout the
war as 'The Most Interesting and Inexpensive House of Entertainment in
London'. Tussaud's was no longer concerned only with carriage customers,
but boasted first and foremost that they were at Baker Street Station and
'in connection with all Train, Tube, Tram and Bus Routes'. Instead of
appealing to 'gentry, gentlemen and ladies', they now claimed to have
'Magnificent Attractions for Young and Old and for the Soldier, Sailor and
Munition Worker'. Their posters no longer stressed a large crowd of royals
but their 'unique war relics', portraits of 'heroes of the war', including the
second Commander-in-Chief of the Allied Forces, General Foch, and
the 'Principal Labour Leaders'. A free film show, 'Topical Moving Pictures',
was also on offer. It was carefully stated that refreshments were 'at controlled
prices'.

This war-time advertisement shows clearly that Tussaud's had moved
into a different age, when it was no longer relevant to boast only about
royal patrons and wealthy visitors, but when it was essential to attract a
mass market. Five of John Theodore's young sons fought in the war, so
there were other reasons than pure marketing to stress the war. An enormous
map of the war was put up in the central hall and used for daily lectures
and updating. The lectures were so popular that they had to be repeated
three times a day. John Theodore also showed war films. The model of the
Kaiser had to be taken out of the exhibition because customers abused it,
but so many soldier visitors complained about the exclusion that it was
repaired and put in a more secure display. Servicemen were encouraged to
visit the exhibition and effectively to treat Marylebone Road as a second

home, which must have materially altered the elitist and snobbish character which successive Tussaud's had imprinted on the exhibition, with ladies' orchestra and the expensive restaurant. Calling the exhibition a 'National Institution' in 1917 meant something very different than it had done in 1840. [67] Tussaud's was no longer a promenade along the plank of time, but was making an effort to be truly a tabloid entertainment.

8

Waxworks in the Age of Film

By the early 1920s the cinema had long since swept away most of the nineteenth-century popular entertainment such as the dioramas and pan-oramas. Tussaud's survived, an odd item of nostalgia, as somewhere to take the children and briefly recapture one's youth. According to W. R. Titterton in 1918, 'Madame Tussaud's has a homely middle-Victorian air ... there is something brave in its persistence, something innocent in its smug ugliness. It is a relic of an age when men played with the mechanical mimicry of life as with a toy, and had not yet discovered it was a monster'.[1] Tussaud's continued as before the war, with an orchestra playing both in the afternoon, when visitors might hear a Gluck overture, 'Mandalay', a foxtrot by Arnheim, or in the evening 'The Waltz of Long Ago' by Berlin or 'Beautiful Doll' by Gilbert.[2] In the years after the First World War Tussaud's annual attendance figures reached a new peak of half a million and rose to 750,000 in 1924,[3] although some newspapers commented that the exhibition had become dingy, particularly the Chamber of Horrors.[4]

In 1918 the Poyser family sold Madame Tussaud Limited to members of another wealthy business family with varied interests, Charles and Arthur Wheeler. The artistic side was still run by John Theodore, who was also an appointed director of the company. His uncle Victor was still involved a little in publicity. Four of his sisters (three unmarried, Maud, Beatrice and Dolly, and one married, always referred to as Mrs Remy) devoted their life to making and repairing costumes. They were paid very modest wages and never achieved senior positions or became directors. One of Joseph Randall Tussaud's daughter's, Mrs Cuthbert, inherited Madame Tussaud's job as paybox cashier until she left in 1968. Things were to change dramatically from the days when more than twenty of the family worked on site. Very few of the next generation, and only a tiny number of John Theodore's ten children, worked in the exhibition. Five of his seven sons fought in the First World War and amazingly, given the high casualty rates of this war, all survived. The eldest, Jack, born in 1895, when John Theodore was thirty-seven, worked in the exhibition before the war, but when he was demobbed emigrated to Canada and did not become involved in wax ventures there.

Frank (1899–1968) worked in the exhibition for a time after the war, but left after disagreements with his father. Hugh emigrated to Australia after war service but may have worked in the studio for a time before he left. In 1931 he was to become the director of a new waxworks in Dublin. Guy (1897–1966) emigrated to Canada and kept well away from waxworks. Another son, Angelo, preferred painting birds to wax models, but eventually he joined the board of directors shortly before his father's death. Gabriel, born in 1900, never worked in the exhibition. Only two of John Theodore's children put in years of service to Tussaud's: Joan, who ran the wardrobe throughout her adult life, and Bernard (1896–1967), who worked there except for a short period.[5] Not a single member of the next and very numerous generation of Tussauds was employed in the exhibition. While this was not an untypical pattern for family businesses in this period, the absence of younger family members weighed heavily on the older generation and also on the vitality of the exhibition.

The interwar years were bleak for Tussaud's. In 1925 a devastating fire destroyed the whole exhibition. There were other problems, including the challenge of cinema and major conflicts between the family and the management. Business and the economy in general took a catastrophic downturn in these years. Even in good times, fire was a perpetual nightmare for a wax show. Two of Louis's exhibitions went up in flames. The Tussaud's exhibition had a close call before the disaster of 1925. On Boxing Day night 1869, when the rooms were packed, there was a gas escape, but fortunately no explosion and no panic. The ceiling space above the main rooms was found to be full of gas. On 25 March 1925, however, almost everything on display was destroyed by a fire, apparently the consequence of a short circuit in the bioscope organ. The wind raked the elegant dome. There were no fire doors and the building was gutted within an hour. Frank Tussaud was the first to the scene and phoned his father at his home in Rickmansworth. Overnight the 'palace of enchantment' became a 'palace of disenchantment' widely displayed in numerous press reports and photographs.

John Theodore's initial guess was that the cost of restoration would be in excess of £250,000. Fortunately the company was insured for £245,000 plus a 'lost profits' policy.[6] The directors settled for a cash payment, which they pocketed. The old company kept its staff and set to work to reconstruct the models. In August 1926 the old company went into liquidation and the new company took over the employees and the reconstruction, making it as near as possible to the design of the building that had been gutted. The membership of the 'new' company was identical to the 'old'. The switch from the old company to a new one meant that no tax was due until 1930.[7]

After the fire there was no thought of innovation, simply imitation. John

Theodore's aim was simply to rebuild the galleries and restock them exactly as they had been. He calculated that it would take thirteen months, finishing in November 1927, to complete the reconstruction, allowing the staff only bank holidays and one week off in the summer. The Tussaud's parrot, Joey, a live exhibit, survived the fire, but only 171 of the 467 models were rescued, and most of them needed extensive repairs. The Chamber of Horrors was less damaged, as were some of the Napoleonic memorabilia, also in the basement but not on display. Fortunately the moulds from which the heads had been made were also stored in the basement and models could be remade. However, only thirty of the old models that needed replacing had complete sets of moulds. John Theodore reckoned that with his assistants it would take seven to eight weeks to have these figures ready for dressing. The studio staff would then turn to repairing the 171 rescued figures, which included the residents of the Horrors, on the assumption that the least badly damaged area would reopen first. The remaining figures, which had to be made anew, had originally been made without specific moulds for their bodies, the norm then but not in 1927, so 270 complete bodies had to be made, including twenty-six completely new figures. For the first time, apparently, an order for over two hundred of these bodies, minus heads, arms and hands, was placed with an outside company, Gems, which was run by Josephine Tussaud. The motive was partly time, but also cost. The price per body was from £3 10s. to £7, including shoes and stockings. This was much cheaper than the price quoted by the Tussaud's studio. Tussaud's, however, did not want people to know they had not done the work themselves and John Theodore swore Gems to secrecy. Replacement costumes were also made by an outsider, the costumier Morris Angel.

Even with this help the studio required twelve workers and four artist-modellers to rebuild the collection. John Theodore's calculations of the cost of reconstruction provide a rare glimpse of wage levels. Weekly wages in the model shop (not counting John Theodore himself) totalled £52 6s. 6d. His son Bernard received a mere £4 4s. a week, while his fellow portrait modellers got £6 5s. and £7 3s. respectively. John Theodore's long suffering four sisters, who were colourists and who also inserted the hair, were each paid a mere £2 10s. each.[8] Yet workers showed enormous loyalty. Two had worked at Tussaud's for forty years and three for thirty.

The exhibition was reconstructed, but 'without much faith in the future'.[9] The new building opened in April 1928 and all living men and women whose models were on show were invited to the opening. The reconstruction had cost £266,921. An indication of how Madame Tussaud's business methods had survived is how close this figure was to original estimates. There were eight thousand visitors on the day they reopened and by October over one million people had seen the main exhibition and 700,000 the Horrors. There was an even greater emphasis on families with children than before 1914. A jungle was created with live donkeys, monkeys and an assortment of mechanical animals. In 1928 the jungle was demolished, to expose a family of squatter rats. Tussaud's also put Sam and Barbara, two stuffed polar bears who had lived at the nearby London Zoo, in the entrance hall to greet young visitors. In 1930 tableaux dedicated to children were set up in the entrance hall, perhaps in response to the success of films. Mickey Mouse sat at the piano and Jack the Giant Killer stood alongside a Red Riding Hood group.

The Chamber of Horrors was not neglected, but there was more debate about the propriety of some models than there had been in pre-war days. The Opium Den, a tableau of East End sailors and their Chinese host, was removed when the Chinese government protested that it misrepresented China, which had fought in the nineteenth century to prevent Britain flooding China with opium grown in India. There was a lucky find in 1930. The original model of a guillotine, supposedly destroyed in the fire, was discovered in a lumber room. After some restoration to replace charred timbers, it was replaced in the Horrors.

The onset of the Great Depression in 1929 left millions of people with endless leisure but very little cash for extras, and attendance at all amusements fell. In addition the fire seems to have been a catalyst for lengthy disputes between 1929 and 1932 on the viability of the business, between John Theodore and Bernard on the modelling side and the owners. At the climax of the row Bernard left temporarily to work for Louis Tussaud's waxworks in Blackpool.

Louis's enterprises were often innovative, but always financially marginal. In 1923 he had again been declared bankrupt, despite his defence that he was an artist and not a businessman. He was not discharged until 1937. In addition to Blackpool he ran a touring show. In 1933–34 he undertook a punishing tour, on the scale of his great grandmother, to Crystal Palace, Birmingham, Liverpool (Casino Ice Rink), Sheffield, Leeds, Manchester, Glasgow, Belfast, Hull, Cardiff, Bristol, Derby, Nottingham, Leicester, Wolverhampton, Coventry and Northampton. He toured major cities, mainly in the industrial heartland of the north and midlands, hunting for the mass market that the Marylebone Road Tussaud's seemed to be ignoring. Few affluent southern towns were included. Louis was far more of an innovator than John Theodore. He included sound effects and up to date illumination techniques in his tableaux, which were set off by reproductions of famous posters. His catalogue made ambitious claims on the scale of his great grandmother.

An Exhibition such as the one embarking now on its momentous and epoch-making [tour] strengthens our book knowledge of the past with the present, and paves the way for the future. One might even in these enlightened days answer the oft-quoted Roman question, 'Quo Vadis?' by the simple phrase 'Know Thyself', for knowledge is power. And in these words lies the whole secret of the educational value of this Exhibition ... This Exhibition is education in tabloid form ... It is a case of beauty applied to art and art to beauty.

Meanwhile the senior Tussaud's waxworks was struggling. There was bickering within the management, notably between John Theodore, the managing director and the general manager, Mr Wild. Criticisms of the exhibition flew around within the organisation. There were complaints that the figures were dingy and out of date, that customers wanted to see more people in the news. John Theodore, by now well past retirement age, was accused of being slow in completing figures, of clinging to tableaux when visitors were no longer interested, and of spending more time on private orders than on work for the exhibition. There was criticism within the management that his expensively cultivated 'newspaper pets' were not providing good copy. More serious were press comments that figures of easily recognised contemporaries, such as the king, George V, were embarrassingly substandard. Leading public figures had also been heard to criticise their wax selves when they visited the exhibition.[10] Customers were bound to wonder whether any of the models really looked like their originals. In an age when photography and film made the features of well-known individuals familiar to customers, a waxworks could not risk displaying poor copies.

The Depression aggravated Tussaud's problems. Attendance figures, which had averaged 591,588 before the fire, were 903,401 in the year to October 1929. The onset of the Depression in that month heralded a decline and in the year to October 1931 only 826,696 visited the exhibition. In 1932 visitor figures fell further by 22 per cent. Net profits, £30,186 in 1920, were only £27,177 in 1932. Arthur Wheeler, a major investor in Tussaud's, lost heavily in Stock Exchange dealings. The directors complained of over taxation, the impact on the entertainment industry of the Depression, restrictions preventing them adding criminals to the Horrors quickly, and the loss of the Napoleonic relics and works of art in the fire.[11]

When they realised that time would not solve their problems, economies were attempted. Staff were made redundant. It seems to have been a case of 'women first'. The Ladies' Orchestra was pensioned off, saving £21 a week. The number of lift and catalogue girls was reduced. In total staff cuts brought down wage costs a little, from £37,537 in the year to October 1929 to £36,162 the next year.[12] Because there were few early customers the exhibition delayed the opening for an hour, to 11 a.m. Advertising and publicity was focused away from the cinema, which lost money, onto the main exhibition. The longer term solution adopted under Norman Wild, who was to remain as chairman until his death in 1952, was to restructure the company, changing its name from Tussaud's (1926) Ltd back to Tussaud's Ltd and cutting dividends from 25 to 10 per cent, and then to 6 per cent. A total of £380,000 worth of new shares were issued.[13]

Reading between the lines of these protracted disputes, it seems clear that one problem was that the exhibition had not taken as much advantage of the mass market as they might have done. In the interwar years Tussaud's seems to have reverted to trying to appeal to an upmarket audience. For instance a new restaurant, complete with dance floor, was opened in 1932 in the depths of the Depression. Prices were steep and hours late. Customers could dance until 11 p.m. to a Duke Ellington style jazz band, kitted out in smart green lounge suits. The Duke was himself actually performing in London when the Tussaud's band began its performances. Its bandleader was Stanley Barnett, who played tenor saxophone and violin. He had previously played in London at the Carlton and Regent's Palace hotels as well as abroad. In 1933 the band made a record, 'Rockin' in Rhythm', the music of which was described as 'hot foxtrot' or 'hot dance'. Tussaud's customers could also enjoy an obligatory set menu dinner. The evening cost 3s. 6d.[14] Bernard would have been hard-pressed to afford such an evening out in his own restaurant on his wages, and it would have been well beyond the means of his sisters.

Emphasis was placed on building up the cinema, a particular favourite of John Theodore. The stress was on the well-heeled customer. The new cinema was decorated in a 'dignified ... late eighteenth-century English style, reminiscent of Adams in Wedgwood blue'.[15] It seated 300 and had a Wurlitzer organ and its own restaurant. Popular contemporary films were shown and the programme changed regularly. The films included Bette Davies in The Marked Woman, Marlene Dietrich in Garden of Allah, Harold Lloyd in Speedy and Flanagan and Allen in Underneath the Arches. Respectability was, as always, paramount. In 1940 Tussaud's assured potential customers, 'All the films shown are viewed and specially selected, thus ensuring to us the most interesting pictures with no objectionable, sordid or unhealthy features, so that our films can be seen and appreciated by young and old'.[16] This was the heyday of children's cinema, yet Tussaud's never tried to attract a junior audience with special Saturday matinees in the style of the cheap mass morning shows in British cinemas.

The Tussaud's recipe, which may have been good for wax in the previous century, was less successful in the cinema business, where competitors imposed few moral hurdles in their choice of films. Between June and

September 1930 just under 174,000 cinema tickets were sold. In September 1930 prices were reduced. The dearest seats came down from 3s. 6d. to 3s., and the cheapest from 1s. 3d. to 1s. The policy was a failure and Tussaud's decided to redecorate the cinema and raise the price. It must have been almost a relief when the cinema and restaurant were destroyed by enemy bombs in September 1940.

The chequered history of monarchy did a little to lift the income of the exhibition. In 1935 special exterior lighting was installed for the Silver Jubilee of George V and Queen Mary. The most successful publicity coup was the abdication of Edward VIII. Edward's speech was relayed throughout the galleries and the press was encouraged to photograph people crowding around the tableau of the royal family while he spoke. Mrs Wallis Simpson was quickly added, complete with red satin evening frock and 'ruby' jewels, with an attendant close by in case this unpopular figure was attacked. She boosted attendance by 10,000 in a fortnight. A coronation group for Edward's successor, George VI, was hastily assembled. Television was in its infancy and in 1937 Bernard appeared on the BBC to demonstrate his work on a model of Neville Chamberlain, soon to be famous (and as rapidly scorned) for naively promising 'Peace in our Time' after his meeting with Hitler over the future of Czechoslovakia. The model of Hitler created a sensation when it was introduced in April 1933, three months after his appointment as chancellor. The model was frequently vandalised and a replacement was made in 1936. It had to be moved to a less prominent position and carefully guarded. In 1942 a British munitions firm in search of orders put up atrocity posters which included a wax model of Hitler on a gibbet. Tussaud's were quick to deny they had made the model, which was probably Louis Tussaud's work. Goering and Goebbels made it into Marylebone Road on the outbreak of war in 1939, Hess a year later. Lenin and Mussolini do not appear to have been waxed, but Stalin was done in 1934. A new portrait of Winston Churchill was needed in 1940 when he became the head of the National government. He had been a member of Tussaud's since 1908, when, a young man in naval uniform, he was a minor player in the Admiralty group. A total of ten Churchill portraits were to be made, one of which in 1965 showed him in retirement as a painter, wearing a large white stetson hat. A model of de Gaulle appeared in 1941, some months after his move to London. Tussaud's were careful to buy a French army uniform from the army supply store in London, complete with a Sam Browne belt and his customary brown shoes. (£67 in total). The wax life of public figures has always been ephemeral. The 'Men Who Won the War' of 1914–18 disappeared in 1934. Herbert Hoover was melted down soon after he was replaced as US president by F. D. Roosevelt in 1933.

Sporting celebrities became increasingly prominent. Before the war there had been tableaux of sporting activities, but these do not seem to have held their place for long, and they did not feature particular individuals, although there were waxworks of a few famous sportsmen. In the interwar years the cult of the sporting personality became established and Tussaud's responded, in particular, to the craze for soccer. In April 1933 Bernard Tussaud modelled the Everton captain, Dixie Dean. Film stars became favourites. Greta Garbo joined the show at the same time as Hitler.

In Paris the Musée Grévin experienced some of the same long-term problems Tussaud's encountered in these years. Safely in the hands of the Thomas family, however, it did not have to endure the internecine squabbles which weakened its rival, but it was not a period of innovation or growth. Even earlier than Tussaud's Grévin actively sought the widest popular audience in its poster campaigns and all-in prices offered through railway companies. The gallery was praised as a 'fairyland',[17] but attendances were variable, 414,393 in 1930, 542,453 a year later. Takings were much higher than twenty years before, 1,600,000 million francs in 1930, over two million francs in 1931. This was an illusory rise, simply the result of inflation and the fall in the value of the franc during the war and subsequently.[18] Grévin continued to function in the Second World War during the German occupation, but almost every item relating to national political history and foreign affairs had to be put in store to avoid controversy. Only the comte de Paris and the duc de Guise survived. The Vichy head of state, Marshal Pétain, replaced George VI on display in 1939 but was removed in 1941. Grévin stuck to scientific development and culture, particularly drama and actors and dancing, especially ballet. It did well to stay open; other entertainments such as the Eiffel Tower were closed.

In 1939 the financial situation of Tussaud's had not improved. Chairing a meeting of shareholders, Sir Thomas Polson reported that in the five years to the end of 1938 net profits were a mere £230,000, out of which £49,600 and £140,000 were paid respectively in debenture interest and tax. £50,000 was borrowed from the bank. Polson was actually congratulated for doing the best that was possible. An area of 333.5 square feet on the north side of Marylebone Road was sold to the Crown Estate for £1150, a curious decision that cannot have done much to relieve the situation.[19] Tussaud's tried to continue as normal on the outbreak of war in 1939, although some moulds were moved out of London for safe storage. The black out, however, keeping all night time lights to a minimum, plus the evacuation of people from London, cut attendance at first. Numbers picked up and, as in the First World War, soldiers on leave were keen visitors. Keeping up to date on the decorations of serving soldiers, such as the generals Eisenhower,

Montgomery and Alexander was difficult, particularly as visitors were inclined to purloin the decorations.

On 9 September 1940 a bomb that wrecked the cinema and did considerable damage to the restaurant destroyed over 350 moulds, many of them historic. But no one was either injured or killed. There was considerable media coverage of the king and queen inspecting the damage and in December Tussaud's reopened. The exhibition limped on, reducing salaries and paying no dividends to shareholders from the beginning of 1941, when a net loss of nearly £9000 was reported. John Theodore died in 1943, leaving nearly £6000, a substantial sum, but not for someone who had headed a leading tourist attraction for nearly sixty years.

Bernard Tussaud was now in sole charge and the fortunes of Tussaud's began to improve. In 1943 their shares began a slow recovery and they made a small profit. Media coverage expanded. In 1943 Mary Wimbush, a well-known actress, played Marie Tussaud in a biographical feature film, *Pinnacle of Fame*. In September the popular radio series 'Appointment with Fear', included a programme, 'Menace in Wax', set in Tussaud's. A famous sculptor, Whitney Smith, made the model of the radio comedian Tommy Handley. During the war the catalogue, still 6*d.*, shrank to a mere twelve-page list of all the models. In 1944 the price of entry was 2*s.* 3*d.*, children 7*d.* and members of the armed forces 1*s.* 9*d.* This made the exhibition more expensive than its nearby competitor, the Zoo, which charged 1*s.* 6*d.* for adults and 6*d.* for children, with a reduction to 1*s.* on Mondays and free entry to members of the forces on Sundays and half price in the week.

Bernard's sister Joan still ran the wardrobe. For many years, until she retired in 1962, Joan undertook the herculean task of maintaining all the models in pristine condition. Her team went into action at 6 a.m. Five models were worked on each day. Their heads and hands were taken off, washed and recoloured. Their hair was washed and reset. The process was complete by the time Tussaud's opened. Every week all the models had a thorough brushing and any white items-lace, shirts, collars or anything light coloured were changed.[20]

With five hundred models to maintain, wartime rationing presented a real headache. Human beings were issued with clothing coupons, which permitted minor purchases of absolutely essential items. The Board of Trade, however, turned down every application for clothing coupons for the Tussaud's models, although some rationed liquid soap was secured for sprucing up costumes and faces. It therefore became even more important than usual to try to obtain a set of typical clothing from the subject. Norman Hartnell came up with copies of his gowns for the king's fast-growing daughters, Elizabeth and Margaret, in time for the Christmas rush of 1943. Tussaud's even ran out of plaster to make the initial moulds for figures. Supplies of fine plaster were restricted to medical use, both during the war and in peacetime when the new National Health Insurance was launched. Eventually in 1947, when Tussaud's persuaded the Board of Trade of the exhibition's potential as a dollar earner, they acquired enough plaster to make new models.

Juggling shortages of cloth, plaster, hair and eyes, Bernard Tussaud was on tenterhooks to know whether Attlee's Labour Party would beat Churchill in the first peacetime election in 1945. For Tussaud's a Labour victory would be a minor disaster, for twice as many new figures would be needed if Attlee won (which he did). Bernard mused that the Tussaud's wardrobe had enough material to kit out the new cabinet in Roman togas and pondered the accompanying labels, Julius Churchill, Mark Attlee, Marcus Bevin, Metullus Cripps etc.[21] Bernard made a wrong guess that the Republican Dewey would win the US presidential election following Roosevelt's death in 1945 and had his model ready. Instead there had to be a rapid meltdown to put President Harry S. Truman on his pedestal. Tussaud persuaded the American Embassy to procure an outfit and Prime Minister Attlee returned from the Washington Conference with one of Truman's suits, which Tussaud's collected from 10 Downing Street. The exhibition even ran out of human hair and glass eyes, especially blue and grey, formerly imported from Germany and Czechoslovakia. They were almost at the point when the choice of whom to model was determined by available eyes, until a European manufacturer decided to relocate his business in Britain. There was also a paper shortage. No catalogues could be printed until 1949, when it was necessary to double the size. By 1952, however, when Elizabeth II succeeded her father, although rationing was still in force, Tussaud's were able to order an exact match for the Tudor rose carpet in the Throne Room at Buckingham Palace plus copies of the chandeliers. Relevant Hartnell gowns were supplied, and the queen's own gown was dramatically shown for the first time on the day of the actual coronation.

Tussaud's survived the Second World War, but the real post-war take-off was when they fully accepted that the future lay in the exploitation of a mass market, in particular the pop and media world. A high point was the inclusion of the Beatles, who attended in person when their wax selves, modelled from life, were put on show to record-breaking crowds. From then on Tussaud's began to be known as a prime attraction for the 'jeans generation'. There was a vast increase in the number of media and sports personalities. 'The Battle of Trafalgar', the biggest and most complex tableau ever made, was opened in 1966 by an admiral of the fleet. It broke new ground, appealing to all the senses. It showed the port side of the *Victory* full size, complete with forty seamen and four guns. Unlike all previous Tussaud's presentations, only Nelson was made of wax and, unlike everything done previously, it was not just a feast for the eyes. There were streaks of sunlight, gunfire, the sound of the sea and all the noises a creaking wooden warship would have made, plus the smell of gunpowder, tar, smoke, even of the sea. In 1967 a 'Heroes Live' section was opened, which included Brigitte Bardot in wax and General de Gaulle, twice life size, in concrete. This new mix of real and fantasy continued. The Beatles used their wax selves, not their real selves, to adorn a record sleeve. Marat and Fouquier-Tinville were lent to the Royal Academy for its 'France in the Eighteenth Century' exhibition in 1968, and the *Victory* tableau was used by a French film company in an historical reconstruction. In the same year Tussaud's agreed to put thirteen of their figures, covering the period 1817–22, in an exhibition at the Royal Pavilion, Brighton.

Gradually, and hesitantly, Tussaud's began to adopt radical changes in their business strategy, the first of which was the Planetarium. The decision not to reconstruct a cinema and restaurant provided the space and in August 1957 the building was complete. The idea had first been put forward in 1938 and was a modern version of the nineteenth-century panoramas, focusing on the sky. Interest in the stars was intensified with the beginnings of the space race between USSR and USA. A working model of the planetary system was projected onto the rounded ceiling. At first a Zeiss machine was used, then a Digistar projector. It represented how the stars actually move in space.[22] Schoolchildren learned something of astronomy, while in 2002 the general public were entertained with 'Wonders of the Universe', a simulated ride through space in which they were given a palpable sense of supersonic movement. The opening of the Planetarium meant that Madame Tussaud's famous 1s. entry fee was finally abandoned. In 1962 the price of admission was raised to 2s. for children, 2s. 6d. for the combined entry to planetarium and waxworks.

Although space was at a premium, Tussaud's insisted on maintaining workshops and the studio within the exhibition. Part of the reason was the need for daily maintenance of the figures. Equally important, sculptors and artists knew at first hand what visitors thought of their work. Tussaud's began to show a positive interest in investing abroad. Each proposal was exhaustively investigated and carefully costed. In 1964 came the first of many visits to America, designed to promote a branch of Tussaud's in an area of high entertainment concentration. In the same year they sent an exhibition of miniatures on tour to Japan and then set it up in Portsmouth next to the *Victory*.

Diversification did not stop inter-family feuds and litigation continued within the family about the use of the name Tussaud. The main rival was still the Louis Tussaud's waxworks, which was related only in name. In 1956 Louis Tussaud had a show in Clacton, but probably their most successful operation remained that in Blackpool. By 1983 the London firm had apparently given up its struggle to try to stop them using the name, for the Louis Tussaud programme for that year had a picture of Madame Tussaud herself on its front cover. Since 1978 sound and animation had been added, similar to Disneyland, all for a mere 30p. For an extra 30p adults could visit the anatomy exhibition, 'inadvisable for those of a nervous or sensitive nature'. In 1986 the Blackpool show paid £15,000 for replicas of the Crown Jewels. Michael Jackson also sat for his own model. Madame Tussaud Ltd was careful to collect all of Louis Tussaud's Blackpool catalogues, usually a modest two pages. They paid an agency to supply any relevant press cuttings from the local paper. In 1959 the Louis Tussaud Company (Blackpool) was also a base for overseas operations including Gems, Niagara, run by a cousin, Josephine Tussaud.

In 1972 Antoinette, the great great great granddaughter of Madame Tussaud, was running a wax show in Brighton and Southend. There was a Tussaud family waxworks in Stratford from 1971 to 1983. An Australian Tussaud's also ran for several years and in 1972 a wax exhibition opened in Copenhagen. With the exception of this last venture, in which the original Tussaud's firm eventually became involved, Tussaud's used all legal means to try to prevent others using the family name.

It is interesting to compare Tussaud's postwar development with that of its Parisian rival. Like Tussaud's, and possibly most entertainment venues, the Grévin exhibition was still small scale in the first two decades after the Second World War, when people had only limited spare cash for amusements. The cinema and a new craze, bingo, drew in the crowds, and television was beginning to cultivate couch potato stay at homes. In 1966 a small travelling show of Grévin waxworks began to tour the French, Belgian and Dutch canals on a specially converted barge. The focus was on French history; among the passengers were Charlemagne and Louis-Philippe, king of the French (1830–48). The canal-barge commander who welcomed visitors on board was successively French chief minister Mendès-France, Churchill and Eisenhower. Apart from this venture, in 1974, like Tussaud's, Grévin was still a relatively small enterprise, with forty-two employees, all working on the original site, with no mention of the theatre, cinema and other additional attractions. Marketing in France, however, as indeed world wide, was about to change. André Malraux, France's leading cultural figure at the time, anointed Grévin with the accolade of an 'historical monument', a must for children. There was an immediate 10 per cent rise in attendance. Leading influential daily papers, such as *Le Monde* and *Le Figaro*, also began to take Grévin seriously. The gallery was recognised as the third most popular museum after Versailles and the Louvre. In March 1975 it was about to welcome its thirty millionth visitor and in 1974 alone there were 500,000 customers, mainly children.[23] (This was actually 42,000 fewer than in 1932 at the height of the Depression, an indication that, despite upbeat publicity, Grévin had been badly affected by the war and the German occupation.)

In 1969 Tussaud's awareness of Grévin as a rival crystallised in a plan to invest in the Paris *musée*.[24] The managing director of Grévin attended the Tussaud's anniversary dinner the following year. In 1971 Tussaud's had a chance of acquiring a controlling interest in Grévin and the Tussaud's managing director Peter Gatacre visited its rival. Admitting that Grévin had potential, he noted that at that time the gallery relied on a provincial market. It had little appeal to sophisticated Parisians and made no attempt to attract foreign visitors. He was shocked to find that the gallery did not open until 1 p.m. Gatacre thought Grévin could be a good investment, but he warned his colleagues that the French regarded the gallery as French property. At the end of 1971 the French Bourse was depressed and Grévin shares were relatively cheap. At this point the Banque Occidentalle pour l'Industrie et Commerce was commissioned secretly to buy shares on Tussaud's' behalf. The latter's target was to acquire 20 per cent of the shares, which would have put them in a commanding position. By September 1972 they had bought 1.5 per cent, by December 2.7 per cent. At that point share prices on the Paris Bourse began to rise. Meanwhile Grévin had realised what Tussaud's were doing and began to buy Tussaud's shares. A year later Tussaud's owned 5 per cent of Grévin shares. By early 1974 Tussaud's had paid out near £57,000 for 7 per cent of Grévin. Realising they still could exercise no influence on the gallery, in February 1975 the Tussaud's directors cut their losses and sold their shares for £40,500 to the Thomas family, which retained financial and managerial control of the gallery.[25] The contest had been a waste of time and money for both firms.

Things were about to change for both companies. Grévin invested in waxworks in Canada and the USA. In 1974 an American competitor launched a wax show at Lourdes, France's leading Roman Catholic shrine. They were disappointed: only 200,000 of the four million pilgrims who went to Lourdes visited the waxworks. Five years later Grévin took it over in partnership with a local family and developed an additional wax show on the life of the saint of Lourdes, Bernadette Soubirous. Their success was ensured when the pope decided to make a centenary visit.[26] In 1975 Grévin also linked up with an American company to put on a show on the first floor of the Eiffel Tower.

In 1984 Grévin acquired the Château Royal at Tours, in which thirty tableaux and 140 models showed the history of Touraine. This went well and other wax-based exhibitions were opened with variable success and survival, all based on the history of their regions: La Rochelle (1989), Mont-St-Michel (1991), St-Jean-de-Luz and Salon-de-Provence (1992). A favourite with the central management was the loss-leader at Yvelines à Elancourt near Paris, the France-Miniature park. A huge map of France was laid out over five hectares with miniatures of the Eiffel Tower and other tourist attractions, plus model farms, typical of different regions. The park was specifically designed to acquaint schoolchildren with their country. Another Grévin offshoot appeared in Montreal at the same time and an exhibition was planned for Monastier in Tunisia. In Paris itself Grévin opened a branch in the new version of Les Halles. The exhibition focused on La Belle Époque, Paris, 1885–1900, with twenty tableaux, relevant accompanying sounds and a model of Victor Hugo with moving lips.[27] It was never profitable and closed in 1996.

One could not imagine anyone getting away from the Marylebone Road with Beckham under their arm, but Grévin lost some models to opportunist thieves, usually in search of publicity. Georges Marchais, the secretary of the Communist Party after the Second World War was stolen, stripped and had 'Moscow' scrawled across his chest by twenty young masked supporters of a right-wing group. They then threw him into the bears' cage in the Jardin des Plantes zoo in Paris. The four brown bears hid in a corner at first, but then began to play with the model. The director of the zoo protested indignantly that his bears were not toys and that a diet of wax was not good for them.[28] In 1981 the former president Valéry Giscard d'Estaing was stripped and François Mitterrand was stolen. Only his badly damaged head was recovered following a daring commando-style raid. On Christmas Day, 1983 the prime minister, Jacques Chirac, left the building in the clutches of five youths. As the cost of making a model was by then around 25,000 francs, this was no small loss.[29]

In 1981 the Montmartre gallery had 634,000 visitors, Lourdes 220,000.[30] By the centenary of its opening the main exhibition had received 45,000,000 people,[31] and before half the centenary year was through one million people had been through the turnstiles.[32] In contrast to Tussaud's, a proportion of these went in free. Grévin even issued complimentary season tickets. Grévin overtook Versailles to become the second most popular museum in Paris after the Louvre. The centenary was celebrated with a champagne reception.

Grévin was a limited company from its inception, but unlike Tussaud's the management and the majority shareholding, remained in family hands. In 1982 Maxime-Gabriel Thomas, the daughter of the founder, had served for fifty years as managing director, while the next managing director was Regis Thomas, the grandson of Gabriel Thomas. Although the Musée Grévin had diversified, the main waxworks was in the doldrums at the end of the twentieth century, with average yearly attendances of 600,000 not much higher than in 1950, and no space to attract more visitors on the Montmartre site. No one wanted to move and finally in 1999 the Asterix company bought up the *musée*. They embarked on a radical makeover, closing the galleries from December 2000 until the summer of 2001. The new management was aware that the Grévin had always failed to match Tussaud's – the *musée* constantly compared itself to Tussaud's, whereas Tussaud's very rarely thought about their Paris rival. The major problems they identified were the separation between customers and models, the Grévin figures had always been distant, and space was limited. The biggest headache were the bottle-neck queues waiting for the traditional *palais des mirages* and the theatre, which was then called the *cabinet fantastique* and gave fifteen minute magic or marionette shows during opening hours. Their solution was to close both and to increase the model population by eighty to two hundred and fifty. Depardieu and other idols were placed in the theatre where touching and close encounter photography, following the example of Tussaud's, was en-couraged. The price of admission soared from 65 francs to 99, twice the cost of a visit to the Louvre. Asterix, renamed Grévin and Company, retained France-Miniature, leaving the regional exhibitions to fend for themselves, but adding an animal park at Le Touquet and an aquarium in St-Malo. Two new theme parks in the Netherlands were acquired in September 2001.[33]

Given their emphasis on history, it is not surprising that Tussaud's enjoy celebrating their own past. In March 1970, Tussaud's held the two hundredth anniversary (a little early) of the establishment of Curtius's *salon* in the Palais Royal. One hundred and fifty living illustrious originals of Tussaud models sat down to dinner in their Grand Hall. In his speech of thanks on behalf of the guests, Earl Mountbatten told his audience how, when he was First Sea Lord, the Russian Fleet visited Portsmouth for the first time. When the sailors were taken on a bus tour of London, all they wanted to see was Tussaud's. The chairman of Tussaud's, Sir Christopher Chancellor, told his guests, a sizeable number of whom were senior members of the diplomatic corps of various nations, that when in 1898 the American ambassador was asked what it was like going to Tussaud's, he had replied that it was like any ordinary English party. Meanwhile the press was entertained to a reception in the entrance hall. To emphasise the Anglo-French character of Tussaud's, the menu of food with very English names (with one forgiveable exception) was written in French: *Consommé Bourbon, Filet de sole Nelson, Noisettes d'agneau Victoria, Pommes de terre Byron* and *Bombe Gladstone.*

In 1970 Tussaud's opened a second exhibition in Amsterdam, where Josephine Tussaud had tried and failed. In Marylebone Road a Grand Hall was completed, based on the design of the assembly rooms in which Madame Tussaud had toured and in 1974 a conservatory, similar to that in the original building, was erected. In 1973 Tussaud's finally made the decision to diversify into other enterprises, as long as they were family daytime amusements. Their first ventures were small-scale. Basing their endeavours on the twin principles of profitability plus respectability, in 1973 they bought Wookey Hole caves in Somerset and a nearby paper mill. A craft centre was opened in the mill and Wookey Hole was transformed into a very useful, naturally temperature-controlled store room for pensioned heads.

In 1973 all this rapid diversification was temporarily halted when the first world oil crisis brought high fuel prices, fuel rationing, and consequent reductions of up to 20 per cent in the numbers of both foreign and British customers to all the exhibitions, and amusements. Another serious problem for all tourist attractions were the frequent IRA. bomb scares and actual bomb blasts. In January 1974 a bomb was discovered in the *Trafalgar* display. In two and a half minutes nearly five hundred people had been escorted off the premises. The five pound bomb exploded, but no one was hurt. The exhibition reopened the next day, but *Trafalgar* was out of action until April.[34]

Business recovered slowly. The numbers of foreign adult visitors began to increase in the mid 1970s, although the directors were alarmed that Tussaud's attracted fewer children.[35] In 1976 annual attendance topped two million for the first time, but the number of English families visiting continued to fall. There were plans to give away children's tickets in the *Daily Mirror, Woman* or through British Rail, in return for free publicity.[36] Early in 1977 Tussaud's launched a promotion scheme in *Woman's Own,* which, with a circulation of 1,500,000, was one of the biggest-selling women's magazines.

Expansion plans were soon renewed. In 1976 Tussaud's hoped to acquire Battle Abbey, but lost out to the Department of the Environment. On a much smaller scale they bought Tolgus Tin, in Cornwall, where tin had been mined for three hundred years, to develop it as a tourist attraction. The directors became very seriously bent on acquiring additional firms, looking for 'star' quality and a return of about 20 per cent on their investment. They calculated that, although there was no guarantee that available spending on leisure activities would actually match the increase in leisure time itself, the acquisition of top quality entertainments would protect any investment Tussaud's made.[37]

In 1977 Pearsons, ATV under Lord Grade and Trident TV all began to manoeuvre to gain control of Tussaud's. While the negotiations were proceeding, Tussaud's itself began to negotiate to buy Chessington Zoo from Pearsons. Towards the end of the year, however, Pearsons gained control of Tussaud's. In 1978 the new firm began to negotiate to buy a chunk of Windsor and Eton railway station to set up a permanent Victorian style exhibition, 'Royalty and Railways'. A lengthy tussle with the local council, horrified by the thought of increased traffic, ensued, but the show opened and ran for a quarter of a century. Towards the end of 1978 they acquired Warwick Castle and one hundred acres of parkland from Lord Brooke for £1,500,000. Some locals were appalled, for the same reasons as the middle classes of Windsor, but Tussaud's hoped that the £7500 they donated to the Birmingham City Museum's plan to buy two Canaletto paintings of the castle would help ease the blow of their schemes for car parks for 1100 cars and sixty coaches and a hotel. The castle proved attractive as a venue for mock battles and private occasions, such as weddings, at £2000 for a two and half hour slot in which the customer could fantasise about owning a real castle. The following year saw abortive plans to buy the Royal Agricultural Hall in Islington. There was talk of Tussaud's presenting an exhibition on Dickens's London there, although the directors of Tussaud's were sceptical what they could contribute beyond the name and some advice.[38] They also considered the purchase of the Savoy Hotel for £50,000,000, but it was agreed that the purchase would have to be accompanied by unwelcome asset stripping and that it would be a major step outside the field of daytime family entertainment. In these years of expansion and talk of further growth, the entertainment market itself remained relatively depressed. The second oil crisis, with increased prices and shortages, reduced attendance at Marylebone Road by 2 per cent. There were fewer foreign visitors and even the Americans were spending less.

Pearsons encouraged Tussaud's to acquire 'projects that fitted in with Madame Tussaud's philosophy'.[39] Never had so much been said about the Tussaud's philosophy. Madame Tussaud herself might have been puzzled, being always very frank about the primacy of profitability, which, in reality was what the concern with 'philosophy' meant. The Tussaud's 'philosophy' was as much invented as real. Tussaud's responded to what they thought was a majority view. The acquisition of Napoleon artefacts reflected a sustained fascination in the emperor in Britain after 1815, while in 1946

Tussaud's refused to buy Nazi relics at a time when they would have caused only disgust.[40]

The 'Horrors' philosophy changed radically, but the alterations may have been provoked less by growing refinement in popular sensibility than by practical necessity. The Chamber of Horrors has always been the single most popular aspect of Tussaud's, but it was criticised (even by *Punch* which had given it its name which the Tussauds themselves did not really like). In 1861 the newspapers were keen to publicise that it had been renamed the Chamber of Comparative Physiognomy, which sounded respectable and unsensational. The new name did not survive but Tussaud's felt obliged to claim that the Horrors had psychological benefits. Even Shakespeare was roped into the defence.

> It will have blood; they say blood will have blood;
> Stones have been known to move and trees to speak;
> Augurs and understood relations have
> By magot-pies and choughs, and rooks brought forth
> The secret'st man of blood.

When crowds stopped the traffic in Baker Street to queue to see Mrs Pearcey and the pram, the 1891 catalogue insisted:

> That there should be a widespread and general interest in the details of great crimes, and a curiosity concerning the personal appearance and surroundings of great criminals, is a fact proven by long experience, and one of which the cause is not far to seek.
>
> Attention is naturally attracted by whatever is unusual and enormous in a crime ... Nor is the contemplation of these criminals without its uses and lessons. It is a wholesome check to pharisaic pride to see how frequently the passion of the murderer, and the capacity for the worst of crimes, have lurked beneath the outward appearance of eminent respectability.

After 1945 Tussaud's themselves wondered whether it was appropriate to make a display of death after the genocide of the war. There were only three new recruits in these years, but this was not because Tussaud's were trying to protect their customers from psychological harm. The new boys were Haigh, Heath and Christie, chosen because their multiple murders were spectacularly and calculatingly violent and vicious. The three wax models drew large crowds. John Haigh (1909–1949), a forger, murdered four women and disposed of them in baths of sulphuric acid. He visited the Chamber the day before his arrest, which suggests that he sought notoriety and hoped to identify where his model would be placed. Haigh was proud that his murders qualified him for the Chamber and insisted that the clothes he wore for his trial were delivered to Tussaud's the day before his execution, so that an accurate model could be on show immediately after his hanging, which it was.

In 1962 some Horrors material was excluded because people complained it was unsuitable for children.[41] In the late 1970s the directors began to worry about whether some of the models were in bad taste.[42] Their solution was to put up signs indicating escape routes for those who were shocked. In reality television inured people to violent sights and it was a change in the law that made a radical review of the Horrors essential. Execution had always been the qualification for entry, except for paying customers. This restriction had been observed with particular care since the Ardlamont Mystery of 1894. Alfred John Monson had been tried but not convicted for the murder of a young pupil, Cecil Hamborough, who, Monson claimed, had accidentally shot himself while they were out hunting. Shortly before Hamborough's death Monson had taken out a life insurance policy for £20,000 on the lad, of which Mrs Monson was the chief beneficiary. Monson claimed that displaying his model near the entrance to the Horrors was defamatory because the murder charge against him was 'not proven'. He failed to prevent Tussaud's displaying his model because it was not actually in the Chamber itself, but he won an action for libel. Although Tussaud's were only ordered to pay one farthing compensation, the lengthy proceedings made them very cautious.

The 1965 legislation abolishing the death penalty for murder threatened to rob Tussaud's of all their future Horrors. In 1974 the Rehabilitation of Offenders Act forbade any reference to existing convictions, which seemed to indicate even imprisoned murderers had to be excluded. Tussaud's were uncertain how to cope and hesitated for several years. Meanwhile the Chamber was becoming embarrassingly out of date and customers were more bored than terrified. In April 1970 the managing director Peter Gatacre expressed his judgement that:

> I do not believed that murderers are interesting since the abolition of capital punishment; even sensational newspapers give them less space; anyway given the nature of the Moors murders ... even if we had no scruples except our showmanship, we would hesitate to depict them.

When Gatacre left, Tussaud's consulted the leading British libel expert, Perin Bowsher QC, whether they would risk libel charges if they included wax models of imprisoned live murderers. Bowsher concluded that Tussaud's would not be caught by the 1974 Act, which only applied to people sentenced to ten years or less. He concluded, however, that 'the overwhelming majority of civilised members of our society will be revolted by the idea of a gallery of modern living criminals'.[43] The chief executive of Tussaud's, Michael Herbert, commented to their solicitor, 'being an "institution" means that we carry a burden of responsibility and Madame Tussaud simply cannot afford to risk being accused of bad taste'. [44]

Finally, under Pearson's ownership all this heart-searching was set aside and the Chamber was renovated in 1980 with new lighting and sound effects – and a prison cell with a number of current imprisoned murderers, notably Donald Neilson, the 'Black Panther', so called because he wore a black hood for his robberies and kidnapping. Neilson kidnapped a young girl and kept her in a series of drainage shafts before hanging her.[45] The Chamber cell also included Graham Young and the Hosein brothers, but looked for all the world like a supermarket check-out queue. Those whose crimes created most outrage were excluded, quite the opposite to previous custom. The Moors murderers were excluded, not because of outrage at the nature of the heinous crimes, but because it was thought that Lord Longford might complain that Myra Hindley's presence in the Horrors would prejudice his case for her release. Only one person wrote opposing the inclusion of live murderers, in this instance the East End gangland killers, the Kray brothers.

Some of the Victorian murderers were relegated to gruesome coffins, although Burke and Hare still dragged a chest full of their latest victim, while Charlie Peace crouched over his violin case containing his house-breaking tools. Gary Gilmore sat in the Utah State prison firing range. The first section also showed different ways people had been executed over the ages, with decaying bits of corpses in cages overhead. Next came a chilling walk through East End streets revealing Mary Kelly, the Ripper's last victim, leaning against a door post, while across the street customers could gaze at the disembowelled body of Catherine Eddow, Jack the Ripper's fourth victim, seen alive just a quarter of an hour before her gruesome death.

Crippen, Haigh and Neville Heath were still in place. The sadistic fraudster Heath, who had killed and mutilated two women, had been installed just twenty minutes after his execution in 1946, but Bernard Tussaud refused to allow the model to wear Heath's RAF tie. Christie also remained. In 1953 John Reginald Christie was installed in a tableau showing the kitchen of 10 Rillington Place, where he had killed six women, and possibly a seventh and her unborn baby – a crime for which her husband, Timothy Evans, was hanged. Also retained was the Californian Charles Manson, and his three girl friends who had helped in the ritual murder of seven victims.

Brought up on repeated examples of violence, real and imaginary, children were apparently scornful of the renovated Chamber. A Tussaud's survey in 1995 revealed that over half those who were questioned complained that the Horrors was not horrible enough, while a third said it was too small.

Tussaud's tried to establish just what they were trying to achieve. The Horrors had to be consistent with Tussaud's policy to project

> real, recognisable PEOPLE in appropriate contexts realistically portrayed; to be differentiated from the competition, to avoid causing distress ... avoid emphasising victims or glorifying violence (like the London Dungeon), but we will not over sanitise or destroy people's fascination, or shy away from being controversial.[46]

Horror was not a thing to be taken lightly. Tussaud's commissioned a report on how people reacted to horror. Violent crime, particularly when the perpetrators looked very ordinary, fascinated people. Eleven million people regularly watched *Crimewatch* and fifteen hundred phoned in during a transmission. *Prime Suspect* and *Cracker* commanded audiences of sixteen million. The Tussaud's specialist, Professor David Carter, noted that human beings started their diet of violence in early childhood with fairy stories such as 'Little Red Riding Hood'. Like fairy stories, the Chamber of Horrors provided a safe environment in which customers could face their fears. Carter concluded that this was healthy in moderation because it was pointless to deny the reality of violence.[47]

The Chamber of Horrors was once more reorganised, this time at a cost of £1,000,000. First, Visions of Hell showed torture and execution through the ages, including Dracula (Vlad the Impaler), then Joan of Arc burned with appropriate sound effects. Opposite her Guy Fawkes waited to die. To the sound of running water a pirate was shown hanged at low tide on the Thames and suspended through three tides while rats devoured him. Newgate bell tolled and Ripper Street survived. Executed and currently imprisoned serial killers were still in line, while customers could watch the judge pass sentence on Christie, who was then hanged. Finally the Chamber returned to the roots of the exhibition as a guillotine swiftly and bloodily did its job. Meanwhile the young Marie Grosholz was sorting through severed heads ready to make her wax models. On the right of the guillotine lay the stabbed Marat, as he had done since Marie first modelled him. As the customers left they could look at more original models, and the death's heads of Louis XVI, Marie-Antoinette, Robespierre and the other revolutionaries. Curiously, whereas elsewhere in the exhibition the emphasis on history was reduced, the opposite was the case in the Horrors. Perhaps this was because at the end of the twentieth century visitors wanted to escape from the violence of their own times.

The views of young people and their parents dictated the redevelopment of the Horrors. Aware that young people were big spenders, Tussaud opened a Rock Circus in Piccadilly in 1989. Its patrons were all young, up to 700,000 of them a year. In 2000 the site was sold and the Tussaud's models were sent on a world tour. Alton Towers, acquired in 1990, was a far more costly but much more successful venture. Transformed into a theme park, it quickly became the second most visited site in the Tussaud-Pearson empire, with two and a half million customers in 1997. Park Aventura near Barcelona was less profitable and was sold in 1997. Tussaud's began to participate in projects in Manhattan, Melbourne, Sydney, and Hong Kong and there were discussions about the development of Stonehenge and participation in the Millenium Wheel. In the contest for customers they recognised that they were competing in a 'time poor, but money rich' society. There was also a dramatic change in how tickets were sold, with a trend away from selling at the door. The object was twofold, to guarantee visits and to avoid a queue. Tickets were sold by phone, through the Internet, or in the case of Port Aventura through a local building society. In 2002 the cafeteria was closed and plans laid to have customers queue inside. (Yet surely the queue had been affirmation of the value of a visit.)

In 1998 Tussaud's were a profitable part of the Pearson portfolio and were negotiating the purchase of the popular Surrey theme park, Thorpe Park, for £15 million. The London waxworks and Alton Towers jostled for the distinction of attracting the most visitors of any tourist business in Britain. Nonetheless the new Pearson chief executive, the American Marjorie Scardino, formerly chief executive of the *Economist*, and most famous for being the mother of the boy star of *The Indian in the Cupboard*, decided that Pearson should focus on their media and publishing empire. It was noted, in the *Financial Times*, also part of Pearson, that the Tussaud's portfolio only produced 7 per cent of Pearson's profits in 1997 and that total attendance had dropped slightly in the year.[48] After prolonged rumours, Tussaud's was put up for sale, being valued at between £350 and £430 million pounds. Pearson had just bought the publisher Simon and Schuster and were keen to reduce a debt of £2 billion. Lazard Brothers, the bankers, themselves part-owned by Pearson, produced an extensive booklet to launch the search for a purchaser in 1998.

There was hot speculation in the press on 24 June 1998 that Tussaud's might be bought by First Leisure, which owned Blackpool Tower and was in process of selling it, including Louis Tussaud's waxworks. The *Guardian* noted that, in planning to sell Tussaud's, Scardino had 'taken on a sacred cow'.[49] In November 1998 none of the predicted bidders, which included Rank, Time Warner and Universal, were willing to pay the price. The buyer was ultimately Charterhouse Development Capital at a cost of £352 million. Expansion continued, the purchase of Thorpe Park was completed and new Tussaud's waxworks opened in Las Vegas in 1999 and New York in 2000.

The Australian touring waxworks were taken fully under the Tussaud's label and moved to Hong Kong.

The ownership of the waxworks and the variety of different firms in the Tussaud's portfolio were vastly different from the *salon* Curtius first opened in the 1770s. Yet the process of creating a model has altered very little. In 2002 Tussaud's calculate that it takes five to six months and costs £20,000 to complete a model. Curtius and Marie had to turn out their revolutionaries and villains within a few days to catch the market. They made and dressed the whole figure. Subsequently the work was divided among the sculptor and a variety of make-up and wardrobe assistants, mostly family members. In the 1970s the managing director, Peter Gatacre, distinguished the sculptor, who made the head and hands, as an artist, from his team, who were artisans. Since the late 1960s there has been a change and now the sculptor has overall responsibility for the look of the whole model, including the body, colouring and hair. However, it is a team effort with involvement from the moulding, wardrobe and hair and colouring departments. There has also been an increased stress that the sculptor is trying to do more than make an exact photographic-style image.

> Our intention is always to produce a *total* impression of the subject that is much more than just the sum of the details. A good sculptor is not necessarily an effective wax sculptor and vice-versa. Some wax figures are potentially fine pieces of sculpture, but ultimately unconvincing waxworks. Some waxworks have a natural craft charm, but their lack of sculptural quality detracts from their excellence.[50]

Unlike in John Theodore's day, senior posts in the Tussaud's studio are no longer gender-specific. The studio itself moved out of the main exhibition to Shepherd's Bush and then to Acton. Since 1987 only running repairs and maintenance have been done on site in Baker Street. The main studio has been run since the late 1980s by a highly-qualified sculptor and painter, Judy Craig, who started work with Tussaud's in 1978. She heads a team of five full-time sculptors and ten freelances, who are called on as needed. Models are made in the traditional way, but with far greater precision and accuracy than a quarter of a century ago. Hence the complete process takes five to six months. Some of the materials have altered: fibreglass to give a light but strong body; acrylic instead of glass for eyes because no one makes glass eyes any more; acrylic also for teeth instead of plaster, wax or sometimes real human teeth in Madame Tussaud's day; and plastic mixed with the wax to make hands stronger and slightly flexible.

Making a model still starts in the traditional fashion with an interview and photo-shoot, if possible at Tussaud's' studio. The sculptor talks to the subject and with a team of cameramen takes hundreds of photographs of all angles and parts of the body, many of them with a telephoto lens. Colour transparencies of eyes and teeth are taken. Modern computer technology is used to translate some of these photographs, a substantial number of which are blown up to life size. Numerous key measurements are noted onto the photographs with dots, many carefully measured from the tragus, the gristly flap in the front of the ear. The photographs begin to look like an advanced case of measles.

Colour matches for skin, hair and eyes are all done at the interview. The subject's teeth are accurately mapped by the most modern dental techniques developed by the Mount Vernon Hospital. Over four days a complete and exact set is made, with each tooth colour-matched. The hands are cast as always from life, but in a new, far more forensic way. The subject slides hands and forearms into a large tub of dental alginate. After a few minutes the arms can be taken out, leaving an unnervingly accurate impression of all the lines, pores and even hair follicles. This mould is filled with plaster to make a 'positive' mould. Then a flexible rubber 'negative' mould is made in two halves from which the final hand and arm is moulded from wax, to which elvex (plastic) is added. The subject's eye colour and fine markings on each eye are noted. Glass eyes are used to match the colour, but the last person in the family in Golders Green who made glass eyes for Tussaud's for generations has now retired, so acrylic eyes are made and painted. Over two days the eyes are built up from the iris outwards. When the scelera is added silk threads are worked in to each eye to show fine veins. Tussaud's ask the subject to provide a pair of shoes, vital to identify the height and exactly how the person stands, and if possible a set of clothing, or details as to where an exact copy can be bought or made.

Production can then begin. The whole operation takes about six months, far longer than during the French Revolution, when such a delay might have meant death for Curtius. Then speed was the essence and total accuracy less vital or possible. In April 2002 the Acton studio was in the middle of producing a tableau of three New York firemen to commemorate 11 September for the New York exhibition for the first anniversary of the atrocity. David Beckham's model was almost complete, ready, it was hoped, for a World Cup display.

The sculptor marks the position of the feet on the floor of the studio and erects an armature, a support made out of scaffold poles and joints. This has to be strong enough to support the clay model, which may weigh up to 150 kilos. Steel and aluminium rods, chicken wire and newspaper are all brought into play where wood and cloth were used in the past. A complete clay model of head, hair and body is developed upon the armature, following the photographs and adding 2 per cent to allow for the shrinkage of the wax. Little clay pimples are added to show the hair line and the position of the eyebrows. The clay hair is removed later, revealing the shape of the skull. This stage takes about twelve weeks. The clay head is made so that it can be lifted off.

Next the head is covered with a fine plaster piece-mould, so called because it is made up of numerous sections, starting with the ear. This mould will be reused to make a new wax head whenever needed. Similar moulds were the most vital part of Madame Tussaud's baggage when she arrived in England and these can still be used today. When the piece-mould is complete the clay interior is broken up and the clay later reused. The plaster head is then bound tightly together, soaked in water and the water wiped away. The interior is filled with a thick layer of a similar mixture of melted beeswax and Japan wax that Curtius used. Three-quarters of an hour later the surplus wax is poured away, leaving a thickness of 5/8 of an inch. After another two hours the plaster piece-mould is removed and the wax head is left wrapped in a blanket to cool slowly overnight.

The real revolution in model-making lies in the body. Until well into the nineteenth century bodies were a total deception, being composed of leather or wood, stuffed around with cloth to make a rough figure. Later bodies were made in plaster, but these were very heavy and extremely fragile. Since the early 1960s accurate fibreglass bodies have been used. The clay is first coated with shellac to prevent the plaster sticking. Then plaster-coated hessian strips are built up on the clay and the whole plaster body divided into two or more pieces. When the plaster is set, the clay model is extracted and discarded for reuse. Fibreglass and resin strips are laid inside the halves of the plaster cast to make the final body. These fibreglass bodies are durable and light. Extra bodies can be easily made for the growing number of Tussaud's exhibitions.

The model is returned to the sculptor who first ensures all join marks from the head are filed away. The wax eyes are burned out and the acrylic ones inserted from the inside and the teeth fitted. Basic skin colour will have been added to the wax. Numerous very thin layers of oil paint are applied over thirty-five hours to colour each head to retain the life-like translucency of wax. In the past water colours were used, but models could not be washed.

The longest single finishing process is hair and, like all the other components, the system has been made far more accurate in the last twenty years. It takes 140 hours to construct a head of hair, even if, as in the case of Beckham, each six inch hair will, at the end, be trimmed with a number one clipper familiar to every young lad. Real hair is still always used, and is inserted into the wax with a needle like a darning needle, one hair at a time. The barbed construction of each hair means that, once inserted, it is permanently fixed with no risk of premature balding. The front section is set in the head, while the rest is made up as a wig to allow for regular washing. If grey hair is needed, a mixture of the right shade of grey and appropriate coloured hair is inserted. In April 2002 the Jubilee wig being made for the queen in the bouffant style of her jubilee portrait contained predominantly silver with a scattering of black.[51]

Although modern materials are used, traditional ones predominate. Basic methods have barely altered, although processes and the final results are now far more sophisticated. Sculptors stress the importance of combinations of figures in tableaux, to convey emotion and atmosphere in addition to appearance. Because the Tussaud's Group now has waxworks in America and Hong Kong, as well as London and Amsterdam, several copies of many models are needed. The two American Tussaud's meant that whole collections had to be made. Twelve new sculptors were engaged to complete the 175 models for New York and 100 for Las Vegas.

For the twenty-first century a radical reworking of the Marylebone Road show was undertaken. A visit was made a total experience. A variety of lighting, from the fairy lights of the 'Garden Party' to the flashing neon ones of 'Behind the Scenes with the Stars' and the traditional chandeliers of the Grand Salon, dazzle the visitor. Everywhere there is sound, starting with the fountain, then celebrities uttering catch phrases and building up to a crescendo of pop tunes. One's eyes are captured by a huge range of video clips. Constantly encouraged to touch, embrace and be photographed with the wax models, the visitors themselves are absorbed into a total experience, to such a degree that distinguishing between wax and reality is hard. Only the royal family are roped off, but it turns out that this is simply a Jubilee game; men dressed as guardsmen march nearby and visitors are 'announced' to and photographed with the wax monarch.

There were fewer changes in the dark, cold, echoing tomb of the Chamber of Horrors, although here too videos and special sound effects make the hanging of Crippen in 1953 and an unnamed victim of the guillotine seem real, for a fraction of a second. The 'Spirit of London', a 'taxi' ride through London's history, opened in 1993, uses moving models on a scale never before seen in Marylebone Road. A complete innovation is the opportunity to tour the studios and see at first hand how models are made. A real revolution (actually a return to how Madame ran things in Baker Street) was the removal of the café to the Grand Salon and its replacement on the ground floor by a new way of queuing inside to the accompaniment of a variety of videos, describing the origins of Madame Tussaud's and major events in the twentieth century.

In 1997 ten million people visited Tussaud's venues, bringing £35 million profit. The waxworks alone attracted 3.3 million visitors, making it the top tourist attraction in Britain that charges an entry fee. Tussaud's had triumphantly negotiated the transformation from middle-class promenade to mass culture.

9

The Appeal of Waxworks

'You perceive that this is some sort of holy of holiest, the nearest Victorians got to a cathedral, with its saints enniched within.'[1] This was a verdict given in 1918, not on a religious shrine but on the Tussaud's waxworks. The history of Tussaud's is more than the story of a family business. The development of waxworks reflects changes in the popular culture of France and Britain. Waxworks were an element of the promenade culture of the late eighteenth and the first half of the nineteenth century; it was an ideal opportunity for a family to engage in rational recreation and display itself. Wax sculpture made itself part of easily understood popular science, contributing a little to fashions such as phrenology and physiognomy. Later, with some setbacks, Tussaud's successfully embraced, and came to play a major rôle in mass family entertainment.

Even a casual visitor to Tussaud's in London, plying the usual tourist route, once within the exhibition cannot help but be affected by a variety of emotions. Even those that are there for a giggle with a group of mates, larking around taking photos of each other next to unlikely celebrity companions, the tomb-like atmosphere of the Chamber of Horrors in the basement still throws a pall of clammy silence over the party. Wax gives both a sense of the permanence of death with the illusion of life and the irrational suspicion that, under the waxen layer, life (or death) is uncannily preserved. The surface has a sheen and appears to glow from within, very like a live person. The slender 'corpse' of Sleeping Beauty, ethereal yet erotic, visibly 'breathes', with the help of electricity. One visitor, a forty-year-old bank official, actually declared undying love for Philippe Curtius's first surviving model and begged to be allowed to work in the gallery to guard her. Tussaud's replied politely that psychological help would be more appropriate.[2]

There is nothing so fascinating for a human being as others of the species. What is gripping about a waxworks like Tussaud's is that the models are full size and the visitor can gaze at celebrities as familiar equals, a dream (or nightmare) come true. The duke of Wellington, a frequent visitor to Tussaud's, was particularly taken with the Chamber of Horrors. His explanation was 'Do not the murderers here represent fact?' Films, and particularly television, have not made 'live' waxworks irrelevant because waxworks allow customers to look at three-dimensional models of the media heroes who dominate the present-day exhibition for as long as pleases them. People can be snapped standing next to a favourite personality.

Why do people like to be photographed with a lump of dressed-up wax? The urge to have a laugh or show their friends that they are an associate of some celebrity, whether the Queen or Dame Edna Everage, is understandable. What of those who are snapped next to a mass murderer? This question was put to Dr Anthony Storr, the famous psychiatrist, who suggested that people are fascinated because they recognise their own capacity for evil. All those photographs taken snuggling up to stars must be a dreadful disappointment. Wax models are not photogenic. The effect of light on wax is very different to its impact on a plaster cast. Wax does not reflect light but absorbs it and it is almost impossible to take a good snap of a wax portrait.

A skimming of wax cuts out the air, preserving anything from jam to statues. In the eighteenth century the statues in the Tuileries Gardens in Paris were coated with coloured wax to protect the stone. The wax layer was stripped off and renewed each year,[3] apparently leaving more sensitive onlookers with a sensation that the skin of the statues was being torn away, a vision of torment and destruction alongside preservation. A layer of wax, like the coating of gold paint on the anti-heroine of James Bond's *Goldfinger*, might as easily mean death as life. The sensation that Tussaud's five hundred models are so many graveyard reliquaries provokes only a momentary shiver among the visitors, no longer raised on old norms of the funereal use of wax. The ages old perception that wax was intimately linked to remembering the dead has, however, not entirely faded. In 1978 Tussaud's were asked to make a wax model of Evita Peron (1919–52), the wife of a former Argentinian president, hugely popular with working people in her life and a cult figure after her death.

A lasting impression on contemporary visitors to Tussaud's is the illusion of truth and realism. Important documents, even now, are stamped with a wax seal to confirm their genuineness. Does some of this seriousness rub off on wax models? Madame Tussaud and her heirs always sought to affirm realism. They surrounded their wax statues with their own possessions, whether murderers or monarchs. From the start in Paris, the wax replica wore either the subject's actual clothes or exact copies. Curtius, and later Madame Tussaud in London, paid large sums to court dressmakers to secure the latter. At Tussaud's two rooms of Napoleonic memorabilia, unsurpassed by anything in Paris, surrounded the emperor's model, all accompanied by signed documents attesting to their authenticity. Probably few visitors paid much attention to Tussaud's claims of to be historically accurate, but more were impressed by the high cost of the memorabilia. The 1850 catalogue boasted:

> It has been the constant endeavour of Madame Tussaud and Sons to bear in mind that exhibitions have a great influence on the public taste, they have, in consequence, spared no expense to give youth an idea of those gorgeous palaces, which fall to the lot of few to possess.[4]

Madame Tussaud believed she provided entertainment, artistic enlightenment, historical education and a place of pilgrimage. She described her Napoleon rooms as a shrine and the contents as relics. Her Wellington tableau was virtually worshipped and other models, including Baden-Powell, founder of the Scouts, were regarded by customers with great reverence. Today the most touched figure is Joanna Lumley, though whether the motive is reverence is anyone's guess. While a rival, Grévin, exploited a wax collection at Lourdes, Tussaud's have always been careful to avoid this type of religious display and to remember that, whatever their origins, they were operating in a Protestant state.

Waxworks have been described as being at the intersection of the culture of museums and commercial spectacle.[5] Wax sculpture certainly became an element in nineteenth-century museums. Small items of wax portraiture, miniatures and small busts were displayed in museums in Germany and in establishments devoted to a mixture of elite and popular culture, such as the Musée Carnavalet in Paris. The Victoria and Albert Museum acquired a collection of wax miniature portraits. Such objects, however, justified their place by their historical credentials. A waxworks was a different matter. Madame Tussaud always called her establishment a museum, and this was justified by Tussaud's by the high proportion of museum-style, unique artefacts. After the loss of many of these items in the 1925 fire, it was referred to simply as 'the Exhibition'. Nineteenth-century visitors may have thought of it as a museum. The period saw the proliferation of museums, which were universally regarded as monuments to bourgeois culture, alongside a kaleidoscopic array of manifestations of popular culture, from circuses to magic lantern shows, providing entertainment appealing to the 'popular classes'. The former were apparently dominated by artistic considerations of good taste, subsidised by taxation; the latter designed as spectacles and driven by commercialism.[6]

Like the civic museums that mushroomed in the nineteenth century, Madame Tussaud aspired to an elite clientele, but in reality attracted a middle-class one, who enjoyed the snobbery of 'mingling with the mighty'.

Very few models were put on pedestals. Tussaud's visitors meandered among almost all the models face to face. Museums, in contrast, made themselves socially exclusive by demanding certain standards of dress and behaviour. Madame Tussaud operated a similar policy by pricing. During her touring days the 'popular classes' were admitted at half-price only at unpopular times. On the other hand, Madame Tussaud and her successors never forgot that the visitors paid their wages. She herself always manned the cash desk, watching the money, but also ensuring her customers were satisfied. She established a Tussaud's tradition never forgotten, that everything had a price.

Actual historical artefacts not only put Tussaud's in a similar league to a museum, it reinforced the wax illusion of reality. Conscious that wax models themselves were not themselves the stuff of museums (the only ancient part is the original plaster mould, which is not on display), Madame Tussaud, following the example of her mentor, Curtius, introduced authentic items. She wanted her exhibition to form part of the historical record, and always displayed documentary authentication for her purchases. Her Napoleon rooms were the real beginning of this development, when the 'new', 'novel', 'modern' wax effigy was mingled with actual things Napoleon had used, even with parts of his body. His real tooth and hair lay close to his waxen image, which was dressed, slept or rode in the emperor's own possessions. A visitor could feel much closer to Napoleon in Baker Street than in Les Invalides, where his remains are housed.

Tussaud's played an important part in shaping the popular image that the British had of the French, in particular the main figures in the Revolution and of course Napoleon. There were the models, their outfits, artefacts and paintings. Visitors carried away with them not only memories but also the Tussaud's catalogue. The first edition in 1803 was dominated by France. There were thirteen pages of biographical detail on Napoleon alone, concluding with an uncompromising condemnation of political violence and dictatorship. In 1822, a year after the emperor's death in exile on St Helena, when Marie was staging a spectacular display of his coronation copied from David's famous portrait, her catalogue recorded, 'he who once could make the mightiest monarchs tremble ... at last became himself an object of pity'.[7] By 1834, as the Napoleonic myth built up, the catalogue became more appreciative.

> No age or country has produced a more astonishing man than Napoleon Bonaparte. Unlike his person, which was small, his mind was that of a giant. Like the eagle, his famous emblem, he towered over the common race of men.[8]

Although the figures themselves may have been maintained unchanging, the Tussaud's interpretation of individuals responded to political circumstances. Robespierre is a fascinating case. In Marie's first catalogue he earned eleven pages.

> It was the idea of his virtue, and the confidence in his principles, that procured him the unbounded esteem of a corrupt age; vested with supreme authority he threw off the character of humanity and became a demon.[9]

By 1861 there was not a whiff of esteem.

> A sanguinary demagogue ... of all the kinds of monsters who figured in the French Revolution none has descended to posterity with a name so abhorred as Robespierre; the crimes he committed were so horrible in nature that they have handed down his character to future ages as the guiltiest of the guilty.[10]

The French edition was more guarded, 'among those figures who gave rise to the French Revolution, none has been more demonised and more deified'.[11]

The early catalogues were sympathetic to the French royal family as individuals, but accepted that the Revolution had been necessary. Little of this altered until 1892, when George Sala rewrote and enlarged the entire catalogue. Marie-Antoinette was revered as a totally innocent heroine. 'There are some stories so dreadful in the immensity of human misery which they reveal – there are some tragedies of which the catastrophe is one of such unmitigated horrors.'[12]

Two major focuses of the Tussaud's exhibition were France and monarchy. In addition to interpreting the French for British audiences, a task for which their visitors believed them eminently qualified, they played a not insignificant part, as self-avowed champions of royalty, in reconciling popular opinion to monarchy. It did not take Madame Tussaud long to make and eulogise a substantial, though not particularly admirable, collection of British royals. When the exhibition settled in Baker Street, the succession of Victoria was a godsend and every possible angle of the young queen and her family was exploited.[13]

Violent crime, the third and most vital element in Tussaud's' success in the nineteenth century, became an 'adjoining room', a 'separate exhibition', finally the Chamber of Horrors. Many customers knew a little of phrenology and physiognomy, popular semi-scientific creeds of the day, but the Tussaud's were careful to allow customers to make connections between these theories and their individual villains, without themselves imposing science or pseudo-science on them. Tussaud's were content to offer fast and accurate representations of recent murderers. Marie's successors were almost as scrupulous as the police in their investigation of crime, attending court hearings, taking notes, making drawings and negotiating the purchase of suitably shocking artefacts. They were so successful that the new genre of novel, the detective mystery, was not infrequently set in Tussaud's or involved wax deceptions. In 1872 Tussaud's announced the recent acquisition of their 'Collection of Instruments of Torture'. They claimed with delight that the previous owner had refused offers from Monsieur Herberte, the long-serving director of French prisons, arguing 'Tussaud's were the first to preserve to history and science relics like these, the most curious in existence'. The collection contained thirty-nine articles of torture, ranging from an iron chair in which

> the victim was seated and sustained by the front bar, then by another vertical bar, while two rings fastened the ankles below; in the upper portion there is a collar for the neck and then another transverse bar passing through the first, and fitted at each extremity with a ring holding the wrists, while underneath the seat is a stove.

Then there was the 'Gressillon' hand-crusher, a mask of ignominy and a hog's mask, either of which could be put over the heads of unfaithful husbands, who were then marched through the street. There was a thumb-screw, tongue pincers and several instruments of torture used the previous year by the government to torment supporters of the Paris Commune.[14] Madame's claim to teach history carried conviction for many of her visitors, even those involved in writing about the past professionally. Hilaire Belloc attested to the serious contribution Tussaud's made to the understanding of history.

> I have known the collection from my very earliest childhood and I may tell you that I have visited it with the special object of recording the immediate physical impressions produced upon contemporaries by various personalities of the French Revolution of which I was writing. I do think it of the highest historical importance.[15]

What was displayed was an intimately corporeal biographical history. The form of the body and the clothes the person had worn were set, as a bee in amber, for eternity, never ageing, never deteriorating. This itself was an illusion. The wax, hair and clothing were regularly cleaned, very frequently if the visitors thought a lot of the person and habitually touched the model. Models were almost weighed down by the quality and quantity of their costumes. You would never see a king without his coronation robes. New paint, new clothing, hair and wax maintained the impression of the subject being everlasting. Wax was one-dimensional history in a three-dimensional mould. Visitors might imagine how the person thought, but the body made no demands on their intellectual faculties in the way in which a written record does. The appeal of wax history is very democratic.

Tussaud's history lessons transcended and denied time. Models were grouped to suit a theme, not chronology. All the kings and queens of England were put together and could have whispered across the centuries in their wax display. Academic historians might mock Tussaud's history, less so now than in the past perhaps, but many British people saw history, particularly their own and that of their closest neighbour France, through Tussaud's eyes. For most people history is biography, the story of famous people, and Tussaud's always excelled in portraying them. The nineteenth-century British press loved history Tussaud-style. On 14 July 1883, when the new Marylebone Road Exhibition opened, the *Daily Telegraph* noted that the new Grévin gallery was useless as a guide to the past, in contrast to Tussaud's, whose figures were so correctly portrayed and dressed that they would be an ideal aid for a teacher. The portrayal of famous people in history at Tussaud's was favourably compared with the most reputable biographical dictionary.[16]

That Tussaud's offered painless history and current affairs instruction with a leavening of fear, was not enough to explain the popularity of the exhibition. Just before Tussaud's moved from Baker Street *Chambers's Journal* devoted a leading article of four and a half columns to 'Wax Humanity'. They dismissed the relevance of simple likeness to celebrities in an age of photographs. No one could be persuaded to pay a fraction what people paid to go to a waxworks simply to look at a photograph album. Nor were they convinced that people went to gaze at the costumes, however gorgeous, costly and correct in detail they were as at Tussaud's. Nor could they believe that English people were enthused by statues, 'most statues of famous men are … unintentional libels in sooty bronze or unmanageable colossal stone'.

The secret of the appeal of wax, in the journalist's view, lay in the liberation of the observer from all normal rules of politeness and consideration of others. Visitors could walk up to a succession of lifelike kings and queens, stare at them, and talk about them frankly for as long as they liked. As royalty came in for criticism in nineteenth-century Britain, the waxworks gave embryonic republicans a chance to let off steam. Then there was the unique chance to go up to a politician, without him being able to buttonhole you with his views. The attraction of wax was 'the similitude of the figures to life'. Yet, the author objected, as if himself addressing one of the models, wax figures were always 'sorry imitations of the reality'. Modellers were reluctant to reproduce the imperfections of their subjects. He exempted only two of Tussaud's figures, Oliver Cromwell, who stood four-square, warts and all, and David Livingstone, convincingly covered in dust, as betokened an explorer: 'the pleasure of delusion is complete'. One of the biggest problems, for painter or modeller, of reproducing human skin tones or texture, was solved in these instances. The silence of apparently talking figures was oppressive; you could never catch the eye of a wax model. The article concluded with a familiar media rant against the Chamber of Horrors – the educated writer disapproved of the fact that this was the biggest attraction of Tussaud's.[17] In 1907 another journalist and writer Max Beerbohm, famous for his caricatures of celebrities, expressed his dislike of the Horrors more passionately:

> What is it that pervades this congress of barren effigies? Why is there an atmosphere so sinister, so subtly exhaustive? They frightened me when I was a little child. In a sense they frightened me again ... I could not tear myself from their company ... the orchestra playing lively tunes did but intensify the gloom and horror of the exhibition ... Had they some devils' power of their own, some mesmerism ... It flashed upon me, as I watched them, they were stealing my life from me, making me one of their own kind.

Even Dickens, who in *All the Year Round* in 1860 remarked that Tussaud's was 'something more than an exhibition, it is an institution', also commented on 'the profound and awful misery of the place, which provides the Englishman with an entertainment which does not make him happy'.

Whether Tussaud's merited moral indignation or feelings of terror, it was perennially popular as a setting for novels, plays and films. Arnold Bennett sent two of his main characters, Violet and Henry, in his 1923 novel, *Riceyman's Steps*, to visit Tussaud's after their wedding breakfast.

> There was no disturbing precocity in the attitude of sightseers, who did not care a fig what 'art' was ... They had the wit to put it in its place and keep it there. 'I'm sure it's a very nice place', Violet observed. There was a spacious Victorianism about the interior and especially about the ornate branching staircase ... 'crowds of respectable people, solid people, no riff-raff, no wastrels, adventurers, flighty persons. It's a very nice place – they're much better than audiences at cinemas'.
>
>   What interest there was in the stories told, and the human side, not the historic importance ... Magna Carta, the foundation stone of British liberty? NO! But the death of Nelson, Gordon's last stand, the girl Victoria getting news of her accession, the execution of Mary, Queen of Scots? Yes, *100 per cent* success everyone.

Bennett acutely summarised the appeal of Tussaud's for many customers. It *was* a decent and safe place to visit, with no risk of being importuned by beggars or worse. Bennett's account of what visitors liked about the artistic side of Tussaud's was also shrewd, including the imposing and obviously expensive entrance hall. Customers related to the humanity of people in the past; details of chronology and 'significant' themes washed over them. Madame Tussaud herself would have approved of Bennett's description of her exhibition. Tussaud's kept assiduous records of such references to their show in the archives ranging from the Grossmiths' *The Diary of a Nobody*, to Graham Greene, – even Paddington Bear, who tries to put his melted chocolate bar in the hand of a model and finds it is a real attendant.

Victorian interest in wax figures was reflected in their frequent appearance in one of the most popular contemporary forms of fiction, the detective novel. Sir Arthur Conan Doyle was the star guest at a dinner held to celebrate the centenary of Madame Tussaud's arrival in Britain. It can be no coincidence that he lodged his own hero, Sherlock Holmes, in Baker Street just around the corner from the Chamber of Horrors. In his tales he used a wax Sherlock Holmes on several occasions to throw his enemies off the scent. Both in 'The Empty House',[18] and in 'The Mazarin Stone', a wax model of Sherlock Holmes (French-made of course) plays a not insignificant role in preserving the great detective's life.

> It was, therefore, an empty room into which Billy, a minute later, ushered Count Sylvius. The famous game-shot, sportsman, and man-about-town was a big swarthy fellow with a formidable dark moustache, shading a cruel, thin-lipped mouth, and surmounted by a long, curved nose, like the beak of an eagle ... As the door closed behind him he looked round him with fierce, startled eyes, like one who suspects a trap at every turn. Then he gave a violent start as he saw the impassive head and the collar of the dressing gown which projected above the armchair in the window ... He took one more glance round to see that there were no witnesses, and then, on tip-toe, his thick stick half raised, he approached the silent figure. He was crouching for his final spring and blow when a cool, sardonic voice greeted him from the open bedroom door:
> 'Don't break it, Count!'[19]

An entire Sherlock Holmes mystery, *The Adventure of the Wax Gamblers*, developed by his grandson from one of Holmes's unsolved cases, was set in the Chamber of Horrors. The playing cards in the hand of a wax gambler are used to convey inside information on guaranteed winners in horse races. The ruse is only discovered when an investigator notices that the cards the model holds have changed.[20]

Fiction writers were invariably intrigued by wax tales of mystery, suspense and horror, never by wax celebrities, however glamorous. *The Waxworks* (1922) by W. L. George told the tale of a young couple visiting a waxworks one rainy afternoon and being scared almost out of their wits.

> Henry Badger rapidly paced the City churchyard; his air of anxiety seemed to overweigh his small, though not unpleasing, features, he was an insignificant

little man, dressed in pepper-and-salt tweeds. His hair was cut very close, except where a love-lock, plastered down with jasmine-oil, trailed over his forehead from under his hard black hat. Whenever he completed the circuit of the churchyard he peered towards the gate through which must come disturbance and romance. Henry Badger was in love, and he could not escape the consequences of his share in our common delight and affliction.

Suddenly brightness overspread his sharp features. It was she! She, in a pink crêpe-de-Chine blouse, disconnected rather than connected with her white serge skirt by a patent-leather belt. Above the pink blouse was an equally pink neck, and a rather pretty face, all soft curves ... her name was Ivy, and she liked to live in harmony.

Henry has been reading *Strange Sights of London* and decides they should visit the docks. An omnibus has just dropped them in totally unknown territory in the East India Dock Road when it starts to rain. Henry sees a battered sign 'To the Waxworks. Mrs Groby, Proprietress'.

Henry seized the door handle, which resisted for a moment. The door jammed, but with a great effort he forced it open. It made a great clatter as he flung it against the wall. Breathless, and wiping their wet faces, the two stood giggling in the hall. Then, feeling alone, suddenly they kissed. The excitement of the run and of the caress sheltered them against an impression which the place imposed upon them only by degrees. They were in the hall of a house, of a house like any other house. There was no noise, except for a slight sound. It felt deserted. The door handle on the right was covered with dust. Nobody had gone into that room for a long time. An unaccountable emotion developed in them. The house was still except that at last they identified the slight sound: far away a tap was leaking. They found themselves listening to the drip which came regularly from the basement ... Ivy began to look about herself with unexplainable anxiety. The darkness of the stairs, the banisters broken in several places, the dusty door handle, stirred in her a vague fear; she looked about her like a cat in a strange place and preparing to flee. As the feeling communicated itself to Henry his manliness revolted. It would be too silly to have the jumps. So he said: 'Ive, since we're here, why not go upstairs and see the show'.

In the attic they find the figures of Charles Peace, Dr Crippen and other murderers and small tableaux.

One of the groups comprised a man and a woman in a pink flanelette dressing-gown. With an expression of pinched determination the murderer was forcing the female figure down into a bath, where a sheet of mica, tinted green, represented water. In the grasp of a bony hand, the female figure held the edge of the bath, wildly raising the other arm, while into her distorted mouth floated the green edge of the water that was to drown her, It was a work of art of indescribable horror. It was as if the snake-like fingers moved, as if in another moment the head would disappear under that still green surface.

With an exclamation Henry turned aside to the other group, that stood dim within the shadow, away from the faint rays that fell through the skylight. This represented a very old woman, lying on her face, her white hair scattered and stained with blood, while kneeling over her, a sandbag still half-raised, was a short man in the clothes of the day, his face set and coated with a horrible scarlet flush.

Now a new sound made them start. It was the growing rain, pattering upon the skylight, as if goblins raced across it. In a sudden desire for union again they kissed, quickly falling apart, as if espied.

They turned away for a moment, fascinated, they did not know how, in this gallery of crime; the still things about them seemed to have a motion, a vibration of their own. They found themselves looking sharply into corners as if something were there after all, as if these were not creatures of wax, but actually poisoners, men and women experienced in violence and still capable of evil ... the second group gained in horror. It was not only the sight of the blood coagulated on the white hair, it was something else, something unnamable. The art of the sculptor had gone too far; here was mere and abominable reality. Real hair, and crouching above, with drooping eyelids, the figure of the murderer, ill-shaven and flushed with health. Something twisted in Ivy's body as she thought that upon the still mask she could discern beads of sweat.

... Then, in the far distance, they heard the front door slam.

The couple tear down the stairs and leave in terror. A pair of policemen on the beat stop the frightened couple. Ivy is convinced the figure clutching the sandbag had moved his arm. The policemen are inclined to believe that someone may have murdered the old woman. She lives alone and rumour has it that she kept all her money in the house. They are, however, dismissive of Ivy's terror.

Back in the attic, the policeman tries to persuade Ivy to touch the figure of the old woman to feel that it really is wax.

'Wax', said the policeman, 'you silly kid. That's only wax. And so's this wax', he added, as he bent down and negligently laid his hand upon the blood-stained white hair. But, in the same movement almost, the policeman jumped up and recoiled, his staring eyes glaring at his hand. For less than a second did he gaze at it; then, with a cry, as if seized by an ungovernable hysteria, he brought down his truncheon upon the head of the kneeling man, which under the blow, scattered into tiny fragments of tinted wax. [21]

The proprietress lay dead and her murderer had fled when Ivy and Henry arrived, pushing a wax model into his place.

Tussaud's may have been the inspiration for linking wax deception and detective skills, but other writers ranged beyond Baker Street. E. Nesbit's

'The Power of Darkness' is set in the Musée Grévin and adapted the apocryphal Tussaud's' tale that spending the night in the waxworks is the ultimate test in manly courage. Edward and Vincent, two old friends, studying art in Paris, fall for the lovely Rose, who, it is rumoured, is actually in love with Edward, but he is too timid to press his advantage. At the end of term, while waiting for their train, they go to the Musée Grévin.

> The Musée Grévin is a waxwork show. Your mind, at the word, flies to the excellent exhibition founded by the worthy Mme Tussaud. And you think you know what waxworks mean. But you are wrong. The Musée Grévin contains the work of artists for a nation of artists. Wax-modelled and retouched till it seems as near life as death is: that is what one sees at the Musée Grévin.
>
> 'Let's look in at the Musée Grévin,' said Vincent ... 'I hate museums', said Edward. 'This isn't a museum', Vincent said, and truly; 'it's just a waxworks'.

They investigate Grévin's version of the French Revolution and of the catacombs in ancient Rome. Later, over a drink, they bet each other, with Rose as the prize, that neither can spend the night in the waxworks. Vincent is confident of winning because he knows from their childhood that Edward is terrified of the dark. Edward agrees to give it a try when he gets back to Paris after the holidays. After Edward has left for his train Vincent decides to make sure he wins by spending that night at the *musée*, and so, after a good dinner, he goes back and settles down to sleep with the wax corpses in the catacombs.

> The silence was intense, but it was a silence thick with rustlings and breathings, and movements that his ear, strained to the uttermost, could just not hear. Suppose, as Edward had said, when all the lights were out these things could move? What if such conditions were present now? What if all of them – Napoleon, yellow-white from his death sleep; the beasts from the amphitheatre, gore dribbling from their jaws ... all were drawing near to him in this full silence.
>
> He felt for his matches and lighted a cigarette. The gleam of the match fell on the face of the corpse in front of him. The light was brief, and it seemed, somehow, impossible to look by its light in every corner where one would have wished to look. The match burned his fingers as it went out. And there were only three more matches in the box.
>
> It was dark again, and the image left on the darkness was that of the corpse in front of him ... His hand reached forward and drew back more than once. But at last he made it touch the bier and through the blackness travel up along a lead, rigid arm to the wax face that lay there so still. People always said the dead were 'waxen'.

Vincent hears other tiny rustles and sighs and decides to use his last three matches to light his path away from the noises to the exit, but in his terror he walks towards them.

> 'Bah', he said, and he said it aloud. 'The silly things are only wax. Who's afraid?'
> His voice sounded loud in the silence that lives with the wax people.
> 'They're only wax', he said again, and touched with his foot contemptuously the crouching figure in the mantle.
> And, as he touched it, it raised its head and looked vacantly, and its eyes were bright and alive. He staggered back against another figure and dropped the match. In the new darkness he heard the crouching figure move towards him. Then the darkness fitted in round him very closely.[22]

The moving figure is Edward, who has missed his train and also decides to win the bet that very night. The story ends well for Edward, who marries the fair lady, but Vincent spends the rest of his days in an lunatic asylum, convinced that all the attendants are made of wax.

Waxworks were not merely the setting for short stories, novels and plays, they are themselves a form of theatre. In the nineteenth century Tussaud's tableaux stimulated the *tableaux vivants* of the live theatre, when human actors imitated wax models. In 1962 Tussaud's made a wax army for a Sadlers Wells performance of Henry V for a live star-studied cast, including Peggy Ashcroft. It consisted of eighty wax heads on dummies, to be carried by forty live extras. In 1969 the Halifax Playhouse performed *1066 and All That* using Tussaud's models, which then 'came to life'. In 1994 a wax life of Madame Tussaud herself was put on in Cardiff and subsequently at the Lyric Theatre, Hammersmith.

Numerous feature films have used Tussaud's. The Chamber of Horrors has been a favourite venue for these. Alfred Hitchcock set part of his 1934 film *Night and Day* in the Horrors. In the same year Bernard Miles spent six nights filming *Midnight at Madame Tussaud's*. The 1936 Katherine Hepburn movie *A Woman Rebels*, based on a feminist novel about the Victorian 'new' woman, featured three scenes at Tussaud's. Tussaud's tableaux have also been used for British and French historical films. In 1946, when the Chamber of Horrors was replicated in a Paris film studio for *Corridor of Mirrors*, Tussaud's lent wax figures and the death masks of Louis XVI and Marie-Antoinette. When the French made a television series on Napoleon and the English, they shot their battle of Waterloo sequence at Tussaud's. The difference between a visit to Tussaud's and theatrical and television presentations is that visitors become part of the waxworks, respond to and consciously interact with the models in their behaviour as well as in their own minds.

The question whether people like wax models because they consider them works of art is more difficult to answer. Until the seventeenth century works of art were commissioned by the very wealthy, usually kings, princes and aristocrats, but also the wealthy bourgeoisie in rich areas such as Holland and the Italian city states. Art was for private consumption, to enjoy in one's own palace, to share with and impress a small group of friends. It was also for public display, mainly in religious ceremonial, in cathedrals and churches, to subdue the passions of the popular classes and gain merit with the Almighty for the rich contributor, although the artisans who built the cathedrals seem to have secured no public recognition. As we have seen, wax had a respected place, particularly on the religious front, in this world.

As trade and commercial development expanded, the numbers of those with spare cash increased and art of all kinds became accessible to a broader range of consumers. In all cultural spheres, from music to painting, and including wax, patronage spread beyond kings, aristocrats and clerics to other wealthy groups. Gradually culture entered a much wider market place, typified by annual public salons, public museums, art galleries and opera houses. The socialist idealist Charles Fourier, for instance, dreamt in the early nineteenth century of utopian communes of just over 1600 people, each with its own opera house. An entrepreneurial approach to art emerged with the rapidly expanding market. Many customers were happy to buy artistic objects which had been cheaply reproduced. The Curtius wax exhibitions and private sales of wax figures satisfied this market. In the eighteenth century high quality wax models, including anatomical ones, were considered collectors' items and works of art.

In the nineteenth century wax models were increasingly disregarded as art. Even the anatomical waxes which were made were inferior and very utilitarian. Until the Musée Grévin opened, waxworks had little appeal in France. By the nineteenth century the proliferation of public galleries, museums and concert halls created a wider audience for artistic endeavour, but comfortably off citizens, while accepting the need to educate the popular classes, were also keen to distinguish between themselves and those they considered their inferiors. Sharp distinctions between 'elite' and 'popular' culture proliferated. As the introduction of public galleries and exhibitions carried the risk that the elite might have to rub shoulders with the popular classes, high entry fees were charged and elaborate measures taken by the museums to keep art for the 'respectable' sector of society. There seems no doubt that what was art became narrowly defined precisely to exclude anything that might appeal to the 'popular' classes.

While Tussaud's successfully made itself a not insignificant element in the promenade culture of the middle classes in the first half of the nineteenth century, there seems little doubt that, as soon as they sought a mass audience, their middle-class clients adopted a more condescending and distant tone towards them. Waxworks were held at arm's length because they were regarded as mechanical representation, particularly as art itself became decreasingly representational. No one doubted that waxworks were part of popular culture, but whether they were art was another matter. The anatomical section of Louis Tussaud's waxworks in Blackpool housed some of Jacob Epstein's much-criticised early sculpture, notably *Jacob, Adam* and *Consummatum Est*,[23] but no one would have thought this made the waxworks an art gallery. Indeed the items were housed in the basement and were relegated there because they themselves were not considered art at the time.

Wax sculptors such as Curtius and later the Tussauds sought recognition as artists by working in other media. Madame Tussaud's grandson, Joseph Randall Tussaud, and his cousin, Francis Babbington, exhibited at the Royal Academy and subsequently made wax casts of these models for the waxworks. So did their sculptor neighbour in Marylebone, Adams Acton, who rented a studio from them. In 1878 Tussaud's displayed a wax cast of Acton's portrait of the caricaturist Cruikshank. Joseph Randall's son, John Theodore, showed a bust of George Augustus Sala, the journalist who compiled the Tussaud catalogue, at the Academy in 1891 and another marble bust of Tennyson two years later. Wax versions were displayed in Marylebone Road.[24]

Wax models as such did not easily fit into definitions of what was art. Few have any indication of who made them and with the passage of time identifying the sculptor can become impossible.[25] Endless wax models can be made from a mould. When is an 'original' wax model *the* genuine article? The Musée Carnavalet in Paris was delighted to claim in 1911 that they had acquired the head that Curtius had made immediately after Robespierre's execution,[26] which at first glance might have seemed to be a relic from the Boulevard du Temple *salon* gone missing for nearly sixty years. In 1911, however, John Theodore Tussaud, modeller in chief of the London exhibition, recorded in his journal that he had given a copy of the Robespierre head to the Carnavalet.[27] We also know that Madame Tussaud had included the head in her luggage in 1802 and it is still in the London Chamber of Horrors. With wax illusion is the only reality. There is no such thing as an original wax.

The plaster mould from which a wax model is cast is, in contrast, original and Tussaud's treasure their old moulds. Madame Tussaud claimed to have brought all of her and Curtius's interesting moulds to Britain and they still survive and are used. From the original mould, wax models are endlessly reproduced. Tussaud's store most of theirs at Acton. Before they sold them, they were also stored in Wookey Hole caves. As long as there was a market for private commissions, Madame Tussaud and other wax sculptors were delighted to sell copies of their work. The ability to renovate and remake wax figures is sometimes regarded as an indication that a wax sculpture does not therefore qualify as a work of art. But painters or their students often make several copies of their work, as do sculptors, and lithographs and modern prints fetch high prices. Old masters are constantly restored. Even exposed forgeries often have a financial value. Wax cannot be dismissed as a work of art because it can be copied, but the only response to a claim that a wax model is an 'original' must be a wry smile.

What of a model's 'props'? There were nearly as many 'original' Marat bathtubs as there were 'true crosses' on which Jesus died. The Eden *musée* in New York claimed to have acquired the original, as also did the Musée Grévin. Another problem with a wax model is that it is a team effort, not the work of one artist. Until recently the body was a rough skeleton. Clothes, make-up, hair, eyes are the work of other craftsmen. Only the original sculptor could be compared with an artist in bronze or stone.[28]

From the Renaissance onwards, sculptors worked in both wax as well as other mediums, often using wax for their preliminary efforts. Degas's famous dancer, of which there is a bronze copy in the Tate, began life in wax, and like a typical Tussaud figure, was dressed in a real tutu.[29] Unless carefully maintained and renovated, however, wax models deteriorate far more rapidly than works in stone or bronze, and thus few old waxes survive.

The fact that the wax was coloured and the models clothed troubled those accustomed to marble, bronze or other naked representations of humanity.[30] The smoothness of wax also offended delicate aesthetes. In 1919 the renowned art historian Roger Fry damned the revolutionary painter David by comparing his painting to a wax model: 'David had to invent for them that peculiarly distressing type of the ancient Roman, always in heroic attitudes, always immaculate, always spotless and with a highly polished "Madame Tussaud" surface.'[31] That the wax sculptor aimed at the most accurate representation of the individual, with no room for artistic licence, also told against wax models. For the cultured elite, wax lacked subtlety and depth. Snobbery was no small element in this value judgement. Wax had too many associations with the fairground and popular entertainment to be accepted as art.

The potential for deception, which was part of the realism of wax, disqualified it as an art form for some observers. A popular early twentieth-century writer of detective stories, Austin Freeman, made a wax sculptor the chief murder victim in his *The D'Arblay Mystery:*

> Wax-work is a fine art, but it differs from all the other fine arts in that its main purpose is one that is expressly rejected by all those other arts. An ordinary

work of sculpture, no matter how realistic, is frankly an object of metal, stone, or pottery. Its realism is restricted to truth of form. No deception is aimed at, but, on the contrary, is expressly avoided. But the aim of the wax-work is complete deception; and its perfection is measured by the completeness of the deception achieved.

Total realism is an integral part of the fun of Tussaud's, from the wax policeman to wax attendants.[32] In 1949 Richard Dimbleby recorded the BBC radio series, 'Down Your Way' in the Chamber of Horrors. Celebrities (presumably not murderers or victims) were invited to dress in the same outfit as their Tussaud's models and visitors were asked to guess which one was real. Wax models are certainly meant to deceive, but does that exclude them as works of art? How many works of art in other mediums are equally intent on trickery, and not merely on the level of Salvador Dali's clocks? Does it matter if the eye is deceived, whether by bronze, wax or paint?

It was not until commentators became concerned that art and culture had been defined too narrowly, and that more 'pop' democratic definitions were vital for marketing if for nothing else, that wax modelling began to be taken seriously, not only as a manifestation of popular culture, but also as art. The Musée Grévin consciously set the trend towards gaining recognition for wax as a medium for artistic expression when two well-known popular artists ran the gallery's workshop. The gallery was accepted as a quintessential reflection of Parisian boulevard culture. Tussaud's was very different. In 1903, when Tussaud's put on a celebrity dinner to celebrate their centenary in Britain, their guests included popular authors of the time like Conan Doyle, Edmund Gosse and W. W. Jacobs, but no artists or sculptors. After the 1925 fire overall planning of new settings, costumes and decorations was put in the hands of the famous artist and art historian Herbert Norris, a recognised master and the author of several books on costume. Norris was keen to make everything as historically accurate as possible. Joan of Arc had to be dressed in the correct suit of armour she would have worn.[33] Norris, however, was an exception.

Sculptors who worked in other materials were reluctant to admit that they had made wax models.[34] Tussaud's wax modellers, on the other hand, trained as sculptors. John Theodore's son, Bernard, and Jean Fraser, their leading sculptor after Bernard's death, learned the trade of wax modelling and undertook five years training at the Slade School of Sculpture. Bernard Tussaud insisted that a wax sculptor needed as much skill as any other artist and that many of the techniques used were identical to those employed by other sculptors. All began with a clay model. The only difference was that a wax sculptor finished his creation in wax, to which he added hair, glass eyes and colouring 'to add to verisimilitude'. Like a portrait painter, a wax sculptor faced the problem that producing a mechanically accurate representation was not enough, there was also a need to capture the character of the subject, perhaps conveyed in a fleeting smile, or the way in which the person's eyes flashed as they spoke. Men were easier to capture in wax than women. Their faces have more clearly defined planes and their characters could be conveyed in a single expression, while a woman's face was more mobile. In his view a good sculptor in wax was as much an artist as any other.[35]

When in 1967 Tussaud's employed the well-known sculptor Arthur Pollen to model Brigitte Bardot, he had no objection to his work being acknowledged.[36] Pollen became excited by the possibilities of wax. Two years before he had written to the world-famous sculptor Sir Henry Moore,

> I had never thought of Madame Tussaud's as something that something could be done about ... the near wizardry of Jean Fraser's [a Tussaud's' sculptor] Audrey Hepburn made my head swim with possibilities. *If* an effigy of Elizabeth II *could be* a genuine likeness, even a shining one, a small wave of wonder and interest in the whole waxwork thing could be started and a form of genuine pop art founded ... Then the possibility that likenesses could be 'expressionist'?

Pollen, however, never had the chance to explore the realistic and expressionist potential of wax as a manifestation of popular culture, because soon afterwards he lost his sight.

Lord Clark, a great expert on culture, was asked to speak at the Tussaud's bicentenary anniversary dinner in 1970. He began: 'The words waxworks and Madame Tussaud's have long been the harshest words that any aesthete could pronounce about a piece of painting or sculpture which displeased him.'[37] He then went on to praise the exhibition, but you might add he had little choice because Tussaud's had invited him to dinner.

Roy Strong, when director of the Victoria and Albert Museum, became a passionate publicist for Tussaud's. In 1966 he wrote, somewhat tongue-in-cheek, 'There is something irresistibly timeless about Tussaud's as though the clock had obstinately stopped at the high noon of Victorian history painting. Even the Beatles seem to have arrived by way of Millais's *Boyhood of Raleigh*'.[38] A year later, he had convinced himself of the cultural merits of the exhibition:

> Are we right in regarding Tussaud's as a travelling side show come to a sudden and unexpected halt in Baker Street? Displayed anywhere else than in the fun fair atmosphere of Tussaud's these would have been recognised years ago as a precious and unique collection. The Battle of Trafalgar as it happened is a new

spectacle, part theatrical, part waxwork, part academic ... Tussaud's, poised midway between Museum and Funpalace, can pioneer in a way denied to public institutions.

Strong became entranced by Jean Fraser's models of Arthur Hitchcock and Malcolm Muggeridge, and particularly by the bullfighter El Cordobes, a model made by James Butler, whose clothes were also made of wax. 'Staggering instances of the tradition of high academic realism at its best which suddenly seems absolutely right within this world of pop.'[39] Influenced by both Pollen and Strong, Henry Moore visited the exhibition shortly after this accolade. Other artists began to visit the exhibition. These gurus of contemporary culture became convinced that Jean Fraser, with her head of Nelson (1966) and her portrait of the lone yachtsman Francis Chichester, had indeed produced likenesses that were 'expressionist'. In 1972 Ian Nairn, another famous figure in the culture industry, observed in an article in the *Sunday Times*:

> The borderline between reality and illusion has disappeared. You are involved in something that is just a semitone away from life – and involved not in the way of personal fantasy, like the cinema. The waxworks act as catalysts between you and the other visitors. Something which modern theatre is attempting with greater pretensions and less success. The actual technique of modelling has altered too; the surfaces have become rougher, proving what the best painters have always known, that a slight distortion – not caricature is more real ... It all adds up to an experience which can be simple fun, or serious instruction, or great art, as it takes you.[40]

An affirmation that wax modelling was now being taken seriously by the academic world as well as by the 'quality' newspapers was the 1973 publication by Oxford University Press of E. J. Pyke's substantial work of historical research into the lives of wax modellers.[41] A further indication that attitudes to wax modelling had changed and that it was now regarded as art was a 1975 conference on wax sculpture held in Florence. A collection of academic papers were delivered and, to the delight of its directors, Tussaud's was the only commercial organisation to be invited. The conference was such a new departure, for Tussaud's as well as for the academic world, that the managing director of Tussaud's, Peter Gatacre, hesitated before he accepted the invitation. The pre-eminence of Tussaud's in the field of wax sculpture was acknowledged by the conference organiser, Dr Maria Luisa Azzoioli, who sought Gatacre's advice and an introduction from him to the curator of the collection of Florentine anatomical waxes at the Wellcome Museum.[42] Gatacre gave two papers, written in conjunction with two colleagues, one on Madame Tussaud's methods,[43] a second on portraiture in the exhibitions of both Curtius and Tussaud.⁴⁴ It was the first time any member of staff had given and published a paper at an academic conference.

A second international conference was held at the Victoria and Albert Museum in 1978 in conjunction with Tussaud's. The organisers were concerned that the first conference had been held in the Natural History Museum in Florence and that the vast majority of papers had been on anatomical waxes, only four representing the artistic qualities of wax as a medium. Roy Strong, the director of the Victoria and Albert Museum, by now a wax enthusiast, opened the proceedings. The world expert on wax modellers, E. J. Pyke, gave a paper in which he explained that, since the publication of his book on wax modellers in 1973, sixty-eight more private wax collections, twenty-nine public ones and sixty-four more wax sculptors, had come to light. There was a tour of the studios at Tussaud's, followed by a champagne reception for eighty participants. Gatacre and Jean Fraser gave talks on making full-size wax figures, but, ironically, not as Tussaud's employees. In June 1976 the directors decided that their managing director no longer fitted into the team.⁴⁵ Jean Fraser protested and went freelance. This sequence of events is indicative of the ambiguous self-image of waxworks, eager to be taken seriously – up to a point.

The Florence conference heralded a flurry of academic interest in wax modelling. A new extended edition of Pyke's dictionary of wax modellers was published in 1981. The duc d'Orléans's extensive collection, which like many other anatomical waxes had gathered decades of dust in Paris museums and the schools of medicine when wax models were superseded by other tools in the study of anatomy, was rescued from long neglect, restored, studied, written about and exhibited.⁴⁶ In 1990 the Musée d'Orsay ran a major exhibition on eighteenth-century and nineteenth-century body parts, including anatomical waxes, Le corps en morceaux, which displayed their elegance in spacious and well-lit surroundings. In the same year the salon for which the young Madame Tussaud had made models was included in an exhibition of Paris theatres during the 1789 Revolution shown at the Bibliothèque Historique de la Ville de Paris.⁴⁷

If the artistic, even academic, qualities of wax sculpture were being appreciated, Tussaud's themselves were encountering a serious problem in finding sculptors, either with craft or artistic skills. There were no more trained family members. It is interesting to speculate why there were no women wax sculptors between Madame Tussaud, who died in 1850, and June Jackson, who was taking a leading role in Tussaud's by 1948. The answer lies partly in the growing formal professionalisation in all skilled jobs. In occupations where a defined scheme of training emerged in the nineteenth century women were excluded from the programme.⁴⁸ Few parents would have been willing to pay for a girl to train, assuming that her adult life would be devoted to raising a family. Changes in the curricula of art schools also prevented men from qualifying to sculpt in wax. Science and art were increasingly divorced. Figurative or imitative art, which involved working from life and learning anatomy, were no longer an automatic part of an art school education, partly because of the daunting cost of obtaining models, partly because of artistic fashion. The collapse of apprenticeship schemes added to the problem. There was a shortage not only of students but also of qualified teachers of figurative sculpture. In 1975, as a solution to the desperate shortage of sculptors qualified to work for them, Tussaud's launched plans to offer prizes, bursaries or subsidies to students in art schools who were willing to train as wax sculptors.[49] In 1977 they offered scholarship funds of £750 at the Royal College of Art. Two of Tussaud's senior managers were appointed to the RCA panel to make the awards. £600 was given to a female painter and £150 to a woman training in ceramics. Both the *Times* and the *Financial Times* commended this initiative.[50] Perhaps in recognition of their efforts in the world of art, in October 1977 forty-nine people applied for posts as trainee sculptors at Tussaud's. Seven were interviewed and two appointed. The problem was not solved. When Tussaud's decided to set up offshoots in Las Vegas and New York they struggled to recruit a dozen extra sculptors to produce the required figures, one hundred and seventy respectively for the two exhibitions. One advertisement yielded fifty replies, but when the twenty-five who seemed most promising were invited to Acton to model a test head, only one produced a result of a high enough quality.

At the beginning of the twenty-first century profitability was paramount for Madame Tussaud Limited, as it had been for Marie Tussaud. Echoing ephemeral media razmatazz came first, recording the more serious aspects of the here and now and recalling the past was perhaps less compelling. Creating the illusion that the visitor was a participant, an actor in a vibrant show rather than a customer, was the unique objective that distinguished the waxworks from other entertainments. Its was achieved even more emphatically in 2002 than ever before. Models and visitors were so intimately physically mingled, and the quality of the figures had reached such sophistication, that the two were almost indistinguishable.

Relics, shrine, topical theatre – the fame of illusion for Tussaud's has always been interactive, something that museums were slow to develop. The paying customers could bounce in the Waterloo coach imagining themselves as the Great Emperor or the Ogre Boney. From 1993 they toured Victorian London on skeleton black cabs – going much faster than a real taxi could travel. In 2002 they could feel as well as see how wax models were made. All the stars that television, film and magazines such as *Hello* had taught them to regard as part of their lives could be studied in detail, and fantasy relationships recorded by photography. Wax adapted itself brilliantly to the fleeting, fickle, ephemeral glamour of pop culture. Tableaux were replaced by visual and audio clips and an actual journey through British history. British royalty was not forgotten. Tussaud's had its own public condolence book after the death of the Queen Mother. The Jubilee was used for an interactive game.

Madame Tussaud herself was still the spiritual president of the exhibition, but her image changed. Tussaud's visitors would not be interested in her improbable claims to have lived at Versailles or to have been imprisoned, shorn for the guillotine, and miraculously released at the end of the Terror. In 2002 she was shown in the Chamber of Horrors as an innocent girl, modelling the victims of the guillotine. What was stressed in the most recent entry in a national biographical dictionary was an impecunious migrant who, by her showmanship, artistry and business acumen, became the most successful businesswoman in the country. 'Her wax self-portrait, made at the age of eighty-one, bears the marks of a hard life and the determination that carried her through. It still presides over the exhibition today.'[51]

An additional appeal of Tussaud's in 2002 perhaps lies in the world scale and variety of entertainment offered, in Britain with the waxworks and planetarium in London, Alton Towers, Warwick Castle, Chessington World of Adventure and Thorpe Park. There are also Tussaud's exhibitions in Amsterdam, Las Vegas, New York and Hong Kong. Madame Tussaud would have been proud of the advertising. In 2001 BT was enlisted, with numerous full-size advertisement urging customers to skip the queue by booking on the phone or on-line. Tussaud's advertising was targeted at children and parents at weak moments when they struggled into their cornflake packets, guaranteeing them free tickets for one junior cereal eater. Madame Tussaud's expectation that she would educate the young was, however, sidelined in the search for the fastest big-dipper and the most vertical descent. Detailed biographical catalogues listing every model gave way to shiny, brightly-coloured self-advertisment, with little real information. Madame's desire to limit entrance to the prosperous middle classes emerged anew; in 2002 an annual family pass cost £219. Admittedly this would take the family to all the Tussaud's venues in Britain, Park Asterix in France and theme parks in Holland, Sweden and Germany. Tussaud's marketing was hard to escape and was an integral part of the itinerary of every organisation running mass tourism. No self-respecting beaver, cub, scout, rosebud, brownie or guide could avoid a visit to at least one of Tussaud's venues and no foreign visitor could return home without tales of the waxworks. Despite revolutionary changes in the structure and size of the business, the waxworks in Marylebone Road was the linchpin of the business and continued to draw the biggest crowds. This all illustrates the triumph of publicity, but does not explain why waxworks have survived the explosion of the visual media which has taken place since Madame Tussaud set sail for England.

This book began by noting that the age-old tradition of modelling in wax has always inspired the onlooker with an awareness of the omnipresence of death, at times linked with a morbid sensuality, and often with a sense of the conflict between truth and falsehood, realism and deception. The Tussaud's waxworks have survived and prospered because they have denied mortality, have rarely acknowledged the erotic potential of wax and have unceasingly and joyously exploited the potential for fun of innocent deception in realistic representation. Tussaud's is no tomb; all of the models, however long dead, affirm their life. Tussaud has always rejected anatomical wax models, which, however instructive, twist death and sex together in an uneasy combination. Sleeping Beauty has undertones of corpse-like eroticism, but to overcome that she ostentatiously 'breathes' and is fully clothed. There is evil and terror, but this is kept under control in the basement. Tussaud's is a reassuring microcosm of successful social order – even more cathartic today than in Victorian times. For many visitors the chance to touch total strangers is compelling, but nostalgia – or to use the more fashionable word memory – may still sell most tickets.

Notes

Notes to Chapter 1: The Origins of Wax Modelling

1. The contents of such a tomb were discovered in 1852 and are now in the museum of archaeology in Naples. I. Schlosser, *Histoire du portrait en cire* (Paris, 1997), p. 16. Schlosser, who died in 1938, ran the well-known Kunsthistorisches Museum in Vienna, which was the first public art museum in the world. His account of the history of wax figures seems to be a more reliable source than many.
2. R. Altick, *The Shows of London* (Cambridge, Massachusetts, 1976), p. 93. Anyone interested in the varied range of different public shows, from art exhibitions to public gardens, should read this book, which is an erudite and entertaining guide. My footnotes will frequently acknowledge my debt and thanks to this volume for information on non-wax entertainment.
3. L. Lambton, *A-Z of Britain*, p. 135.
4. R. Richardson, *Death, Dissection and the Destitute* (London, 1987).
5. L. Deer, 'The Doctor and the Waxworks: Wax Models and the Teaching of Anatomy in Britain in the Eighteenth and Nineteenth Centuries', *International Conference on Wax-Modelling*, Victoria and Albert Museum, 1978.
6. The illustrated catalogue available at the exhibition has a summary sheet in English.
7. The Josephinium was renovated in the 1960s. The collection was restored by the sculptor Willy Kaner and the present catalogue was created. E. Lesky, 'The Viennese Collection of Wax Models in the Josephinium', *Biblioteca della revista di storia delle scienze mediche e naturali*, 20 (1977), *Atti del I congresso internazionale sulla ceroplastica nella scienza e nell'arte* (Florence, 1975).
8. A glance at the illustrations in M. Lemire, *Artistes et mortels* (Paris, 1990) will confirm this opinion.
9. F. Cagnetta, *International Conference on Wax-Modelling*, Victoria and Albert Museum, 1978.
10. J. Clair (ed.), *L'âme au corps arts et sciences, 1793–1993* (Paris, 1993).
11. Lemire, *Artistes et mortels*.
12. L. Nead, *Victorian Babylon: People, Streets and Images in Nineteenth-Century London* (New Haven and London, 2001), p. 178.
13. Deer, 'The Doctor and the Waxworks'.
14. See below, Chapter 6.

15. How did these nubile wax lovelies fit into eighteenth-century debates on the role of women? They seem to conform to Rousseau's maxim in *Emile* that women should confine themselves to breast feeding their offspring and providing their early education. He was not happy that wealthy educated women were spending time running *salons* and influencing politics. In the French Revolution a tiny minority of women and a few men demanded that women should have equal rights with men. By the 1820s protests against the 'Venuses' began to appear in the press, although these were more indicative of moral outrage than protests about the passivity of the wax models.

16. L. Jordanova, *Sexual Visions: Images of Gender in Science and Medicine between the Eighteenth and Twentieth Centuires* (Hemel Hempstead, 1989), pp. 44–55.

17. J. Timbs, *Curiosities of London Exhibiting the Most Rare and Remarkable Objects of Interest in the Metropole with Nearly Sixty Years of Personal Recollections* (London, 1868), p. 35.

18. T. Frost, *The Old Showmen, and the Old London Fairs* (London, 1874), p. 31. For the survival of traditions see M. Judd, '"The Oddest Combination of Town and Country": Popular Culture and the London Fairs, 1800–1860', in J. K. Walton and J. Walvin, ed., *Leisure in Britain, 1780–1939* (Manchester, 1983), p. 22.

19. Altick, *The Shows of London*, p. 50.

20. W. Wordsworth, *The Prelude*, vii, 'Residence in London', in W. J. Brown, ed., *The Fourteen Book Prelude* (Ithaca and London, 1985), p. 156.

21. John Evelyn's diary quoted in Altick, *The Shows of London*, p. 50.

22. I. Schlosser, *Histoire du portrait en cire* (Paris, 1997), pp. 116–17.

23. L. Claretie in *L'intermédiare des chercheurs et curieux*, 27 (1877), p. 511.

24. J. Adhémar, 'Les musées de cire en France: Curtius, le banquet royal, les têtes coupées', *Gazette des Beaux Arts*, 92 (1978), pp. 206–7.

25. Clarétie, *L'intermédiare des chercheurs et curieux*, 27 (1877), p. 51.

26. A. Ward, *A List of Waxes in the Victoria and Albert Museum* (London, 1978).

27. Both the Victoria and Albert Museum and the Wallace Collection have good examples of these models.

28. R. Reilly, *Josiah Wedgwood* (London, 1992), p. 193; G. Le Breton, 'Essai historique sur la sculpture en cire', *Académie de Rouen: Classe de Belles Lettres* (1894), p. 295.

29. E. J. Pyke, 'A Biographical Dictionary of Wax Modellers', *Biblioteca della revista di storia delle scienze mediche e naturali*, 2 (1977), p. 572, 'Atti del I congresso internazionale sulla ceroplastica nella scienza e nell'arte' (Florence, 1975).

30. E. J. Pyke, *A Biographical Dictionary of Wax Modellers* (Oxford, 1973), p. 55.

31. *Daily Telegraph*, 14 July 1883.

32. Sylvester's handbill, Guildhall Museum; quoted in Altick, *The Shows of London*, p. 54.

33. K. A. Eustace, 'A Handlist of Waxes in the Victorian and Albert Museum' (1978), typescript, Madame Tussaud's Archives.
34. 'Seventeenth- and Eighteenth-Century Wax Shows', Madame Tussaud's Archives.
35. Altick, *The Shows of London*, p. 54.
36. A. Guépin, 'Faits divers', 1833 (a brief diary of main events in his life) in Guépin papers, Archives Départementales, Loire Atlantique 19J4.

Notes to Chapter 2: The Wax Salon

1. 'Madame Tussaud's Life in France', Lady Chapman's notes for Edward Gatacre. (Madame Tussaud's Archives, n.d.). Lady Chapman was the first full-time Tussaud's archivist. She not only organised the archives but also set to work to check details about the origins and history of the firm. She wrote several books about Madame Tussaud using the published memoirs.
2. Archives Nationales, Z1J1169.
3. A. Monester, *Les grands affaires criminelles* (Paris, 1988), pp. 98–99.
4. Illustrations survive in the Musée des Arts et Traditions Populaires in Paris.
5. M. Willson Disher, *The Greatest Show on Earth* (London, 1937).
6. R. W. Isherwood, *Farce and Fantasy: Popular Entertainment in Eighteenth-Century Paris* (Oxford, 1986), p. 171.
7. Orléans family papers, Archives Nationales, R4.821*.
8. *Tableau du nouveau Palais Royal* (Paris, 1788), p. 97.
9. The first mention of his *salon* was in the *Journal de Paris*, 8 December 1784.
10. *Almanach général de tous les spectacles de Paris* (Paris, 1791), p. 266; 'A propos du cabinet de Curtius ...', manuscript notes, Papiers Farge, 1, 'Le Palais Royal', fol. 57, Bibliothèque Historique de la Ville de Paris, MS 1650.
11. L. Fontaine, *History of Pedlars in Europe* (Cambridge, 1996), p. 76.
12. E. and J. Goncourt, *Histoire de la société française pendant la Révolution* (Paris, 1854), p. 233.
13. Goncourt, *Histoire de la société française pendant la Révolution*, p. 233.
14. L.-S. Mercier, *Tableau de Paris*, 12 vols (Paris, 1782–88), iii, p. 42.
15. Isherwood, *Farce and Fantasy*, p. 161.
16. *Affiches, annonces et avis divers*, 7 February 1783.
17. *Aventures parisiennes: almanach nouveau, galant, historique, moral et chantant sur les plus jolis airs, mélangé de nouvelles chansons, d'anecdotes plaisants, de contes, d'épigrammes, de bons mots etc* (Paris, 1784).
18. *Almanach général de tous les spectacles de Paris*, p. 266.
19. A. F. Cradock, *Journal de Madame Cradock: Voyage en France, 1783–1786*, trans. O. Delphin-Baileyguier (Paris, 1896), pp. 5–6, 59–60. I am grateful to Madame Eveline Léver, the biographer of Marie-Antoinette, for drawing my attention to Mrs Cradock's eulogy of the *salon de cire*.
20. F. W. J. Hemmings, *The Theatre Industry in Nineteenth-Century France* (Cambridge, 1993), p. 80.

21. *Journal encyclopédique ou universel* (December 1777), vii, part 3 and viii, parts 1 and 3; Papiers Farge, MS 1650, pp. 33, 35; *Journal de Paris* (8 December 1784), 'Curtius au Palais Royal'.

22. Theveneau de Morande, *Le vol plus haut ou l'espion des principaux théatres de la capitale* (Memphis, 1784 [place of publication to escape censor; almost certainly published in Paris]); Théveneau de Morande, *Gazette Noire* (1784).

23. Watin (1787), p. 115. Author's translation for all almanachs.

24. E. V. Gatacre and L. Dru, 'Portraiture in *Le Cabinet de Cire de Curtius* and its Successor, Madame Tussaud's Exhibition', *Biblioteca della revista di storia delle scienze mediche e naturali*, 20 (1977), pp. 62–64, extract from *Atti del i congresso internazionale sulla ceroplastica nella scienza e nell'arte* (Florence, 1975).

25. E. V. Gatacre and J. Fraser, 'Madame Tussaud's Methods', *Biblioteca della revista di storia delle scienze mediche e naturali*, 20 (1977), p. 640, extract from *Atti del I congresso internazionale sulla ceroplastica nella scienza e nell'arte* (Florence, 1975).

26. F. Hervé, *Madame Tussaud's Memoirs and Reminiscences of France: Forming an Abridged History of the French Revolution* (London, 1838), p. 16.

27. Hervé, *Madame Tussaud's Memoirs*, p. 16–17.

28. Mercier, *Tableau de Paris*, iii, p. 42.

29. J. Adhémar, 'Les musées de cire en France: Curtius, Le banquet royal, les têtes coupées', *La Gazette des Beaux Arts* (1978), pp. 206–7.

30. F. M. Mayeur de Saint-Paul, *Le chroniqueur désoeuvré, ou l'espion du Boulevard du Temple*, 2 vols (London, 1782–83), p. 135. What happened to the small erotic models? I got some dusty answers when I scoured fashionable antique shops in Paris some years ago asking if they had ever seen such items.

31. *Almanach général de tous les spectacles de Paris* (Paris, 1791), p. 266.

32. *Madame Tussaud and Sons Catalogue* (1846), pp. 29–30.

33. Mayeur de Saint-Paul, *Le chroniqueur désoeuvré*, i, p. 109–10.

34. Archives Nationales, Z1J1169, 6 August 1787.

35. Hervé, *Madame Tussaud's Memoirs*, pp. 1, 22–57.

36. Archives Nationales, O1.3787, O1*3789.

37. Mayeur de Saint-Paul, *Le chroniqueur désoeuvré*, pp. 135–36.

38. *Le désoeuvré mis en oeuvre ou le revers de la médaille.*

Notes to Chapter 3: Revolutionary Paris

1. O. Krakovitch, 'La répresssion des imprimeurs sous Napoleon', unpublished paper, French Institute, London, 14 February 2000.

2. Le Sueur, 'Fifteen Scenes of the French Revolution', are still a very prominent feature of the Carnavalet Museum's representation of the Revolution. The paint is mixed with gum, and the images, including those of the two wax busts, project from the canvas, almost as if the picture itself was made partly with wax. An equally famous picture in the same series was Le Sueur's depiction of men hacking at the Bastille walls during its demolition.

3. Among the best known of recent popular accounts in English is S. Schama, *Citizens: A Chronicle of the French Revolution* (London, 1989), pp. 378–83. Schama is not alone in mistakenly thinking that Curtius still had a *salon de cire* in the Palais Royal on 12 July 1789.

4. P. Curtius, *Services du sieur Curtius, vainqueur de la Bastille depuis le 12 Juillet jusqu'au 6 Octobre 1789 à la Nation* (Paris, 1790), pp. 6–7.

5. Curtius, *Services du sieur Curtius*, pp. 8–9.

6. M. Willson Disher, *The Greatest Show on Earth* (London, 1937), pp. 59–61.

7. H.-J. Lusebrink and R. Reichardt, *The Bastille: A History of a Symbol of Despotism and Freedom*, trans. N. Schurer (Durham, North Carolina, and London, 1997).

8. 'Réponse du président de l'Assemblée Nationale aux citoyens Curtius et Cubin-Bonnemère, qui venaient de faire hommage de la dernière pierre de la Bastille sur laquelle ils avaient fait graver le plan de cette forteresse maintenant démolie', 18 November 1790, Archives Nationales C46, no. 446.

9. Jacob Elie was the standard-bearer of the infantry of the queen; Pierre-Augustin Hulin was the director of the queen's laundry. Like Lafayette both had fought in the American wars.

10. H. E. Hinmann, 'Jean-Louis David et Madame Tussaud', *Gazette des Beaux-Arts* (1965), p. 333.

11. G.-L. Duval, *Souvenirs de la Terreur de 1788 à 1793* (Paris, 1841), i, pp. 288–93; A. Dumas, (ed) *Mémoires de J.-F. Talma* (Paris, 1849), iii, pp. 103–4.

12. O. Browning, ed., *The Despatches of Earl Gower, the Despatches of Mr Lindsay and Mr Munro and the Diary of the Viscount Palmerston* (Cambridge, 1885), p. 271.

13. M. Lemire, *Artistes et mortels* (Paris, 1990), p. 96.

14. *Almanach général de tous les spectacles de Paris et la province pour l'année 1791* (1791), p. 266.

15. Lemire, *Artistes et mortels*, p. 90.

16. *Almanach général de tous les spectacles de Paris et la province pour l'année 1791* (1791), p. 266.

17. *Le panthéon des philanthropes ou l'école de la Révolution: almanach orné de jolies gravures* (Paris, 1792); *Les aventures parisiennes: almanach nouveau, galant, historique, moral et chantant sur les jolis airs* (Paris, 1784); *Les délices du Palais Royal* (Paris, 1786).

18. Comité du Salut Public, Armée du Rhin, Archives Nationales, AF II, 247, 248, 249.

19. *Archives Parlementaires*, 57, p. 542.

20. *Moniteur Universel*, 23 November 1793.

21. H. E. Hinmann, 'Jean-Louis David et Madame Tussaud', *Gazette des Beaux-Arts* (1965), pp. 335–37.

22. Charles Dickens, *All the Year Round*, 7 June 1860.

23. *Archives Parlementaires*, 54, p. 715.

24. *Almanach général de tous les spectacles de Paris et de la province pour l'année 1792* (1792), ii, p. 307.

25. V. R. Schwartz, *Spectacular Realities: Early Mass Culture in Fin-de-Siècle Paris* (Berkeley, California, 1998), p. 93.

26. Lemire, *Artistes et mortels*, pp. 91–95.

27. C. Jones, *The Longman Companion to the French Revolution* (Harlow, 1988), p. 114; D. Greer, *The Incidence of the Terror in the French Revolution* (Cambridge, Massachusetts, 1935); F. Furet, 'Terror', in F. Furet and M. Ozouf, *A Critical Dictionary of the French Revolution* (Cambridge, Massachusetts, and London, 1989), pp. 137–50.

28. In a strange reversal, after the fire at Tussaud's in 1925 a theatrical prop company apparently supplied a replacement model guillotine for the exhibition.

29. D. Gerould, *Guillotine: Its Lore and Legend* (New York, 1992), pp. 31–28. A detailed account can be read in D. Arasse, *La guillotine et l'imaginaire de la Terreur* (Paris, 1987), trans. C. Miller, *The Guillotine and the Terror* (London, 1989).

30. Arasse, *La guillotine et l'imaginaire de la Terreur*, trans. Miller, *The Guillotine and the Terror*, pp. 140–41.

31. M. Heard, 'Paul de Philipstal and the Phantasgamoria in England, Scotland and Wales', *New Magic Lantern Journal*, 7 (1997).

32. E. G. Robertson, *Mémoires récréatifs, scientifiques et anecdotiques*, 2 vols (Paris, 1831–33).

33. 'Cabinet of Curcius and Optic of Zaler', *Calcutta Gazette*, 4 December 1794; *Madras Gazette*, August 1795, Madame Tussaud's Archives.

34. F. Hervé, *Madame Tussaud's Memoirs*, pp. 292–93.

35. G. Wittkop-Menardeau to Lady Chapman, 1970, Madame Tussaud's Archives.

36. Curtius's will in Archives de Paris, DQ10.521.

37. 2 frimaire an IX, Archives de la Préfecture de la Police, A (A) 242/165–69, 177–79.

38. A. Martelli, 'Felice Fontana and the Creation of Anatomical Figures in Wax and Wood', *Biblioteca della revista di storia delle scienze mediche e naturali*, 20 (1977); *Atti del I congresso internazionale sulla ceroplastica nella scienza e nell'arte* (Florence, 1975).

39. J. Hossard, ' Laumonier et l'école des cires anatomiques de Rouen', *Biblioteca della revista di storia delle scienze mediche e naturali*, 20 (1977), pp. 413–20; *Atti del I congresso internazionale sulla ceroplastica nella scienza e nella'arte* (Florence, 1975).

40. Delecluze, p. 343–46, cited in Lemire, *Artistes et Mortels*, p. 98.

Notes to Chapter 4: The Travelling Wax Exhibition

1. *Birmingham Gazette*, 13 February 1797, Madame Tussaud's Archives.

2. R. Reilly, *Josiah Wedgwood* (London, 1992), p. 277.

3. Marie Tussaud to François Tussaud, 9 June 1803, Madame Tussaud's Archives.

4. T. C. Davis, *The Economics of the British Stage, 1800–1914* (Cambridge, 2000), p. 17–18.

5. The deaths' heads of the king and queen were listed for the first time in the 1865 catalogue, *Madame Tussaud and Sons' Exhibition Catalogue Containing Biographical and Descriptive Sketches of the Distinguished Characters which Compose their Exhibition and Historical Gallery* (1865), p. 40.

6. *Biographical Sketches of the Characters Comprising the Cabinet of Composition Figures Executed by the Celebrated Curtius of Paris and his Successor* (Edinburgh, 1803), p. 42.

7. *Biographical Sketches*, p. 13.

8. *Biographical Sketches*, p. 53.

9. K. Carpenter, *Refugees of the French Revolution: Emigrés in London, 1789–1802* (Basingstoke, 1999), provides a lively and well-informed account of the experiences of the émigrés in London, but makes no mention of Madame Tussaud.

10. M. Weiner, *The French Exiles, 1789–1815* (Woking and London, 1960), p. 113.

11. F. Hervé, *Madame Tussaud's Memoirs and Reminiscences of France: Forming an Abridged History of the French Revolution* (London, 1838). Hervé was an established writer whose earlier books included *A Residence in Greece and Turkey*.

12. R. Altick, *The Shows of London* (Cambridge, Massachusetts, 1987), p. 382.

13. T. Standage, *The Mechanical Turk: The True Story of the Chess-Playing Machine that Fooled the World* (London, 2002).

14. Altick, *The Shows of London*, p. 299. The model was wrecked by a bomb during the Second World War. Its reputation, recorded by many visitors including John Keats, was such that it was restored and is now on view in the Victoria and Albert Museum, which has even produced a souvenir tiger pen. (Thanks to my research student Miss Isobel Brooks for noting this.)

15. Advertisements for Philipstal's 1801 season at the Lyceum, 1 October 1801, British Museum, 4445 46.

16. Paul de Philipstal of the Lyceum in the Strand, a patent, *Annual Register*, 20 January 1802, vol. 44, p. 7771.

17. J. Barnes, *Optical Projection: The History of the Magic Lantern from the Seventeenth to the Twentieth Century* (St Ives, 1970), p. 28.

18. A. Leslie, *Mrs Fitzherbert*, p. 126.

19. Quoted in A. Leslie and P. Chapman, *Madame Tussaud: Waxworker Extraordinary* (London, 1978), p. 112.

20. Letter to her family in Paris, 25 April 1803, Madame Tussaud's Archives.

21. It is amusing that in 1925 a periodical devoted to the long lost cause of the Bourbon Legitimism bemoaned the loss of the wax royal group dining at Versailles in a fire that destroyed the whole of the Tussaud's exhibition, lauding the figures as 'relics' and a '*chapelle funéraire*'. V. Doli, 'A propos de l'incendie du Musée Tussaud', *La Legitimité: revue d'histoire mensuelle. Organe de la survivance roi-martyr*, January-September 1925, p. 103.

22. U. Kornmeier, 'Madame Tussaud's First Exhibition in England, 1802–1803',

Object: Postgraduate Research in the History of Art and Visual Culture, October 1998, pp. 45–61.

23. Dictated letter to her husband, 'my beloved', 9 June 1803, 'Madame Tussaud in England', Madame Tussaud's Archives.

24. Marie Tussaud to François Tussaud, 28 July 1803, Madame Tussaud's Archives.

25. Copy of the original and a translation, Madame Tussaud's Archives.

26. 9 June 1803, Madame Tussaud's Archives.

27. 10 October 1803, Madame Tussaud's Archives.

28. Marie Tussaud to François Tussaud, March 1804, Madame Tussaud's Archives.

29. Marie Tussaud to François Tussaud, 20 June 1804. Madame Tussaud's Archives.

30. P. Chapman, *Madame Tussaud in England* (London, 1992), p. 33.

31. *Dublin Evening Post; Faulkner's Dublin Journal*, June 1804, Madame Tussaud's Archives.

32. *Biographical and Descriptive Sketches* (1818), p. 5.

33. 'Heads Modelled from Life', Madame Tussaud's Archives (list is incomplete and has errors).

34. L. Warwick, *Theatre Un-Royal or "They Call them Comedians": A History of the Theatre, Sometimes Royal, Marefair, Northampton* (1806–84 and 1887), p. 81.

35. Each town has it own file in the Tussaud's Archives, each with clippings from relevant newspapers, handbills and, if available, a picture of the assembly rooms which Marie hired.

36. *Biographical Sketches of the Characters Comprising the Cabinet of Composition Figures Executed by the Celebrated Curtius of Paris and his Successor* (Edinburgh, 1803), pp. 41, 42.

37. *Biographical and Descriptive Sketches of the Whole-Length Composition Figures and Other Works of Art, Forming the Unrivalled Exhibition of Madame Tussaud, Niece to the Celebrated Curtius* (Cambridge, 1818); also Boston, 1819 ('adjoining room').

38. *Biographical and Descriptive Sketches of the Distinguished Characters which Compose the Unrivalled Exhibition of Madame Tussaud* (Duffield, 1830).

39. Victor Tussaud to John Theodore Tussaud. The first of a series of letters, this one undated, but it is likely that they were all written after 1901, recording his memoirs of his grandmother, for which John Theodore paid his uncle and then used the material, unacknowledged, in his own *The Romance of Madame Tussaud's* (London, 1920).

40. *Coventry Mercury and Warwick Advertiser*, 12 June 1831.

41. Altick, *The Shows of London*, p. 177.

42. Altick, *The Shows of London*, p. 276.

43. B. Comment, *The Panorama* (London, 2001), offers a comprehensive and beautifully illustrated account of these popular entertainments.

44. P. T.-D. Chu and G. Weisberg, *The Popularization of Images: Visual Culture under the July Monarchy* (Princeton, 1994).

45. I am indebted to Altick, *The Shows of London*, for most of this section on rival attractions to Tussaud's.

46. R. Reilly, *Josiah Wedgwood* (London, 1992), p. 210.

47. *Derby Mercury*, 24 November 1819, Madame Tussaud's Archives.

48. Altick, *The Shows of London*, p. 151.

49. Tussaud Ledgers, Madame Tussaud's Archives.

Notes to Chapter 5: The Baker Street Bazaar

1. In J. M. Crook, *The British Museum* (London, 1972), p. 53.

2. R. Altick, *The Shows of London* (Cambridge, Massachusetts, 1976), pp. 25–32.

3. D. J. Sherman, *Worthy Monuments: Art Museums and the Politics of Culture in Nineteenth-Century France* (Cambridge, Massachusetts, 1989), p. 25.

4. Sherman, *Worthy Monuments*, p. 118.

5. *Times*, 28 March 1834.

6. Poster advertising 'the Musical Promenade', Gray's Inn Road, in J. T. Tussaud, *The Romance of Madame Tussaud's* (London, 1920).

7. G. Abbott, *The Book of Execution: An Encyclopedia of Methods of Judicial Execution* (London, 1994), pp. 254–69.

8. M. Judd, '"The Oddest Combination of Town and Country": Popular Culture and the London Fairs, 1800–60', in J. K. Walton and J. Walvin, ed., *Leisure in Britain, 1780–1939* (Manchester, 1983), p. 20.

9. P. Chapman, *Madame Tussaud's Chamber of Horrors: Two Hundred Years of Crime* (London, 1984), pp. 43–46.

10. Tussaud's Ledgers, Madame Tussaud's Archives, Acton. The earliest full ledgers date from 1833. Madame's notebooks, in her own writing, for some of her early tours, detailing daily expenditure and income also exist in the archives.

11. John Theodore Tussaud, handwritten note, 1917, 'Baker St Bazaar file', Madame Tussaud's Archives.

12. *Colburn's Kalendar of Amusements* (London, 1840).

13. *Literary Museum*, reprinted in Tussaud's 'testimonial' poster for the Duffield Exhibition, Madame Tussaud's Archives.

14. 'First Group: The Coronation of his Majesty George IV', *Biographical and Descriptive Sketches of the Distinguished Characters Which Compose the Unrivalled Exhibition of Madame Tussaud* (Duffield, 1830).

15. 'Tussaud's Reputation', archivist's notes, 1966, Madame Tussaud's Archives.

16. Colburn's Kalendar of Amusements (London, 1840).

17. Chapman, *Madame Tussaud's Chamber of Horrors*, p. 68.

18. Chapman, *Madame Tussaud's Chamber of Horrors*, p. 79.

19. *Biographical and Descriptive Sketches of the Distinguished Characters Which Compose the Unrivalled Exhibition of Madame Tussaud* (Duffield, 1830).

20. *Bell's Weekly Messenger*, 3 December 1815.

21. Altick, *The Shows of London*, p. 235.

22. M. Marrinan, 'Historical Vision and the Writing of History at Louis-Philippe's Versailles', in P. T.-D. Chu and G. Weisberg, ed., *The Popularization of Images: Visual Culture under the July Monarchy* (Princeton, 1994), pp. 113–43;

A. J. Tudesq, *L'élection présidentielle de Louis-Napoleon Bonaparte, 10 décembre 1848* (Paris, 1965), p. 16.

23. P. Mansel, *Paris between Empires, 1814–52* (London, 2001), pp. 369–72.

24. S. Normington, *Napoleon's Children* (Stroud, 1993), p. 115.

25. *Exhibition de Madame Tussaud et fils, 58 Baker Street, Portman Square*, Madame Tussaud's Archives.

26. *Biographical and Descriptive Sketches of the Distinguished Characters Which Compromise the Unrivalled Exhibits of Madame Tussaud, Niece of the Celebrated Curtius* (London, 1843), p. 33.

27. *Chambers's Edinburgh Journal*, 3 June 1843, Madame Tussaud's Archives.

28. W. Bullock, *The Military Carriage of Napoleon Buonaparte Taken after the Battle of Waterloo* (London, 1815).

29. *Chambers's Edinburgh Journal*, 3 June 1843, Madame Tussaud's Archives.

30. *Chambers's Edinburgh Journal*, 3 June 1843.

31. Defused by recent Tussaud archivists and eager antiquarians.

32. W. Wheeler, *Catalogue of Pictures and Historical Relics* (Madame Tussaud's, 1901), pp. 22–24.

33. F. Hervé, *Madame Tussaud's Memoirs and Reminiscences of France: Forming an Abridged History of the French Revolution* (London, 1838), p. 472.

34. Hervé, *Madame Tussaud's Memoirs*, p. 491.

35. Victor Tussaud, Madame Tussaud's grandson, to his nephew, John Theodore, n.d. (but definitely post-1901), Madame Tussaud's Archives.

36. *Daily Telegraph*, 14 July 1883.

37. A. de la Poer, 'Phaeton's Chariot(s): The Mystery of Napoleon's Waterloo Carriage', *Military Illustrated*, March 1991, pp. 14–19.

38. J. Mead (publisher), 'Madame Tussaud's Exhibition of Wax-Work', in *London Interiors* (London, 1841), pp 136–40.

39. *Madame Tussaud and Sons' Exhibition Catalogue Containing Biographical and Descriptive Sketches of the Distinguished Characters Which Compose their Exhibition and Historical Gallery* (1840).

40. Charles Dickens's *The Old Curiosity Shop* was serialised in 1840 when Madame Tussaud, the original Mrs Jarley, was no longer travelling. This extract is from the Wordsworth Classics edition (1995), pp. 197–238, which also includes several illustrations of the proprietress and her collection of figures.

41. Widow Castile to François Tussaud, 27 August 1841, 'Baker St Bazaar' file, Madame Tussaud's Archives.

42. Joseph and François Tussaud to their father, François Tussaud, 30 December 1844, 'Baker St Bazaar' file, Madame Tussaud's Archives.

43. François Tussaud to his father, François Tussaud, 26 May 1846, 'Baker St Bazaar' file, Madame Tussaud's Archives.

44. François Tussaud to his father, François Tussaud, 14 March and 29 June 1848, 'Baker St Bazaar' file, Madame Tussaud's Archives.

45. *Annual Register*, 16 April 1850.

46. *Times*, 17 April 1850.

47. *Illustrated London News*, 20 April 1850.

48. Harcourt Jackson, 'Drama of "Dead Man's Curse"', *Sunday Chronicle*.

49. 'Madame Tussaud's Grandsons', *Times*, 29 March 1885.

50. A blue plaque to Madame Tussaud, who also lived there for a time, was placed there in 2001.

51. Madame Tussaud's Archives.

52. Victor Tussaud, second letter of memoirs to his nephew, John Theodore Tussaud, n.d., Madame Tussaud's Archives.

53. B. Moran, *The Footpath and Highway: or Wanderings of an American* (Philadelphia, 1853), pp. 217–18; quoted in Altick, *The Shows of London*, p. 336.

Notes to Chapter 6: Wax Rivals

1. D. S. Kerr, *Caricature and French Political Culture, 1830–1848: Charles Philipon and the Illustrated Press* (Oxford, 2000), pp. 141–42.

2. J. Clair, ed., *L'âme au corps arts et sciences, 1793–1993* (Paris, 1993).

3. J. Hossard, 'Laumonier et l'école des cires anatomiques de Rouen', *Biblioteca della revista di storia delle scienze mediche e naturali*, 20 (1977), pp. 413–20; *Atti del I congresso internazionale sulla ceroplastica nella scienza e nell'arte* (Florence, 1975). Hossard was the curator of the Musée Flaubert.

4. G. Ongaro, 'The Anatomical Wax Models by Felice Fontana in the Anatomical Museum of Montpellier', ibid.

5. M. Lemire, *Artistes et mortels* (Paris, 1990), pp. 345–63.

6. No one seems to have anticipated Tom Sharpe's *Wilt* option and combined the anatomical and the mechanical at the sordid end of the market as an alternative to the risks involved in using live prostitutes; or, if such operations existed, no records survive.

7. Lemire, *Artistes et Mortels*, p. 101.

8. F. Hervé, *Madame Tussaud's Memoirs and Reminiscences of France: Forming an Abridged History of the French Revolution* (London, 1838), p. 438.

9. A. von Kotzebue, *Mes souvenirs de Paris (1804)*, translated as *Travels from Berlin, through Switzerland to Paris in the Year 1804*, ii, p. 143.

10. Kotzebue, *Travels from Berlin*, p. 243.

11. F. J. Gall, *Sur les fonctions du cerveau et sur celles de chacune de ses parties, avec des observations sur la possibilité de reconnaître les instincts, les penchans, les talens, ou les dispositions morales et intellectuelles des hommes et des animaux, par la configuration de leur cerveau et de leur tête*, 6 vols (Paris, 1822–25).

12. 'Cabinet de Cire', Larousse, *Dictionnaire Universelle* (1904).

13. A. Corbin, *Women for Hire: Prostitution and Sexuality in France after 1850* (Cambridge, Massachusetts, 1990), p. 248.

14. Lemire, *Artistes et mortels*, p. 341.

15. *Literary Gazette*, 31 December 1825, p. 843, quoted in Altick, *The Shows of London* p. 339.

16. 'Madame Hoyo's Grand Collection of Wax Work ... Portsmouth', Madame Tussaud's Archives.

17. Their artistic qualities were revisited in the 1980s; see Chapter 9.

18. *The William Bonardo Collection of Wax Anatomical Models* (Christies, 2001), p. 6.

19. *Bodyworlds*, by G. von Hagens, Brick Lane, London, 2002.

20. A substantial number of his works survive in the Victoria and Albert Museum.

21. Beverley and Sheffield, 1817, Madame Tussaud's Archives.

22. www.Princess Charlotte.

23. 'Not to be Equalled in the World', Madame Tussaud's Archives.

24. 'Passing of Wales "Madam Tussaud" ', *World's Fair*, 10 October, 1936, Madame Tussaud's Archives.

25. 'Last Week but One of the Splendid Collection of Wax Figures.' He was not of the same family as the former British Prime Minister, John Major.

26. 'By Permission. Just Arrived from Italy', Madame Tussaud's Archives.

27. 'Signor Francesco's Extensive and Magnificent Collection', Madame Tussaud's Archives.

28. *Reynolds' New Exhibition Catalogue, c.* 1910 and *c.* 1920, Madame Tussaud's Archives.

29. N. Brazier, *Histoire des petits théâtres de Paris*, 2 vols (Paris, 1838), pp. 187–88.

30. A. Challamel, *L'ancien Boulevard du Temple* (Paris, 1873), p. 44.

31. Larousse, *Dictionnaire Universelle* (Paris 1902); J. Adhémar,'Les musées de cire en France: Curtius, le banquet royal, les têtes coupées', *Gazette des Beaux Arts*, 92 (1978), pp. 210–11.

32. *Le Temps*, 2 June 1888.

33. V. R. Schwartz, *Spectacular Realities: Early Mass Culture in Fin-de-Siècle Paris* (Berkeley, California, 1998), includes a chapter on the role of the Musée Grévin in the popular culture of late nineteenth-century France. Almost all of the information that follows on the *musée* is gleaned from the substantial collection of material, catalogues and newspaper articles in particular on the gallery in the Bibliothèque Historique de la Ville de Paris (*Actualités*). I am very grateful to their librarian, Geneviève Madour. The Grévin archives and the gallery were closed after the gallery was sold to Asterix in 1999 and the archives did not reopen when the gallery itself was relaunched in June 2001. There have been two popular accounts of the *musée*, one by Cézan (1947), the other by Baschet (1982). In 2001 a doctoral thesis on the *musée* was written by N. Saez-Guerif. I am very grateful to Jean-Noel Luc for allowing me to see this unpublished work.

34. A.-V. de Walle,'Musées de Cire', *Les veillées des chaumières* (1952).

35. Eden *musée* catalogue and three posters (n.d.), *Actualités*, Bibliothèque Historique de la Ville de Paris.

36. *New York Recorder*, February 1894.

37. 'How Fleeting Fame Is', *New York Recorder* (1890).

38. *The Advertiser*, 16 December 1910.

39. 'Eden Gallery de Paris', 1880.

40. *Le Temps*, 9 June 1882.

41. N. Saez-Guerif, 'Le Musée Grévin, 1882–2001: cire, histoire et loisir parisien' (unpublished *thèse pour le doctorat d'histoire*, Université de Paris IV, Sorbonne, 2001)', i, pp. 184–87.

42. The Bibliothèque Historique de la Ville de Paris has a collection of Grévin catalogues from the early days to 1958.

43. Rapport du conseil d'administration, *La Vie Financière*, 1 May 1911.

Notes to Chapter 7: From the Great Exhibition to the First World War

1. They were made by the artist N. Montanari. J. Timbs, *The Curiosities of London* (London, 1868), p. 819.

2. B. Silliman, *A Visit to Europe in 1851* (New York, 1853), ii, p. 432.

3. R. Altick, *The Shows of London*, p. 464.

4. C. Hobhouse, *1851 and the Crystal Palace* (London, 1950).

5. Victor Tussaud, Madame Tussaud's grandson, to his nephew, John Theodore Tussaud n.d. (but post-1901), Madame Tussaud's Archives.

6. *Madame Tussaud and Sons' Catalogue*, January 1852, pp. 18–19, Madame Tussaud's Archives.

7. *Resumé biographique et descriptif des personnages et des monuments historiques qui composent les galéries sans rivales de Madame Tussaud et ses fils. Reliques de l'Empereur Napoléon* (1851). The copy of this catalogue in the Tussaud's Archives was a gift of Mlle Thomas, managing director of the Musée Grévin, in February 1969. Madame Tussaud's Archives.

8. 1852 catalogue.

9. Victor Tussaud to John Theodore Tussaud, 23 February 1903, Victor Tussaud file, Madame Tussaud's Archives. Presumably the late emperor he mentions was Alexander III.

10. Letter from Francis Knollys, 22 July 1889, Madame Tussaud's Archives.

11. Phillip Burne-Jones to John Theodore Tussaud, 24 May 1904, Madame Tussaud's Archives.

12. Henri Wallon, in C. Seignobos, *La révolution de 1848 à le second empire (1848–1859)*, vol. 6 of E. Lavisse, *Histoire de la France contemporaine depuis la Révolution jusqu'à la paix de 1919* (Paris, 1921), p. 134 (author's translation).

13. H. Spencer, *Principles of Psychology* (London, 1855).

14. 1873 catalogue.

15. Louisa Kenny (Tussaud), Joseph Tussaud's daughter, notebook, Louisa Kenny file, Madame Tussaud's Archives.

16. 'London Sketches: A Waxwork Exhibition', *Illustrated London News*, 30 March 1872.

17. 'Sketches at Madame Tussaud's', *Illustrated Sporting and Dramatic News*, 11 October 1884.

18. 'Toilettes at Madame Tussaud', *Society*, 15 June 1882.

19. F. M. L. Thompson, *The Rise of Respectable Society: A Social History of Victorian Britain, 1830–1900* (London, 1988), p. 260.

20. J. Walvin, *English Urban Life, 1760–1851* (London, 1984), pp. 144–45; D. Cooper, *The Lesson of the Scaffold* (London, 1974).

21. J. Walvin, *Leisure and Society* (London, 1978), pp. 19–28.

22. Altick, *The Shows of London*, p. 485.

23. National Provincial Bank ledger for 1866–67, Baker Street Bazaar file, Madame Tussaud's Archives.

24. Walvin *Leisure and Society*, p. 65.

25. D. Kift, *The Victorian Music Hall: Culture, Class and Conflict* (Cambridge, 1996), p. 176.

26. J. Timbs, *Curiosities of London: Exhibiting the Most Rare and Remarkable Objects of Interest in the Metropole with Nearly Sixty Years of Personal Recollections* (London, 1868), pp. 819–20.

27. E. Walford, *Old and New London: A Narrative of its History, its People and its Places* (London, n.d., but perhaps 1883), iv, pp. 419–20. The account includes a most unlikely picture of Madame Tussaud.

28. Fragments of Joseph Randall Tussaud's diary, Madame Tussaud's Archives. Each family member has a file in the archives.

29. Joseph Randall Tussaud to H. Brockington, the builder responsible for the new Tussaud's building, 19 July 1884, file 1884–1925, Madame Tussaud's Archives.

30. The main establishment was at 58 Baker Street, now demolished and renumbered 59. Madame also lived at 12 Wellington Road (now 24), London NW8, where, since 2001, there has been a blue memorial plaque.

31. 'Odd, even sinister' was how Lady Chapman described the brothers' calculations in a letter to the Tussaud's' managing director E. V. ('Peter') Gatacre, 7 February 1973. Baker St Bazaar file, Madame Tussaud's Archives.

32. General file, 1929–39, includes a lithograph of the Gothic Granary, Madame Tussaud's Archives.

33. Were the panels Thornhill originals? The catalogue always mentioned that they had been restored by a Mr Holden of Holborn in the eighteenth century. In 1965 the Tussaud's archivist, Lady Chapman, found a crumbling section in storeroom, apparently rescued after the 1925 fire, but Edward Croft-Murray, the British Museum expert, did not think that this very dilapidated remnant dated from the eighteenth century or that it could have been the work of Thornhill. Madame Tussaud's Archives.

34. *Daily Telegraph*, 14 July 1883.

35. 'Madame Tussaud's Grandsons', *Times*, 29 March 1885.

36. 19 July 1884, Exhibition 1884–1925 file, Madame Tussaud's Archives.

37. For instance in *Photographic Views of Madame Tussaud and Sons' Exhibition* (n.d. but 1893–94).

38. Documents of the new companies in Madame Tussaud 1888 Ltd file, Madame Tussaud's Archives, copied from originals in Public Record Office.

39. W. Allsop ran a wax show in Portsmouth in 1849, one in Bristol from 1850 in the Royal Albert Rooms, a show in the Teutonic Rooms, Lime Street,

Liverpool around 1864, and another in Liverpool in 1887, 'Nineteenth-Century Wax Exhibitions', Madame Tussaud's Archives.

40. Frank Tussaud to E. V. Gatacre, January 1968. Madame Tussaud's Archives.

41. *Evening Post*, also *New York Herald*, 8 February 1889, Madame Tussaud's Archives.

42. John Theodore Tussaud's file, Madame Tussaud's Archives.

43. *Morning Post*, 18 July 1889; *Leeds Journal*, 10 August 1889; John Theodore Tussaud's file, Madame Tussaud's Archives.

44. For instance the catalogue for his 1933–4 tour was headed 'Tussaud's Travelling Waxworks Exhibition. Entirely New and Novel Presentation of Waxworks. No Connection with Madame Tussaud Ltd', Madame Tussaud's Archives.

45. *Photographic Views of Madame Tussaud's Exhibition*, Madame Tussaud's Archives.

46. A view expressed by W. Besant in 1903 in his *As We Are and As We May Be*, p. 55 quoted in Bailey, *Leisure and Class*, p. 105.

47. *Daily News*, 12 June 1884; *'England': A National and Conservative Weekly Newspaper for All Classes*, 14 June 1884; *Penny Illustrated Paper*, 14 June 1884; *North-Western Gazette: Marylebone and Hampstead News*, 14 June 1884.

48. 'Special Press Invitation to View Six Tableaux Illustrating *Story of a Crime*', 15 December 1891, Madame Tussaud's Archives.

49. 'Chez Madame Tussaud', *Punch or the London Charivari*, 28 September 1889.

50. 'The Million', *Ladies Pictorial*, 12 August, 1893.

51. *Madame Tussaud's Exhibition*, catalogue for 1917, p. 51.

52. Bailey, *Leisure and Class*, pp. 129–31.

53. 'Studies in Wax: Some Masterpieces at Madame Tussaud's', *Sketch*, 3 January 1894, pp. 535–36.

54. *Chambers Journal of Popular Literature, Science and Art*, 26 November 1881, pp. 753–55, Madame Tussaud's Archives.

55. *Hampstead Express*, 3 January 1891.

56. *City Press*, 3 January 1891.

57. P. Chapman, *Madame Tussaud's Chamber of Horrors: Two Hundred Years of Crime* (London, 1984), p. 117.

58. J. T. Tussaud, 'My Characters', *Strand Magazine*, p. 196.

59. R. Austin Freeman, *The D'Arblay Mystery* (London; repr. 1988). I am very grateful to my colleague Dr Sam Barnish for showing me a not inconsiderable number of instances where detective mysteries made use of wax mystification.

60. 'The Million', *Ladies Pictorial*, 12 August 1893.

61. J. T. Tussaud, 'My Characters', p. 189.

62. *Moonshine*, 30 November 1889.

63. M. Pugh, *The Pankhursts* (London, 2002).

64. C. Thorpe, *The Children's London* (London, several editions, e.g. 1901 and 1905).

65. Baker Street Bazaar file, Madame Tussaud's Archives.

66. L. Macdonald, *1914: The Days of Hope*, p. 41.

67. *Daily Herald*, 4 August 1917.

Notes to Chapter 8: Waxworks in the Age of Film

1. W. R. Titterton, *London Scenes* (London, 1918).
2. Madame Tussaud's, Exhibition Orchestra 'Programme of Music', price 1*d*. (1924?), Madame Tussaud's Archives.
3. *Morning Post*, March 1925.
4. *Graphic*, 22 October 1927.
5. Extensive, detailed, but incomplete family trees exist in the archives.
6. *Morning Post*, 1925.
7. J. Wild (Inspector of Taxes) v. *Madame Tussaud's (1926) Ltd, Accountant. Tax Supplement*, 2 July 1932, p. 288, Madame Tussaud's Archives.
8. J. T. Tussaud, 'Procedure Suggested for Reinstating and Producing the Necessary Models for the New Tussaud's Exhibition to be Opened at Christmas 1927', 1926–28 reconstruction period file, Madame Tussaud's Archives.
9. E. V. Gatacre and L. Dru, 'Portraiture in *Le Cabinet de Cire de Curtius* and its Successor, Madame Tussaud's Exhibition', *Biblioteca della revista di storia delle scienze mediche e naturali*, 20 (1977), extract from *Atti del I congresso internazionale sulla ceroplastica nella scienza e nella'arte* (Florence, 1975), p. 633.
10. 3 January 1929, report to directors, appendix A, general file 1929–39, Madame Tussaud's Archives.
11. No. 1. report to the directors of Madame Tussaud Ltd, n.d. but spring 1932, Madame Tussaud's Archives.
12. General file 1929–1939, Madame Tussaud's Archives.
13. A. H. Lee (secretary) to shareholders, 27 November 1933, legal file, Madame Tussaud's Archives.
14. Sandy Forbes, 'Tussaud's Dance Orchestra', Madame Tussaud's Archives.
15. *Cinema*, 2 May 1928, Madame Tussaud's Archives.
16. Cinema file, Madame Tussaud's Archives.
17. *L'Art Vivant*, 15 November 1929.
18. *L'Information*, 27 February 1932.
19. Meeting of shareholders, 13 December 1939, Madame Tussaud's Archives.
20. 'Clothing the Models', 1940s, Madame Tussaud's Archives.
21. R. Edds, 'Coupons for the Cabinet', *c.* 1947, Madame Tussaud's Archives.
22. U. Concannon and T. Grafton, 'A Star Theatre', *Astronomy Now* (1998), pp. 4–5.
23. J. F. Colomer, 'Du boulevard au management', *Le Figaro* 7 March 1975.
24. N. Saez-Guerif, 'Le Musée Grévin, 1882–2001: cire, histoire et loisir parisien' (unpublished *thèse pour le doctorat d'histoire*, Université de Paris IV, Sorbonne, 2001).
25. Tussaud's minute books, Madame Tussaud's Archives.
26. *Le Figaro*, 15 March 1979.
27. *Le Monde*, 21 April, 1981.
28. *Le Monde*, 1 February 1980.
29. *Quotidien de Paris*, 8 June 1982.
30. *Quotidien de Paris*, 7 June 1982.

31. *Le Figaro*, 12 February 1985.

32. *Le Monde*, 9 June 1982.

33. Saez-Guerif, 'Le Musée Grévin 1882–2001', ii, pp. 641–49.

34. Minute book, 22 February 1974, Madame Tussaud's Archives.

35. Minute book, 12 October 1976, Madame Tussaud's Archives.

36. Minute book, 8 December 1976, Madame Tussaud's Archives.

37. Minute book, 3 August 1978, Madame Tussaud's Archives.

38. Minute book, 8 March 1979, Madame Tussaud's Archives.

39. Minute Book, 22 February 1979 Madame Tussaud's Archives.

40. General 1929–39 file, Madame Tussaud's Archives.

41. Minute book, 19 September 1962, Madame Tussaud's Archives.

42. Minute Book, 23 May 1979, Madame Tussaud's Archives.

43. 'Opinion' 2 February 1979, Madame Tussaud's' Archives, Chamber of Horrors correspondence file.

44. Michael Herbert to G. U. Mason, 15 February 1979, Madame Tussaud's' Archives, Chamber of Horrors correspondence file.

45. P. Chapman, *Madame Tussaud's Chamber of Horrors: Two Hundred Years of Crime* (London, 1984), p. 250.

46. Caroline Packman, 'Redevelopment Briefing Document', October 1998.

47. David Carter, *Horror: Continuing Attraction and Common Reactions*.

48. *Financial Times*, 24 June 1998.

49. *Guardian*, 24 June 1998.

50. 'Tussaud's' Reputation', n.d., Madame Tussaud's Archives.

51. I am very grateful to Judy Craig, the Head of Portraits of the Tussaud's Studios, for generously giving up her entire afternoon to show me all the processes now used, and enlightening me about developments since she joined the studio in 1978, which was then above the exhibition near Baker Street. See also Judy Craig, 'The Portrait Making Process at the Tussaud's Studios', Madame Tussaud's Archives.

Notes to Chapter 9: The Appeal of Waxworks

1. W. R. Titterton, *London Scenes* (London, 1918).

2. Madame Tussaud's Archives.

3. M. Warner, 'Waxworks and Wonderlands'.

4. Tussaud's catalogue, 1850.

5. V. R. Schwartz, 'Museums and Mass Spectacle: The Musée Grévin as a Monument to Modern Life', *French Historical Studies*, 19 (1995), p. 8: V. R. Schwartz, *Spectacular Realities: Early Mass Culture in Fin-de-Siècle Paris* (Berkeley, 1998).

6. D. J. Sherman, *Worthy Monuments: Art Museums and the Politics of Culture in Nineteenth-Century France* (Cambridge, Massachusetts, 1989).

7. Manchester catalogue, 1834, p. 8.

8. 1834 catalogue, p. 6.

9. *Biographical Sketches* (Edinburgh, 1803), p. 44–53.

10. 1861 catalogue, p. 35.

11. 1851 catalogue, p. 35.

12. George Augustus Sala, *Madame Tussaud and Sons Exhibition Catalogue* (London 1892), pp. 72–80.

13. *Biographical and Descriptive Sketches of the Distinguished Characters Who Comprise the Unrivalled Exhibition of Madame Tussaud* (1838).

14. *Madame Tussaud and Sons' Catalogue: Collection of Instruments of Torture* (1872).

15. Belloc to John Theodore Tussaud, 7 May 1920, John Theodore Tussaud file, Madame Tussaud's Archives.

16. *Daily Telegraph*, 14 July 1884.

17. *Chambers Journal of Popular Literature, Science and Art*, 26 November 1881, pp. 753–55. Madame Tussaud's Archives.

18. A. Conan Doyle, 'The Empty House', *The Return of Sherlock Holmes*, p. 447.

19. A. Conan Doyle, 'The Mazarin Stone', *The Case-Book of Sherlock Holmes*, p. 816.

20. A. Conan Doyle and J. Dickson Carr, *The Exploits of Sherlock Holmes* (New York, 1999).

21. W. L. George, 'Waxworks', in J. Symons, *Strange Tales from the Strand Magazine* (Oxford, 1992), pp. 96–106.

22. E. Nesbit, 'The Power of Darkness', ibid., pp. 342–55.

23. S. Tucker, 'Fifty Years of Lazarus', *New College Record* (2001), pp. 49–50.

24. Gatacre and Dru, 'Portraiture in *Le Cabinet de Cire de Curtius* and its Successor, Madame Tussaud's Exhibition', *Biblioteca della revista di storia delle scienze mediche e naturali*, 20 (1977), pp. 617–38; extract from *Atti del I congresso internazionale sulla ceroplastica nella scienza e nell'arte* (Florence, 1975), pp. 629–32.

25. E. J. Pyke, 'A Biographical Dictionary of Wax Modellers', *Biblioteca della revista di storia delle scienze mediche e naturali*, 2 (1977), p. 572; *Atti del I congresso internazionale sulla ceroplastica nella scienza e nell'arte* (Florence, 1975).

26. 'La semaine Parisienne', *Petit Parisien*, 27 March 1911.

27. John Theodore Tussaud, *Chronicle*, 1911.

28. Gatacre and Dru, 'Portraiture in *Le Cabinet de Cire de Curtius* and its Successor, Madame Tussaud's Exhibition'.

29. 'Tussaud's Reputation', n.d., Madame Tussaud's Archives.

30. I. Schlosser, *Histoire du portrait en cire* (Paris, 1997).

31. R. Fry quoted in Gatacre and Dru, 'Portraiture in *Le Cabinet de Cire de Curtius* and its Successor, Madame Tussaud's Exhibition'.

32. R. Austin Freeman, *The D'Arblay Mystery* (London, 1926), pp. 224–25.

33. H. Norris, 'How I Dressed Them', *Souvenir of Exhibition* (1928), pp. 19–21.

34. Gatacre and Dru, 'Portraiture in *Le Cabinet de Cire de Curtius* and its Successor, Madame Tussaud's Exhibition', p. 627.

35. B. Tussaud, 'The Famous and the Infamous' (despite the pencilled '*c.* 1938', this lengthy article was clearly written at the earliest in the 1950s. He refers to 'this atomic age'. Madame Tussaud's Archives.

36. M. A. Kelly, *My Old Kentucky Home, Goodnight* (1978).

37. Gatacre and Dru, 'Portraiture in *Le Cabinet de Cire de Curtius* and its Successor, Madame Tussaud's Exhibition', p. 627.

38. Roy Strong, *Times*, 5 July 1966.

39. Roy Strong, *Times* and *Spectator*, 1967.

40. Ian Nairn, *Sunday Times*, 31 December 1972.

41. E. J. Pyke, *A Biographical Dictionary of Wax Modellers* (Oxford, 1973); supplement, (London, 1981).

42. Dr Maria Luisa Azzoioli to Peter Gatacre, 23 October 1974, Madame Tussaud's Archives.

43. E. V. Gatacre and J. Fraser, 'Madame Tussaud's Methods', *Biblioteca della revista di storia delle scienze mediche e naturali*, 2 (1977); *Atti del I congresso internazionale sulla ceroplastica nella scienza e nell'arte* (Florence, 1975).

44. Gatacre and Dru, 'Portraiture in *Le Cabinet de Cire de Curtius* and its Successor, Madame Tussaud's Exhibition'.

45. Tussaud's Minute Books, 22 June 1976, Madame Tussaud's Archives.

46. M. Lemire, *Artistes et mortels* (Paris, 1990).

47. G. Radicchio and M. Sajous d'Oria, *Les théâtres de Paris pendant la Révolution* (Paris, 1990).

48. P. M. Pilbeam, *The Middle Classes in Europe, 1789–1914* (Basingstoke, 1990), pp. 101, 206–7.

49. Tussaud's minute books, 10 December 1975, Madame Tussaud's Archives.

50. Minute book, 24 May 1977, Madame Tussaud's Archives.

51. Undine Concannon, 'Madame Tussaud', *Dictionary of National Biography* (1985).

Bibliography

MADAME TUSSAUD'S ARCHIVES

Tussaud's have a considerable archive, with most original documents stored in their studio and copies in Marylebone. They have no full-time archivist and no space for researchers.

A substantial collection of catalogues survive at Tussaud's and there are also some at the Victoria and Albert Museum. In 1803 (for Edinburgh) Madame Tussaud produced her first catalogue, *Biographical Sketches of the Characters Comprising the Cabinet of Composition Figures Executed by the Celebrated Curtius of Paris and his Successor*. Until the Second World War catalogues provided not only a full list of all the figures and where they were located in the exhibition, but also biographical sketches, sometimes extensive ones. Catalogues were designed to be informative and to stress the serious educational and historical purpose of the collection. They also paid their way: about half of the almost eighty-page catalogue consisted of advertising. The title altered from time to time, although the basic format did not. During her touring days, Madame Tussaud published individual catalogues for each town she visited. In the Bristol edition of 1831 came the first mention of the 'separate room'. In 1838 the roles of Joseph and Francis were acknowledged for the first time, in *Biographical and Descriptive Sketches of the Distinguished Characters which Comprise the Unrivalled Exhibition of Madame Tussaud and Sons* (1838). A French edition appeared in 1851 to celebrate the Napoleon Shrine, *Résumé biographique et descriptif des personnages et des monuments historiques qui composent les galéries sans rivales de Madame Tussaud et ses fils. Reliques de l'Empéreur Napoleon* (1851). In 1872 the purchase from France of a substantial torture collection was announced in a separate catalogue, *Madame Tussaud and Sons' Catalogue: Collection of Instruments of Torture*. In 1892 the text of the catalogue was extensively revised for the first time by a well-known journalist, George Augustus Sala, as *Madame Tussaud and Sons: Exhibition Catalogue*. Only minor changes were made between 1892 and 1925. A limited number of photographs of the exhibition and exhibits began to appear and in the 1890s a brief photographic introduction of the exhibition was published, *Photographic Views of Madame Tussaud and Son's Exhibition.* In 1901 a catalogue of the Napoleonic relics was printed, W. Wheeler, *Catalogue of Pictures and Historical Relics.* Illustrated children's catalogues appeared from time to time.

There are an extensive run of minute books. Files recording the development of the exhibition are organised chronologically and thematically. There are separate files for each town visited during the touring years. Each Tussaud involved in the exhibition has a file or files. There are also general files organised chronologically, plus files for each main figure depicted in the exhibition.

Notable features are photocopies of Madame Tussaud's letters to her family in 1803–5 and various notes made by family members, especially Victor and John Theodore Tussaud.

PARIS ARCHIVES

A small amount of information on Philippe Curtius and his exhibition can be found in various Paris archives and museums. His will survives in the Archives de Paris (DQ10.521). The Carnavalet Museum has a bust of Curtius and a number of illustrations of his exhibition. The Archives Nationales has a little information on Curtius's role during the Revolution and the Archives de la Préfecture de la Police a few files on the Boulevard du Temple exhibition.

Information on what was in the Curtius exhibition and what people thought of it in the 1780s and 1790s can be obtained from contemporary almanacs, a list of which follows:

Affiches, annonces et avis divers (Paris).

Almanach du Palais-Royal (Paris, 1785).

Almanach général de tous les spectacles de Paris et la province (Paris, 1791).

Aventures parisiennes: almanach nouveau, galant, historique, moral et chantant sur les plus jolis airs, mélangé de nouvelles chansons, d'anecdotes plaisants, de contes, d'épigrammes, de bons mots etc. (Paris, 1784).

Dulaure, J.-A., *Nouvelle description des curiosités de Paris* (Paris, 1785, 1787, 1791).

Grand Carteret, J., *Les almanachs français: bibliographie-iconographique, 1600–1895* (Paris, 1896).

Le panthéon des philanthropes ou l'école de la Révolution (Paris, 1792).

Les délices du Palais-Royal (Paris, 1786).

Mayeur de Saint-Paul, F. M., *Le chroniqueur désoeuvré, ou espion du boulevard du Temple* (London, 1782–83).

Mayeur de Saint-Paul, F. M., *Tableau du nouveau Palais-Royal*, 2 vols (Paris, 1788).

Mercier, L.-S., *Spectacles des boulevards* (Paris, 1782).

Mercier, L.-S., *Tableau de Paris*, 12 vols (Paris, 1782–88).

Prudhomme, L.-M., *Révolutions de Paris*, 16 vols (Paris, 1789–93).

Tableau du nouveau Palais-Royal (Paris, 1788).

Théveneau de Morande, C., *La gazette noire par un homme qui n'est pas blanc: ou oeuvres posthumes du gazetier cuirassé* (Paris, 1784).

Thiery, L.-V., *Almanach du voyageur à Paris* (Paris, 1783–87).

Thiery, L.-V., *Guide des amateurs et des étrangers voyageurs à Paris*, 2 vols (Paris, 1786–87).

CONTEMPORARY NEWSPAPERS AND PERIODICALS

All the Year Round
Chambers's Journal of Popular Literature, Science and Art
Gazette des Beaux Arts
Household Words
Illustrated London News
Illustrated Sporting and Dramatic News
Illustrated Times
Journal de Paris
L'Artiste
L'Illustration
L'Intermédiaire des Chercheurs et Curieux
Les Beaux-Arts
Penny Illustrated Paper
Penny Magazine
Punch
Strand Magazine

SECONDARY WORKS

Abbott, G., *The Book of Execution: An Encyclopedia of Methods of Judicial Execution* (London, 1994).

Abrahams, A., 'The Egyptian Hall, Piccadilly, 1813–1873', *Antiquity*, 42 (1906), pp. 61–4, 139–44, 225–30.

Adburgham, A., *Shopping in Style: London from the Restoration to Edwardian Elegance* (London, 1979).

Adhémar, J.,'Les musées de cire en France, Curtius, le banquet royal, les têtes coupées', *Gazette des Beaux Arts*, 92 (1978), pp. 202–14.

Albert, M., *Les théâtres des boulevards, 1789–1848* (Paris, 1902).

Altick, R., *The Shows of London* (Cambridge, Massachusetts, 1976).

Altick, R., *Victorian People and Ideas* (London, 1974).

Arasse, D., *La guillotine et l'imaginaire de la Terreur* (Paris, 1987), trans. C. Miller, *The Guillotine and the Terror* (London, 1989).

Arnold, D., *Re-presenting the Metropolis: Architecture, Urban Experience and Social Life in London, 1800–1940* (Aldershot, 2000).

Ayton, R., *A Voyage around Great Britain Undertaken in the Summer of the Year 1813*, 8 vols (London, 1814–25).

Bachaumont, L. Petit de, *Mémoires secretes pour servir à l'histoire de la république des lettres en France*, 36 vols (London, 1763–89).

Bailey, P., *Leisure and Class in Victorian England: Rational Recreation and the Contest for Control, 1830–1885* (London, 1978).

Bann, S., *The Clothing of Clio: A Study of the Representation of History in Nineteenth-Century Britain and France* (Cambridge, 1984).

Banville, T. de, *Mes souvenirs* (Paris, 1883).

Barnes, J., *Optical Projection: The History of the Magic Lantern from the Seventeenth to the Twentieth Century* (St Ives, 1970).

Baschet, R., *Le monde fantastique du musée Grévin* (Paris, 1982).

Beaver, P., *The Crystal Palace, 1851–1936: A Portrait of Victorian Enterprise* (London, 1970).

Bertrand, M. (ed.), *Popular Traditions and Learned Culture from the Sixteenth to the Twentieth Centuries* (Saratoga, 1985).

Besant, W., *As We Are and As We May Be* (London, 1903).

Blagdon, F., *Paris as it Was and as it Is: or A Sketch of the French Capital Illustrative of the Effects of the Revolution*, 2 vols (London, 1803).

Bratton, J. S. (ed.), *Music Hall. Performance and Style* (Milton Keynes, 1986).

Brazier, N., *Histoire des petits théâtres de Paris*, 2 vols (Paris, 1838).

Breton, le G., 'Essai historique sur la sculpture en cire', *Académie de Rouen: classe de Belles Lettres* (Rouen, 1894).

Brown, F., *Theatre and Revolution: The Culture of the French Stage* (New York, 1980).

Browning, O. (ed.), *The Despatches of Earl Gower, the Despatches of Mr Lindsay and Mr Munro and the Diary of the Viscount Palmerston* (Cambridge, 1885).

Bruno, G., *Streetwalking on a Ruined Map* (Princeton, 1993).

Bullock, W., *The Military Carriage of Napoleon Buonaparte Taken after the Battle of Waterloo* (London, 1815).

Cain, G., *Anciens théâtres de Paris: le boulevard du Temple, les théâtres du boulevard* (Paris, 1906).

Carlson, M., *The Theatre of the French Revolution* (Ithaca, New York, 1966).

Carpenter, K., *Refugees of the French Revolution: Emigrés in London, 1789–1802* (Basingstoke, 1999).

Carr, J., *The Stranger in France: or A Tour from Devonshire to Paris* (London, 1807).

Cézan, C., *Le Musée Grévin* (Paris, 1947).

Challamel, A., *L'ancien Boulevard du Temple* (Paris, 1873).

Chamfort, S.-R.-N., *Tableaux historiques de la Révolution française*, in *Oeuvres complètes*, 5 vols (Paris, 1824–25).

Chapman, P., *Madame Tussaud's Chamber of Horrors: Two Hundred Years of Crime* (London, 1984).

Charney, L., and Schwartz, V., *Cinema and the Invention of Modern Life* (Berkeley and London, 1995).

Chu, P. T.-D., and Weisberg, G. (eds), *The Popularization of Images: Visual Culture under the July Monarchy* (Princeton, 1994).

Clair, J. (ed.), *L'âme au corps arts et sciences, 1793–1993* (Paris, 1993).

Clark, T. J., *The Painting of Modern Life* (Princeton, 1984).

Cole, F. J., 'History of Anatomical Museums', in *A Miscellany Presented to J. M. McKay* (Liverpool and London, 1914), pp. 302–17.

Comment, B., *The Panorama* (London 2001).

Cook, C., and Stevenson, J., *The Longman Handbook of Modern British History, 1714–2001* (London, 2001).

Cooper, D., *The Lesson of the Scaffold* (London, 1974).

Corbin, A., *Women for Hire: Prostitution and Sexuality in France after 1850* (Cambridge, Massachusetts, 1990).

Cowtan, R., *Memories of the British Museum* (London, 1872).

Cradock, A. F., *Journal de Madame Cradock: voyage en France, 1783–1786*, translated and edited by O. Delphin-Baileyguier (Paris, 1896).

Crook, J. M., *The British Museum* (London, 1972).

Cunningham, H., *Leisure in the Industrial Revolution, c. 1780 – c. 1880* (London, 1980).

Curtius, P., *Services du Sieur Curtius, vainqueur de la Bastille depuis le 12 Juillet jusqu'au 6 Octobre 1789 à la nation* (Paris, 1790).

Davidoff, L., *The Best Circles: Society, Etiquette and the Season* (London, 1973).

Davies, A. B., 'Thomas-Louis-Jerome Auzoux and the Papier Mâché Anatomical Model', *Biblioteca della revista di storia delle scienze mediche e naturali*, 20 (1977), pp. 257–80; *Atti del I congresso internazionale sulla ceroplastica nella scienza e nell'arte* (Florence, 1975).

Davis, T. C., *The Economics of the British Stage, 1800–1914* (Cambridge, 2000).

Deer, L., 'Italian Anatomical Waxes in the Wellcome Collection: The Missing Link', *Biblioteca della rivista di storia delle scienze mediche e naturali*, 20 (1977), pp. 281–98; *Atti del I congresso internazionale sulla ceroplastica nella scienza e nell'arte* (Florence, 1975).

Delgado, A., *Victorian Entertainment* (Newton, Abbot, 1971).

Desmond, S., *The Edwardian Story* (London, 1949).

Détournelle, A., *Aux armes et aux arts! Journal de la société républicaine des arts* (Paris, 1794).

Disher, M. Willson, *Circuses and Music Halls* (London, 1942).

Disher, M. Willson, *The Greatest Show on Earth* (London, 1937).

Doli, V., 'A propos de l'incendie du Musée Tussaud', *La Legitimité: revue d'histoire mensuelle. Organe de la survivance roi-martyr* (1925).

Doré, G., and Blanchard, J., *London: A Pilgrimage* (London, 1872).

Dowd, D. L., *Pageant-Master of the Republic: Jacques-Louis David and the French Revolution* (Lincoln, Nebraska, 1948).

Dowd, D. L., 'Art and the Theatre during the French Revolution: The Role of Louis David, *Art Quarterly*, 23 (1960), pp. 2–22.

Dreyfous, M., *Les arts et les artistes pendant la période révolutionnaire* (Paris, 1906).

Dumas, A. (ed.), *Mémoires de J.-F. Talma* (Paris, 1849).

Dumazedier, J., *Towards a Society of Leisure*, trans. by J. S. McClure (London, 1967).

Dumur, G. (ed.), *Histoire des spectacles* (Paris, 1965).

Duval, G.-L., *Souvenirs de la Terreur de 1788 à 1793* (Paris, 1841).

Dyos, H. J., and Wolff, M., *The Victorian City: Images and Reality* (London, 1973).

Eustace, K. A., 'A Hand List of Waxes in the Victorian and Albert Museum', typescript (1978), Madame Tussaud's Archives.

Farge, A., *Vivre dans la rue à Paris au XVIIIe siècle* (Paris, 1979).

Farge, R., 'Les délices du Palais Royal: almanach de 1786', *Société d'Iconographie Parisienne*, 30 January 1914.

Faucheur, T., *Histoire du boulevard du Temple depuis son origine jusqu'à sa démolition* (Paris, 1863).

Feldman, D., and Stedman Jones, G. (eds), *Metropolis: London Histories and Representations since 1800* (London and New York, 1989).

Fleichsmann, H., *La guillotine en 1793 d'après des documents inédits des Archives Nationales* (Paris, 1908).

Fontaine, J. P., *La vie tumultueuse d'Alfréd Grévin* (Paris, 1993).

Fontaine, L., *History of Pedlars in Europe* (Cambridge, 1996).

Freeman, R. Austin, *The D'Arblay Mystery* (London, 1926).

Frost, T., *The Old Showmen and the Old London Fairs* (London, 1874).

Furet, F., and Ozouf, M., *A Critical Dictionary of the French Revolution* (Cambridge, Massachusetts, and London, 1989).

Gall, F. J., *Sur les fonctions du cerveau et sur celles de chacune de ses parties, avec des observations sur la possibilité de reconnoître les instincts, les penchans, les talens, ou les dispositions morales et intellectuelles des hommes et des animaux, par la configuration de leur cerveau et de leur tête*, 6 vols (Paris, 1822–25).

Gatacre, E. V., and Fraser J., 'Madame Tussaud's Methods', *Biblioteca della rivista di storia delle scienze mediche e naturali*, 20 (1977); *Atti del I congresso internazionale sulla ceroplastica nella scienza e nell'arte* (Florence, 1975).

Gatacre, E. V., and Dru L.,'Portraiture in *Le Cabinet de Cire de Curtius* and its Successor, Madame Tussaud's Exhibition', *Biblioteca della rivista di storia delle scienze mediche e naturali*, 20 (1977), pp. 617–38; *Atti del i congresso internazionale sulla ceroplastica nella scienza e nell'arte* (Florence, 1975).

Gaxotte, P., *Paris au XVIIIe siècle* (Paris, 1967).

George, M. D., *Hogarth to Cruikshank: Social Change and Graphic Satire* (London, 1969).

Gerould, D., *Commemorations* (Princeton, 1994).

Gillis, J., and Purdue A. W. (eds), *The Civilisation of the Crowd: Popular Culture in England, 1750–1900* (London, 1984).

Godechot, J., *The Taking of the Bastille, July 14th 1789* (New York, 1970).

Golby, J. M., *Guillotine: Its Lore and Legend* (New York, 1992).

Goncourt, E. J. A., and J. A., *Histoire de la société française pendant la Révolution* (Paris, 1854).

Granville, Mary (Mrs Delany), *Autobiography and Correspondence*, 2 vols (London, 1862).

Greer, D., *The Incidence of the Terror in the French Revolution* (Cambridge, Massachusetts, 1935).

Hackett, C. J., 'A List of Medical Museums of Great Britain, 1949–50', *British Medical Journal*, 16 June 1951, pp. 1380–83.

Halem, G. A. von, *Blicke auf einen Theil Deutschlands, der Schweiz und Frankreichs bey einer Reise vom Jahre 1790*, 2 vols (Hamburg, 1791).

Hamilton, P., and Hargreaves, R., *The Beautiful and the Damned: The Creation of Identity in Nineteenth-Century Photography* (Aldershot, 2001).

Harrison, J. F. C., *The Early Victorians, 1832–51* (1971).

Hayley, R. M. *The Memoirs of Madame Tussaud: Her Eventful History* (London, 1878).

Heard, M., 'Paul de Philipstal and the Phantasgamoria in England, Scotland and Wales', *New Magic Lantern Journal*, 7 and 8 (1997).

Hemmings, F. W. J., *Culture and Society in France, 1789–1848* (Leicester, 1987).

Hemmings, F. W. J., *Theatre and State in France, 1760–1905* (Cambridge, 1994).

Hemmings, F. W. J., *The Theatre Industry in Nineteenth-Century France* (Cambridge, 1993).

Hervé, F., *Madame Tussaud's Memoirs and Reminiscences of France: Forming an Abridged History of the French Revolution* (London, 1838).

Hervey, C., *The Theatres of Paris* (London, 1846).

Heulhard, A., *La foire Saint-Laurent: son histoire et ses spectacles* (Paris, 1878).

Higgins, E. L. (ed.), *The French Revolution as Told by Contemporaries* (1939).

Hinmann, H. E., 'Jean-Louis David et Madame Tussaud', *Gazette des Beaux-Arts* (1965), pp. 331–37.

Hobhouse, C., *1851 and the Crystal Palace* (London, 1950).

Hossard, J., 'Laumonier et l'école des cires anatomiques de Rouen', *Biblioteca della rivista di storia delle scienze mediche e naturali*, 20 (1977), pp. 413–20; *Atti del I congresso internazionale sulla ceroplastica nella scienza e nell'arte* (Florence, 1975).

Houghton, W. E., *The Victorian Frame of Mind, 1830–1870* (New Haven and London, 1957).

Hugot, E., *Histoire littéraire, critique et anecdotique du théâtre du Palais-Royal, 1784–1884* (Paris, 1886).

Huyssen, A., 'Monument and Memory in a Postmodern Age', *Yale Journal of Criticism*, 6 (1993), pp. 249–61.

Isherwood, R. M., *Farce and Fantasy: Popular Entertainment in Eighteenth-Century Paris* (Oxford, 1986).

Jones, C., *The Longman Companion to the French Revolution* (Harlow, 1988).

Jones, P. (ed.), *The French Revolution in Social and Political Perspective* (London, 1996).

Jordanova, L. *Sexual Visions. Images of Gender in Science and Medicine between the Eighteenth and Twentieth Centuires* (Hemel Hempstead, 1989).

Jordanova, L., and Matlock, J., 'Censoring the Realist Gaze', in Cohen, M., and Prendergast, C. (eds), *Spectacles of Realism* (Minneapolis, 1995).

Jourdan, A., *Les monuments de la Révolution, 1770–1804: une histoire de la représentation* (Paris, 1997).

Jouy, E. de, *L'hermite de la Chaussée d'Antin: ou observations sur le moeurs et les usages parisiens au commencement du XIXe siècle*, 5 vols (Paris, 1813–17).

Kerr, D. S., *Caricature and French Political Culture, 1830–1848: Charles Philipon and the Illustrated Press* (Oxford, 2000).

Kift, D., *The Victorian Music Hall: Culture, Class and Conflict* (Cambridge, 1996).

Kotzebue, A. von, *Mes souvenirs de Paris* (1804); translated as *Travels from Berlin, through Switzerland to Paris in the year 1804*, 3 vols (London, 1804).

Lavallée, J., *Letters of a Mameluke: or A Moral and Critical Picture of the Manners of Paris*, 2 vols (London, 1804).

Lemaistre, J. G., *A Rough Sketch of Modern Paris: or Letters on Society, Manners, Public Curiosities, and Amusements in the Capital* (London, 1803).

Lemire, M., *Artistes et mortels* (Paris, 1990).

Lesky, E., 'The Viennese Collection of Wax Models in the Josephinium',

Biblioteca della rivista di storia delle scienze mediche e naturali, 20 (1977); *Atti del I congresso internazionale sulla ceroplastica nella scienza e nell'arte* (Florence, 1975).

Leslie, A., and Chapman P., *Madame Tussaud: Waxworker Extraordinary* (London, 1978).

London Interiors: A Grand National Exhibition of the Religious, Regal and Civic Solemnities, Public Amusements, Scientific Matters and Commercial Science of the British Capital Beautifully Engraved on Steel from Drawings Made Expressly for this Work, by Command of Her Majesty Published by Joseph Mead, 2 vols (London, 1841).

Lunel, E., *Le théâtre et la Révolution* (Paris, 1909).

Lusebrink, H. -J., and Reichardt, R., *The Bastille: A History of a Symbol of Despotism and Freedom*, trans. N. Schurer (Durham, North Carolina, and London, 1997).

McCormick, I., *Popular Theatres of Nineteenth-Century France* (London, 1993).

McLellan, A., *Inventing the Louvre: Art, Politics, and the Origins of the Modern Museum in Eighteenth-Century Paris* (Cambridge, 1994).

Malcolmson, R. W., *Popular Recreations in English Society, 1700–1850* (Cambridge, 1973).

Mansel, P., *Paris between Empires, 1814–52* (London, 2001).

Marchandieu, J. N., *L'Illustration, 1843–1944: Vie et mort d'un journal* (1987).

Margetson, S., *Fifty Years of Victorian London: From the Great Exhibition to the Queen's Death* (London, 1969).

Martelli, A., 'Felice Fontana and the Creation of Anatomical Figures in Wax and Wood', *Biblioteca della rivista di storia delle scienze mediche e naturali*, 20 (1977); *Atti del I congresso internazionale sulla ceroplastica nella scienza e nell'arte* (Florence, 1975).

Metzner, P., *Crescendo of the Virtuoso: Spectacle, Skill and Self-Promotion in Paris during the Age of Revolution* (Berkeley, California, 1998).

Moran, B., *The Footpath and Highway: or Wanderings of an American* (Philadelphia, 1853).

Monester, A., *Les grands affaires criminelles* (Paris, 1988).

Nead, L., *Victorian Babylon: People, Streets and Images in Nineteenth-Century London* (New Haven and London, 2001).

Nochlin, L., *The Politics of Vision: Essays on Nineteenth-Century Art and Society* (London, 1991).

Nora, P., *Les lieux de mémoire*, 7 vols (Paris, 1984–93).

Norris, H., *The Evolution of European Dress through the Earlier Ages*, 4 vols (London and Toronto, 1924–38).

Ongaro, G., 'The Anatomical Wax Models by Felice Fontana in the Anatomical Museum of Montpellier', *Biblioteca della rivista di storia delle scienze mediche e naturali*, 20 (1977); *Atti del I congresso internazionale sulla ceroplastica nella scienza e nell'arte* (Florence, 1975).

Pilbeam, P. M., 'A Forgotten Socialist and Feminist: Ange Guépin', in M. Cornick and C. Crossley (eds), *Problems in French History* (Basingstoke, 2000), pp. 64–80.

Pilbeam, P. M., *The Middle Classes in Europe, 1789–1914* (Basingstoke, 1990).

Piozzi, Hester (Mrs Thrale), *The French Journals of Mrs Thrale and Dr Johnson*, ed. M. Tyson and H. Guppy (Manchester, 1932).

Premuda, L., 'The Waxwork in Medicine', *Images*, 48 (1972), pp. 17–24.

Pugh, M., *The Pankhursts* (London, 2002).

Py, C., and Ferenczi, C., *La fête foraine d'autrefois: les années 1900* (Lyon, 1987).

Pyke, E. J., *A Biographical Dictionary of Wax Modellers* (Oxford, 1973); supplement (London, 1981).

Pyke, E. J., 'A Biographical Dictionary of Wax Modellers', *Biblioteca della rivista di storia delle scienze mediche e naturali*, 20 (1977), pp. 569–72; *Atti del I congresso internazionale sulla ceroplastica nella scienza e nell'arte* (Florence, 1975).

Radicchio, G., and Sajous d'Oria, M., *Les théâtres de Paris pendant la Révolution* (Paris, 1990).

Reilly, R., *Josiah Wedgwood* (London, 1992).

Renouvier, J., *Histoire de l'art pendant la Révolution consideré principalement dans les estampes* (Paris, 1863).

Richardson, R., *Death, Dissection and the Destitute* (London, 1987).

Roberts, W., 'The Visual Rhetoric of Jean-Louis Prieur', *Canadian Journal of History*, 32 (1997), pp. 415–36.

Robertson, E. G. *Mémoires récréatifs, scientifiques et anecdotiques*, 2 vols (Paris, 1831–33).

Root-Bernstein, M., *Boulevard Theater and Revolution in Eighteenth-Century Paris* (Ann Arbor, Michigan, 1984).

Rosenblum, R., and Janson, H. W., *Art of the Nineteenth Century: Painting and Sculpture* (London, 1984).

Royle, E., *Modern Britain: A Social History, 1750–1997* (London, 1987).

Saez-Guerif, N., 'Le Musée Grévin 1882–2001: cire, histoire et loisir parisien', unpublished *thèse pour le doctorat d'histoire*, Université Paris IV, Sorbonne, 2001).

Schama, S., *Citizens: A Chronicle of the French Revolution* (London, 1989).

Schiebinger, L.,'Skeletons in the Closet: The First Illustrations of the Female Skeleton in Eighteenth-Century Anatomy', in Gallagher, C., and Laqueur, T., *The Making of the Modern Body* (Berkeley and Los Angeles, 1987), pp. 42–82.

Schlosser, I., *Histoire du portrait en cire* (Paris, 1997).

Schwartz, V. R., *Spectacular Realities: Early Mass Culture in Fin-de-Siècle Paris* (Berkeley, 1998).

Schwartz, V. R., 'Museums and Mass Spectacle: The Musée Grévin as a Monument to Modern Life', *French Historical Studies*, 19 (1995), pp. 7–26.

Seignobos, C., 'La révolution de 1848: le second empire (1848–1859)', in Lavisse, E. (ed.), *Histoire de la France contemporaine depuis la Révolution jusqu'à la paix de 1919* (Paris, 1921).

Sherman, D. J., *Worthy Monuments: Art Museums and the Politics of Culture in Nineteenth-Century France* (Cambridge, Massachusetts, 1989).

Silliman, B., *A Visit to Europe in 1851* (New York, 1853).

Spencer, H., *Principles of Psychology* (London, 1855).

Standage, T., *The Mechanical Turk: The True Story of the Chess-Playing Machine that Fooled the World* (London, 2002).

Steegman, J., *Consort of Taste, 1830–1870* (London, 1950).

The William Bonardo Collection of Wax Anatomical Models (Christies, London, 2001).

Thompson, C. J. S., 'Anatomical Manikins', *Journal of Anatomy*, 59 (1925) pp. 442–25.

Thompson, F. M. L., *Gentrification and the Enterprise Culture: Britain, 1780–1980* (Oxford, 2001).

Thompson, F. M. L., *The Rise of Respectable Society: A Social History of Victorian Britain, 1830–1900* (London, 1988).

Thompson, P., *The Edwardians: The Remaking of British Society* (London, 1975).

Thorpe, C., *The Children's London* (London, 1901, 1905).

Tickner, L., *The Spectacle of Women: Imagery of the Suffrage Campaign, 1907–1914* (London, 1987).

Timbs, J., *Walks and Talks about London* (London, 1865).

Timbs, J., *Curiosities of London: Exhibiting the Most Rare and Remarkable*

Objects of Interest in the Metropole with Nearly Sixty Years of Personal Recollections (London, 1868).

Titterton, W. R., *London Scenes* (London, 1918).

Tussaud, J. T., *The Romance of Madame Tussaud's* (London, 1920).

Tussaud L. *The Romance of Madame Tussaud's: A Romantic Novel* (1937).

Valpy, R., 'A Short Sketch of a Short Trip to Paris in 1788', *Pamphleteer*, 3 (1814), pp. 490–552.

Vatout, J., *Histoire du Palais-Royal* (Paris, 1829).

Vogler, R. A., *Graphic Works of George Cruikshank* (New York, 1979).

Waites B., Bennett T., and Martin G. (eds), *Popular Culture: Past and Present* (London, 1982).

Walford, E., *Old and New London: A Narrative of its History, its People and its Places*, 6 vols (London, 1873–78)

Walton, J. K., and Walvin, J. (eds), *Leisure in Britain, 1780–1939* (Manchester, 1983).

Walvin, J., *English Urban Life, 1760–1851* (London, 1984).

Walvin, J., *Leisure and Society, 1830–1950* (London, 1978).

Ward, A., *List of Waxes in the Victoria and Albert Museum* (London, 1978).

Warner, M., *Monuments and Maidens: The Allegory of the Female Form* (London, 1985).

Watson, E., edited by W. C. Watson, *Men and Times of the Revolution* (New York, 1851).

Weiner, M., *The French Exiles, 1789–1815* (Woking and London, 1960).

Williams, R., *Culture and Society, 1780–1950* (London, 1958).

Wolff, J., and Seed, J., *The Culture of Capital: Art, Power and the Nineteenth-Century Middle Class* (Manchester, 1988).

Yates, E., *The Business of Pleasure*, 2 vols (London, 1865).

Index